Evil in Modern Myth and Ritual

E V I L

in Modern Myth and Ritual

RICHARD STIVERS

THE UNIVERSITY OF GEORGIA PRESS

ATHENS, GEORGIA

Copyright © 1982 by the University of Georgia Press,
Athens, Georgia 30602
All rights reserved
Printed in the United States of America
Designed by Richard Hendel
Set in Baskerville

Library of Congress Cataloging in Publication Data

Stivers, Richard.
Evil in modern myth and ritual.
Bibliography: p.
Includes index.
1. Social ethics.   2. Deviant behavior.
3. Good and evil.   I. Title.
HM216.S765   302.5   81-21907
ISBN 0-8203-0617-7   AACR2
ISBN 0-8203-0618-5 (pbk.)

CONTENTS

ACKNOWLEDGMENTS

This book was hewed out of the ideas of Jacques Ellul, Mircea Eliade, Paul Ricoeur, Victor Turner, and Roger Caillois. My indebtedness to these seminal thinkers will become obvious in the following pages.

Those who read one or another of the several drafts of the manuscript and made helpful suggestions include: Edmund Dougan, Andrew Greeley, Martin Marty, Walter Mead, Raymond Schmitt, and Charles Snyder. T. David Brent helped me to see that I needed to ground my analysis of the sacred in social institutions. John McGuigan encouraged me in the midst of my torment about whether my manuscript would ever be published. To him I owe a very special debt.

Ellen Harris did a splendid job of copyediting my book. University of Georgia Press assistant director .and editor Charles East demonstrated confidence in my work and guided its evolution into a book with sensitivity and with courtesy. The University of Georgia Press has restored my faith in the publishing industry, at least in the scholarly end of it.

The expert typing of Irene Taylor, Sue Melton, and Pam Martin deserves recognition; all three completed their work faster than I had any right to expect.

Finally, I wish to thank my wife, Janet, and my sons, Mark and Michael, for accepting the burden this book imposed upon them. Their presence and affection helped to draw me out from the extreme inwardness of writing a book.

Evil in Modern Myth and Ritual

INTRODUCTION

The following study should be confused neither with a metaphysics of evil nor with a theology of evil. My concern is with the social construction of evil, that is, with how modern societies (in a partly unconscious way) create evil as a category of the sacred and how symbols, myths, and rituals of evil are related to this. Furthermore, I am interested in how modern societies provoke individuals to commit evil actions. Our attention will concurrently be on how evil is perceived and constructed, on why it is committed, and on the dialectic between the two.

Sociologists who analyze deviant behavior once studied it with little regard for the symbolic and moral dimensions of the behavior. For the past two decades, however, they have increasingly turned their attention to the rules by which behavior is gauged deviant. Now morality, laws, and beliefs are considered as problematic as the deviant behavior once was.

Still sociologists studying deviance have in practice generally failed to distinguish between sacred and secular rules. If the basis of social order in primitive societies was the cultural configuration of the sacred, symbol, myth, and ritual, then to understand evil one would be required to place it in this context. If, however, myth and ritual have disappeared in modern societies, deviance can be studied as a purely secular phenomenon. Consequently, sociologists have left the analysis of sacred rules and their violations to anthropologists and historians of comparative religion, who, whether by design or not, have generally omitted an analysis of the societal conditions that contribute to the commission of such evil actions. To be fair, it is legitimate to raise the question of whether deviant behavior was as problematic in primitive societies as it is modern societies.

If modern societies are far from being secular and if the sociological study of the causes of deviant behavior is still worthwhile, then combining the approaches of anthropology and comparative religion with that of sociology might prove illuminating. Because cultural anthropologists and historians of religion have tended to emphasize culture in explaining human motivation while sociologists have tended to emphasize social structure, once again a combination of approaches might prove fruitful.

This book, then, is not about all forms of deviance; it is about violations of sacred rules in modern societies as manifested in symbol, myth, and ritual and about how the structure of modern societies unwittingly provokes such evil actions. The book is intended for an audience of sociologists, anthropologists, students of religion, folklorists, and, in short, anyone interested in the subject of evil. I hope to show, among other things, that the promise of the social science lies as much in interdisciplinary inquiry as in specialized research.

By way of introduction, let us briefly consider how the concepts of the sacred, symbol, myth, and ritual are interrelated. Following the work of Eliade, I would prefer to consider them as a cultural configuration. It is a matter not of "imposing" these concepts upon social reality but rather of using them because the subjective meanings people attribute to their actions justify this use. Unlike positivists, who employ concepts as if they were objective, universal, and ahistorical, I will attempt to be sensitive to the ways in which the *forms* that the sacred, symbol, myth, and ritual have assumed in the modern world have changed. To assume that this cultural configuration will appear in modern societies as it did in primitive societies is certainly to miss their adumbrations today.

Hence my approach is nominalistic, perhaps phenomenological at times. This book is an interpretative essay and as such is not essentially empirical research. It builds upon the work of other writers and studies. The assertions in Chapter 2 about what is sacred in modern culture will probably appear presumptuous and unfounded to many. Instead of hard evidence I appeal to the reader's experiences and impressions and hope that I make a plausible case.

The sacred is, among other things, that to which we attribute ultimate value; it is, following Eliade, perceived as power and reality. It forms the basis of the moral and social order, separating good from evil. Both that which is holy and that which is defiling are sacred. The holy can be referred to as the sacred of respect and that which is defiling as the sacred of transgression. The sacred, then, is ambiguous in value. The sacred keeps us on the level of the concrete, for while it is usually viewed as a spiritual power, it is nonetheless a power embedded in material reality.

Myths are often stories about the origin of the world and what is sacred in it and about the origin of evil and its elimination. Myth transports us to the abstract level as a fictive account of what is sacred. Symbols are compacted myths, sacred metaphors that imply larger mythical stories. A symbol of evil is the *form* evil assumes given the prevailing myth. Sacredly transgressive actions are the *content* of evil. Rituals are the reenactment of myths, the putting of theory into practice. Rituals are ways of appeasing the sacred and making its power work for man. Because in most creation myths good emerges from evil, order from chaos, societies have rituals celebrating both order and chaos.

To summarize briefly, evil can be sacred (sacred of transgression). When it is so, symbols and myths that imply or explain the origin and elimination of evil grow up around it. Rituals of transgression permit the commission of evil actions as a reenactment of the chaos (evil) immediately preceding creation (good). The sacred needs myth and ritual as its theory and practice. Therefore, we must consider evil simultaneously as sacred, symbol, myth, and ritual to understand its full cultural significance.

CHAPTER ONE

Advertising and the Media: The Cultural Origins of Modern Myth and Ritual

We shall not expect to understand other people's ideas of
contagion, sacred or secular, until we have confronted our own.
MARY DOUGLAS
Purity and Danger

It is commonplace today to point out that sociology and, to a large extent, all of the social sciences share in their origin and development a commitment to science and progress—a belief that "man has come of age."[1] One consequence of this assumption is to reason that because primitive man lived in a world of myth and ritual, modern man does not. Mythical knowledge, then, is inferior to scientific and historical knowledge; moreover, the two types of knowledge are mutually exclusive. Even those who are not committed to the myth of progress find it difficult to perceive what is mythical and ritualistic today, in part because the context and circumstances of myth and ritual are so markedly different from what they have been at other times and in other places. Even an observer as astute as Mircea Eliade has not seen the fullness of myth and ritual in industrial societies. In his fascinating book *Myth and Reality*, Eliade has a chapter "Survivals and Camouflages of Myths." And although his analysis is excellent as far as it goes, the implication is that the myth that hangs on somewhat precariously today in historiography and the mass media is but a pale reflection of its historical counterpart.[2] I hope to show that this society and societies like it are anything but secular, or, to put it more precisely, that our society is secularized only in respect to what was *previously* sacred.

Myth and ritual need not be supportive of social structure, as Victor Turner has observed.[3] They can and often do assume the guise of antistructure. In his brilliant book *The Ritual Process*, Turner notes that for most British social anthropologists (and for most American sociologists) social structure has meant "relationships between statuses, roles, and offices" which combine to form a segmented and hierarchical society. The social has been identified with what transpires between individuals caught in the web of social structure. Turner, on the other hand, has demonstrated that there is a form of the social he calls "communitas" whereby individuals enter into spontaneous communion with one another, sometimes in ecstatic and mystical ways. Those creating a situation of communitas treat each other as equals, thus defying structural expectations. Communitas involves cognitive and emotional identification—a feeling of being one in all and all in one. Often, but not necessarily, communitas occurs in a liminal context. Following Van Gennep's seminal work on rites of passage, Turner describes the liminal as a transitional state, a condition of betwixt and between, the process of becoming. In abandoning the old status and before assuming the new status, one is in a liminal state. A period of liminality is sometimes marked by rites of status reversal in which lower- and upper-class members exchange roles or by rites of transgression in which the sacred taboos are violated. The question of the transgression of taboos in the sacred festival raises even more questions for the sociologists of deviance than does that of communitas.

The point of the discussion is that adopting a purely social-structural approach and emphasizing only the conscious aspects of the social will lead one to miss the unconscious side of deviance. Equally misleading, of course, would be to view deviance only from the standpoint of myth and ritual, the structural in Claude Levi-Strauss's sense of the term. The issue, then, is between social scientists who emphasize conscious structure and those who emphasize unconscious structure. I will attempt to move toward a theory of sacredly transgressive action that integrates conscious and unconscious social structures.

Conscious versus Unconscious

Sociologists have tended to shy away from the unconscious largely because it could not be directly observed and because they did not know how to study it sociologically. Moreover, symbolic interactionism, which defines the formation of the self as a conscious process, appealed to prodemocratic, liberal sentiments. It better fit the assumptions of American ideology to see the self emerge in a rational way sensitive to one's family and peer group.

Unconscious processes can be inferred, as Sigmund Freud so brilliantly demonstrated in works such as *The Interpretation of Dreams* and *The Psychopathology of Everyday Life*. And their collective manifestations can be studied, as symbolically oriented social scientists have shown. Of course a serious problem emerges if one considers the unconscious to be a self-contained entity, a thing. Rather it makes more sense to use the word unconscious as L. L. Whyte has—as an adjective, not a noun. For him there are only mental processes (about which we know painfully little), which range from unconscious to conscious:

> *Conscious* will be used to mean *directly present in awareness* (or immediately known to awareness). This adjective will be applied only to discrete *aspects* or brief *phases* of mental process. No distinction will be made between "conscious" and "aware." Except for a few doubtful extreme cases (e.g., processes of logical or mathematical deduction) there appear to be no causally self-contained processes of which all aspects directly enter awareness. "Conscious" is a subjective term without, as yet, (i) interpretation in terms of physiological structure, or (ii) explanation of its function. *Unconscious*, in the term "unconscious mental processes" will be used to mean all *mental* processes except those discrete aspects or brief phases which enter awareness as they occur. Thus, "unconscious mental processes" (or the "unconscious," for short) is here used as a comprehensive term including not only the "subconscious" and "preconscious," but all mental factors and processes of which we are not immediately aware, whatever they be: organic or personal tendencies or needs, memories, processes of mimicry, emotions, motives, intentions, policies, beliefs, assumptions, thoughts, or dishonesties.[4]

For Whyte, then, unconscious is a broad term and conscious a narrow one.

Problems arise, however, when one moves from the psychological to the sociological level. Do we posit the existence of a collective unconscious analogous to a collective conscience and a collective mind? Only, if like Freud or like Peter Berger and Thomas Luckmann we remain dialectical, can we speak of a collective unconscious.[5] That is, the relationship of individual to society is one in which the individual both is formed by and forms society. The collective exists because the individuals who compose it possess a sense of the collective, but, in turn, collectively held attitudes and collective actions determine individual attitudes and actions. Thus we can talk about collectively unconscious not merely in the aggregate sense, that is, the sum total of the individuals' unconscious mental processes within a group, but also in the sense that what does not surface to consciousness in the group is unlikely to enter the awareness of the individual.

My position is that side by side with modern instrumental rationality embedded in technology exist mythology and a system of rituals, which to a large extent escape our conscious awareness. Primitive man had an intuitive sense of the sacred but was without a concept of the sacred, whereas modern man has a concept of the sacred (which he applies to every period but the modern) but no intuitive sense of the sacred.

Arnold Gehlen appears to be making the same point in his criticism of Freud's theory of the unconscious when he claims that psychoanalytical theory applies better to modern man than to primitive man.[6] Primitive man may have lacked a critical reflectiveness, but his experiences were intuitive and unitary, not fully conscious but not deeply unconscious either. Modern man, by contrast, is capable of both and, indeed, tends to vacillate between the extremes of consciousness and unconsciousness. Moreover, there is some evidence that the cumulative impact of technological rationality causes the modern mind in compensation to become more deeply unconscious. There are a number of reasons why modern man is unconscious of his devotion to certain sacred phenomena.

The first is the image that modern man holds of himself. Committed to progress, rationality, and science, he thinks that he has outgrown the irrationality of primitive man as expressed in myth and ritual. If modern man is religious, he imagines himself to be so without the aid of magic and superstition. His commitment to science and technology is perceived to be solely a rational one.

The second reason is that technology blocks our conscious understanding of its actual workings.[7] Each new form of technology as an extension of man himself produces an added burden on the central nervous system, which, in turn, diverts perception away from the stress that this technology creates for us by increasing the tempo of life. When we forget that these extensions are our own creations, they become part of objective reality, something to which we adjust by becoming their servomechanisms. Thus technology would also prevent our recognition that we experience it as sacred. Our experience of the sacred is thereby rendered an unconscious one.

The third reason is that the technology that is used on humans makes a largely unconscious appeal. Human techniques are most efficient when they can control man's irrational, unconscious impulses.[8] Various psychological techniques, especially advertising and television, are quite effective in this regard. Hence the very man who part of the day rationally employs techniques is also irrationally affected by the human techniques of others. Yet because technique demands little of our own rationality, its overall impact is not to make us more rational as its users but to make us more irrational as its victims.

From a Literate Back to an Oral Culture

There is little disagreement, I think, that the mass media, television in particular and especially television advertising, have had a profound effect upon us. The media have become our verbal environment, at once encapsulating the higher learning into formulas and clichés and centralizing folk or popular culture. In order to get at how the media create a mythical and ritualistic environment we need first to explore the difference between an oral and a literate culture.

An oral culture, one without the written word, is a culture in which conscious reflection is, if not impossible, at least difficult. Literacy, as Walter Ong has often remarked, is a tool for establishing distance between the knower and the object of his knowledge.[9] Once the sentence, the paragraph, the story has been written, one can reflect on it, think about the ideas represented in language. An oral culture, on the other hand, effects an immediate relationship between the knower and thing known; it brings about less an intellectual than an emotional relationship. Thus one can talk about people in an oral culture possessing an immediate emotional relationship with each other and with nature. Oral language is a means, then, of binding man to man and man to nature. This relationship is both sympathetic and uncritical.

The oral culture is principally a closed system of myth and ritual. Myth is a call to ritual enactment; therefore, oral culture is action-orientated. Literate culture, by contrast, lends itself to reflection and intellectualization, which in turn make it a more open system. In a literate culture, individuality and freedom are a consequence of consciousness; in an oral culture, group cohesiveness and identity are a result of the unconsciousness that myth induces.

An oral culture, essentially a purveyor of myths, is a repository of commonplaces, clichés, aphorisms, and slogans, all of which are told repeatedly. Repetition, then, is one of the key characteristics of a culture that is primarily oral. As Ong has noted, "The noetic processes of primary orality . . . are formulaic and rhapsodic rather than analytic." [10] The repetition of mythical formulas serves many purposes: (1) the retention of culture, for without writing a culture must be "spoken" to be maintained in memory; (2) affective identification with sacred values; (3) obedience to authority. Hence an oral culture is conservative, that is, geared toward the conservation of its sacred values through the myths that effect identification and the rituals that dramatically guide one to the proper actions.

Finally, a culture of primary orality is one with multiple and separate realities. [11] The mythical and ritualistic world is not checked over against the empirical world. This explains in part why the efficacy of rituals is not measured in primitive societies. The rationale for a culture's religious beliefs does not lie *outside* these beliefs but *inside* them, as Clifford Geertz has shown. [12] Ritual enactment of mythical beliefs is itself the proof. Seeing sacred happenings dramatically reenacted in the immediate presence of one's peers produces and reaffirms awe, emotional identification, and ultimately belief itself. The world of myth and ritual is a world more real than that of empirical reality, for the entire empirical world is *contained* in the myth of origins or of creation. If primitive man periodically performed rituals that were believed to accomplish the re-creation of the world, then why would one need to use this empirical reality, dependent as it is upon ritual, to act as a check upon the efficacy of the ritual? For the true believer, the thought never entered his mind.

In a literate culture the distinction between knower and thing known (subject and object), between idea and referent, opens the possibility for one to be critical of ideas. How do they relate either to transcendent reality or to empirical reality? In oral cultures ideas are uncritically related to empirical reality because the ideas are essentially religious; moreover, the religious ideas, as it were, bring about empirical reality.

Ong suggests that modern cultures are primarily literate and only secondarily oral. He acknowledges that radio and to a certain extent television and movies are oral forms of communication but points out that each of these forms is dependent upon scripts. Furthermore, the literacy rate in modern societies is extremely high and the number and kinds of reading materials continue to proliferate. Nonetheless, following Marshall McLuhan and Edmund Carpenter, I maintain that our culture is primarily oral and visual and only secondarily literate. That the overwhelming majority of people spend much more time watching television and listening to the radio than they do reading serious books is well known. While it is true that the mass media are dependent upon scripts, their impact upon listeners is essentially the same as that of the spoken word in oral cultures—*unconscious*.[13] The media, our most pervasive aural and visual environments, do not make an appeal to our conscious, rational minds; rather their appeal is emotional and unconscious. We do not reflect on programs; we experience them. We relate to the images and sounds of the media in much the same manner primitive man related to the images and sounds of his rituals.

The mass media[14] exhibit the same characteristics earlier attributed to the myth and ritual of a primarily oral culture in that they (1) form a closed system; (2) repeat commonplaces and clichés; and (3) form a separate system.

The mass media are a closed system in the sense that they rule out the individuality and freedom that only the written word can provide. The mass media make a fundamental appeal to the unconscious. In this way they rule out the freedom that can ensue from the exercise of reason. Too often in modern culture freedom is identified with the options that consumers are given—the freedom to purchase a yellow Buick with a complete sound system rather than a red Buick with an AM radio. Inasmuch as people increasingly turn away from serious books toward escapist fare and toward the mass media they come more to resemble the general types portrayed in advertising and the media. As Max Horkheimer and Theodore Adorno noted, the "culture industry" produces stereotypical humans for us to emulate who represent general and abstract tendencies but who nevertheless exhibit a kind of pseudoindividuality.[15] Differences in matters of accidental detail we mistake for individuality. Thus the mass media force us to resemble the images they serve up to us in part by creating an illusion of freedom through consumer choice.

The repetition of the mass media overlaps with the previously mentioned tendency to portray life in a general and abstract way. For it is the simple, general, and abstract pattern which can most readily be communicated over and over again. It is not merely the repetition of the same advertisement or even television reruns but, more important, the convergence of ads, television shows, and movies about certain proven stereotypes, "formulas for success."[16] The audience has a vague feeling of déjà vu in watching and listening to the media, not so much at the manifest level of specific situations and characters but more at the deeper level of plot and character types. One gets a distinct feeling of sameness. The repetition is not merely aesthetic, however; it is also moral. Advertising, which informs and partly determines the content of media programming, attempts to compress within a single image[17] or set of images certain desirable actions: to buy certain products and to engage in a consumer-orientated lifestyle. This lifestyle represents a living out of certain sacred values.

Finally, the media with varying degrees of success constitute separate systems. As we have seen, primitive man did not check the efficacy of his myths and rituals against empirical reality. Carpenter reports that informal research conducted on college students indicated that when confronted with an inconsistency between the media's report of an event and what actually happened, the students either accepted the inconsistency uncritically or tended to doubt reality.[18] The students were content that television and the other media were inwardly satisfying; that a media report might prove inaccurate could only be regarded unconsciously as an affront to the profound reality that the media represent. There are indications that some children "associate the ability to think with television."[19] The authority of family and community has been supplanted by that of the media.

Daniel Boorstin maintains that the content of the media is our popular or folk culture. Historically, folk cultures were decentralized and spontaneous; the modern folk culture is centralized and planned—it is a "creature of advertising, and in a sense it *is* advertising." As Horkheimer and Adorno have noted, the "culture industry" is fused with both advertising and entertainment. Advertisements have a profound impact upon us in their promulgation of a consumer-orientated lifestyle. The other side, of course, is that advertisements are a mirror of reality. As McLuhan observed, "The historians and archeologists will one day discover that the ads of our time are the richest and most faithful daily reflections that any society ever made of its entire range of activities.[20]

The relationship of the media to advertising is symbiotic. Carpenter has called attention to how advertising can affect media programming, not just because "he who pays the piper calls the tune," but also because those who write scripts for magazines and television are often told to look at the ads as a guide for what to write.[21] In a sense, media programming is an advertisement for the advertisements.

Advertising and Sociology

Advertising and the media have been compared to an oral culture; it is my contention that sociology (and I use the term here to include popular sociology, analysis of public opinion, and academic sociology) is the part of what is left of our literate culture which most embodies the mythical themes of the media and advertising. As McLuhan has observed: "Ads are not meant for conscious consumption. They are intended as subliminal pills for the subconscious in order to exercise a hypnotic spell, especially on sociologists."[22] Why does he single out sociologists? There are several reasons, I think—our methodologies, our theories, and the fact that we tend to study modern societies.

Raymond Aron once called sociology the "consciousness of industrial society." I do not know if he intended this statement to have two meanings, dialectically related. Yet this is the way I propose it be un-

derstood. Sociology at one and the same time informs industrial society about its behavior patterns and public opinion and is a reflection
in its methods and theories of the deepest mythical beliefs of industrial society. Positivistic sociology is incapable of a radically reflective
stance; it is doomed to describe and reinforce what is. As Max Horkheimer observed, positivistic sociology merely replicates on an intellectual level what a capitalistic, technological society is doing on economic, political, and social levels.[23] Moreover, insofar as it depends
upon questionnaires and interviews it is bound to take at face value
other people's explanations of their own behavior and the behavior of
others. And because most people's attitudes are an ideological reflection of existing social arrangements, whether sociology studies the objective or subjective side of social life, it reinforces social "reality."

Auguste Comte, founder of modern sociology, perfectly illustrates
the argument thus far. Comte believed in Human Progress, a theory
of history whose final stage was a utopian, industrialized society. Sociologists (social scientists) were to be the spiritual and moral guides in
our quest for utopia. Sociologists would use scientific methods to acquire "positive" knowledge in order to build the "positive" society.
The positive theory and methodology were as important as the utopian future in Comte's view; the former were a means to the latter.

Comte foresaw sociologists charting out the "normal" course of
progress. In this view the normal replaces the moral, for evolutionary
progress is a natural, continuous process of improvement. Sociologists, in studying behavior patterns and public opinion, could provide
us with a precise measure of the normal.

Embarrassed by Comte's too-obvious religiosity, positivistic sociologists today have publicly abandoned the idea of a utopian future but
have retained the positive methods and theories for apprehending
reality. Their commitment to Comte's utopian future has gone underground. Theory-building, grand theories which contain once-and-
for-all definitions of human nature and history, and the use of in-
ferential statistics to correlate attitudes all represent an attempt to
ferret out, to externalize, and to measure the normal. Sociological
knowledge thus acquired becomes a tool of advertising and the political state, which can better manipulate us as a result.

Insofar as advertising both makes use of sociological data and influences the people whose opinions sociology samples, it has created a

self-contained mythical universe. Advertising creates needs, titillates our desires and passions, and presents general human types to be emulated and mythical values to be believed. But it has to have a certain empirical base to begin with. This is where sociology comes in. Sociology naïvely tells the advertising industry (and government for that matter) what impact its propaganda is having upon our behavior and attitudes. A positivistic sociology can do no more than dutifully report on public opinion, which both creates and is created by advertising. This, I presume, is why McLuhan suggests that advertising works most effectively on the sociologists, pollsters, and public opinion analysts. They help to disseminate the good news of advertising through their popularized research reports and to provide the advertising industry with an overall sense of its effectiveness.

Sociology is the literate part of our mixed popular culture that most helps to spread the mythical values of advertising.

Levels of Discourse

The discourse to follow will be weaving back and forth among three levels: (1) oral culture in the form of the mass media and advertising; (2) literate culture in the form of sociology; and (3) ritualized patterns of social action. Chapter 2 will draw upon many examples from advertising and the media in its discussion of the sacred in modern culture. The principal reason is, as we will see later, that the sacred is always concrete. The media and advertising enable us to see images and hear sounds of what is sacred. Chapters 3 and 4, on symbol and myth, will concentrate on sociology as our literate popular culture even though examples from advertising and the media will be employed from time to time. The major reason for this is that the fullest and most detailed expressions of symbols and myths of evil will be found in the literate side of culture. Those found in advertising will be more diffuse and less rational.

In Chapter 5, on ritual, the level of emphasis will be on ritualized patterns of social action, although once again examples from the mass media will be used. Moreover, I will set forth a typology of modern rituals that range from those that are dramatically enacted to those that are fully and spontaneously lived out. In Chapter 6, which centers on rituals of transgression, the emphasis is placed on social action, principally because I am interested here in the impact of social structure on human action.

The following is a model that interrelates the different levels that have been discussed:

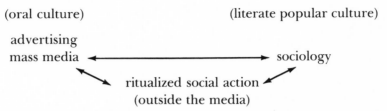

(oral culture)   (literate popular culture)

advertising
mass media ⟵————————————⟶ sociology
                ritualized social action
                (outside the media)

Myth and ritual exist on two separate levels—inside and outside the media. In primitive societies myth and ritual took place on only one level—outside the media. This would suggest that modern man experiences the world in a more fragmented, disjointed way. It is perhaps less possible for modern man to live entirely in the closed, autonomous world of the media than it was for primitive man to live in his unified world of myth and ritual, a world not yet seriously questioned by technology.

CHAPTER TWO

The Sacred of Transgression:
A Festival of Sex, Violence, Drugs,
and Revolution

We distinguish Good and Evil, but in our hearts,
we know they form an entity.
ROBERT MUSIL
The Man without Qualities

Carl Becker once remarked that the more brutal the present becomes, the more we tend to live in the past and the future or, he might have added, lose ourselves in ecstasy. Religious ecstasy is perhaps most identified with the cult of Dionysius, which, among other things, involved the transgression of sacred taboos. Sex, violence, role reversal, the consumption of enormous amounts of food and drink—in short, almost every excess—was permitted or, better yet, demanded during the Dionysian festival. Historians of comparative religion tell us that such festivals are nearly universal, that is, they exist in every society in which myth and ritual abound. Upon hearing this we smile, assuming that in our "demythologized" world myth and ritual, especially those of transgression, exist only in memory. But what if, despite our lack of awareness of it, we still live a mythical and ritualistic existence? Preposterous as it may seem to the scientist and technician, it is a hypothesis capable of being tested, for the sacred from which myth and ritual are nourished always leaves imprints.[1]

Concepts Related to the Sacred of Transgression

The sacred of transgression, specifically when evil is institutionalized in the sacred festival, represents a dialectic of deviant behavior and social control, a form in which deviant behavior becomes social control and social control becomes deviant. Now this dialectic has not been totally neglected by sociologists, but it has invariably been presented in muted form. The related concepts to follow fail to distinguish between secular and sacred situations in which rule violations are institutionalized.

In his classic work *American Society*, Robin Williams, Jr., formulated the concept of the "patterned evasion of norms," a situation in which "a publicly accepted norm is covertly violated on a large scale with the tacit acceptance or even approval of the same society or group, at least so long as violation is concealed."[2] It was difficult, however, in certain situations to distinguish an evasion of a norm from an alternative norm, a norm that is "widely accepted or acquiesced in, although of lower cultural value than the ideal but nominal standards."

Later Williams described the process in the emergence of a "large-scale" patterned evasion of norms:

1. For reasons functionally important to the social structure and the main value systems, a certain activity, thing, belief, etc., is prohibited and widely condemned.
2. But a large proportion of the socially powerful, and otherwise functionally essential, members of the relevant adult population demand the prohibited element.
3. Normative consensus is insufficient to prevent this demand from arising or to deter considerable numbers of individuals from catering to it.
4. But consensus is great enough to prevent a public repudiation of the norm itself. (This fact derives from 1 above.)
5. Many of those who violate or evade the norm hold "essential" status in the social system; there is accordingly a strong resistance to wholesale punishment. (See 2 above.)
6. Hence, the situation is handled by: (a) public affirmation of the norm; (b) covert acceptance of widespread violation and evasion; (c) periodic token or "ritualistic" punishment, and/or

punishment of those whose arrears unavoidably become public.[3]

For example, Prohibition resulted in a flourishing illicit drink trade, and societal condemnation of extramarital sex encourages prostitution.

The concept of the patterned evasion of norms places heavy emphasis on the evasion's being covert, that is, concealed from the public and not flaunted. It also suggests that the audience tacitly accepts the violation. The concept of the sacred of transgression, on the other hand, suggests that the transgressions are overt and are not tactfully ignored. For, as we will soon see, the transgressions have mythical importance in the sustenance of social order.

Synonymous with Williams's concept is Robert Merton's notion of the "institutionalized evasion of institutional rules." Merton defined two situations in which the institutionalized evasion of institutional rules might occur: "when practical exigencies confronting the group or collectivity (or significantly large parts of them) require adaptive behavior which is at odds with long-standing norms, sentiments, and practices or correlatively, when newly-imposed requirements for behavior are at odds with these deep-rooted norms, sentiments, and practices."[4]

In the former case, that of "cultural lag," a tension exists between a new social structure and certain traditional cultural norms so that the institutionalized evasion is quite likely the precursor of norms more congruent with the new structure. And in the latter case, that of "cultural conflict," a conflict ensues between a new set of norms and the previous but now disestablished norms, which are, however, still deeply ingrained (new norms versus traditional norms). Cultural-lag theory, which has previously been analyzed, has always expressed modern man's belief in technical progress by intimating that morals and politics are the cause of most social problems because they do not keep up with changes in the material, technical infrastructure. Cultural conflict theory was often used to explain the deviant behavior of immigrants, who brought with them a "presenting culture" in part at odds with American culture.

Whereas Williams was stressing the covert nature of transgression and its tacit approval, Merton seems to be emphasizing the transitory nature of conflict; for the major implication of cultural lag and cultural conflict is that the old (usually a moral norm) must give way to the new (whether social structure or a moral norm) because the latter is more functional.

The overarching similarity between the concepts beyond the obvious one of terminology (patterned evasion versus institutional evasion) is that both are cast in functionalist terms. For the functionalist, meaning resides in consequence—an act's meaning is its consequences—and not in human purpose. Williams sees the patterned evasion of norms acting to prevent a fatal rupture in the homeostasis of the social organism. Because in Merton's view cultural lag and cultural conflict are transitory, they are not overly detrimental to the social equilibrium. In both concepts the contradiction is muted either because it is covert or because it is short-lived. More difficult for a functionalist would be central and (more or less) permanent conflicts whose meaning could not be gauged exclusively by their consequences.

The final concept to be considered was formulated by Philip Rieff, who has been working toward a theory of culture for several decades. In the *Triumph of the Therapeutic* he introduced the concept of cultural remission. In Rieff's opinion, "culture is another name for a design of motives directing the self outward, toward those communal purposes in which alone the self can be realized and satisfied." The major functions of a culture are:

> (1) to organize the moral demands men make upon themselves into a system of symbols that make men intelligible and trustworthy of each other, thus rendering also the world intelligible and trustworthy; (2) to organize the expressive remissions by which men release themselves, in some degree, from the strain of conforming to the controlling symbolic, internalized variant readings of culture that constitute individual character.[5]

More practically, culture is a set of moral demands that include both controls and remissions. Cultural controls are authoritative definitions of what should and should not be done; cultural remissions are institutionalized releases from the controls. The releases are usually delimited and institutionalized to the point that they become the "unwitting part" of culture. In this respect sublimation represents the model of remission. What is sublimated, for example, sexual aggression, obviously contradicts a society's taboos against violence and sex, but what surfaces after sublimation, for example, mildly erotic dancing, does not overtly violate the taboos. In general the remissions do not contradict the controls, but when they do, the culture's integrity is threatened. "Whenever a releasing symbolic increases its jurisdiction to the point where it no longer serves to support the incumbent moral demands, but rather contradicts them, that culture is in jeopardy. Such freedoms were signatures on the death warrant of previous cultures."[6]

Rieff, like Williams and Merton, does not envisage as a matter of course a contradictory situation in which an overt act that violates an audience's norm is likewise openly institutionalized by that audience or, in Rieff's own terms, a situation in which an act is concurrently transgression and remission. Moreover, he suggests in the above quotation that should the remissive side of culture come to contradict the controls or interdicts, the culture is threatened. But this is exactly what the sacred of transgression provides for—transgression within, not outside, the existing social order.

The Sacred and the Profane Identified

The Technology/Sex Axis

If we live in a sacral world, exactly what is sacred? Following Jacques Ellul, I maintain that the relation between technology and sex on the one hand and between the nation-state and revolution on the other hand are sacred today.[7] Other relations are still sacred—for example, money and its transgression—but not nearly so intensely. The above are the major axes of the sacred.

Modern man is in awe of technology in exactly the way primitive man was in awe of nature. It is both security and threat. Technology is our succor: it guarantees our future, solves our problems, provides happiness, is the creator of order, yes, is even our new nature. Yet it threatens that future, for is it not technology that has provided nuclear weapons of total destruction? Likewise, in solving our problems, it inadvertently creates new problems—pollution and war, for example. Again, as the creator of order it gives rise to disorder through its repressive effects. Finally, as man's new nature it does not invariably enhance his self-esteem. Witness the plethora of advertisements in which man is invidiously compared to a machine. What am I armed with a shovel compared with a snow-blower?

Just as telling is man's tendency to depict himself as *homo faber*, to see his history as the history of technological achievements. As Rieff once noted, our preoccupation with progress and evolution goes hand in hand with a scorn for the past. Didn't history, *real* history, begin with the Industrial Revolution? Eliade's research on comparative religions has demonstrated that some societies only turn to their supreme god in cases of dire emergency.[8] But today every new fact, every new situation unregulated by technology, is an emergency. Communist and capitalist alike turn in supplication to technology to solve their social problems.

For the individual, technology provides happiness in the form of consumer goods and services. Advertising is an epiphenomenon of these goods and services; its existence is justified by its ability to make us buy. It turns goods and services into spiritual values. The American lifestyle is gradually becoming ascendant even in Communist countries. Technology is the world's great provider today. How could we resist considering it sacred?

Perhaps the clearest indicator of the sacred regard for technology is our preoccupation with questions of "how to." Technology is concerned not merely with how to produce a more efficient automobile or how to combat inflation: human techniques—techniques applied to control man—are omnipresent. From *How to Win Friends and Influence People* to *P.E.T.* to *How to Be Born Again*, the concern with technique is dominant.[9] Child-rearing, marital compatibility, the pursuit of happiness, success, and power—virtually every action and goal that used to be regulated by morality is now in the process of being regulated by technique. In a world to be adjusted to on the one hand and manipulated on the other hand, "how to" does not so much supplant "why" as it amalgamates it to itself. "How to" is meaning and purpose.

We are often told that science takes away a sense of mystery because it lays bare reality. But that is true at the theoretical level and for the individual scientist. At the level of application and operation, science actually induces a sense of the mysterious and even the occult. For who but the specialist and technician (and even here one is limited to his own specialty and his particular know-how) understands the inner working of machines, computers, bureaucracies, and the almost infinite number of techniques?

Immediately, however, objections are raised that technology could hardly be sacred with so many people criticizing and poking fun at it. But this reassuring view shows little insight into man's relationship to the sacred. Humor is a way of defending oneself against the sacred. Hysterical and contagious laughter in church has always been rather common. And who has not momentarily turned against his god in the face of continued adversity?

But what about sex? Is it as readily evident that sex is sacred? Yes, I think so. Just as writers have discussed the technologizing and politicizing of society, Maurice North claims that we are now confronted with the "sexualization of everything." [10] Explicitly, or more often implicitly, love is portrayed as erotic love or at least as dependent upon sex. Our sex manuals and textbooks tell us that over 50 percent of the population suffer from sexual problems. Marital happiness is contingent upon sexual adjustment. Even old people are not left alone, for popular magazines admonish them to maintain an active sex life in part for health reasons. Successful people, we are told, generally have a strong interest in sex. "Early to bed, late to rise, makes one healthy, wealthy, and wise" might well be the new slogan of the sex generation. No book sells like a book about sex, and our popular magazines invariably contain several articles about it. Pornography is an enormously successful business today. Children "need" scientific sexual education in the same way that decades ago children "needed" moral instruction about sex. Our concern is more with normal and scientific sexual adjustment than with "moral" sexual behavior. Many formerly immoral sexual practices—premarital sex, extramarital sex, homosexuality, and group sex—are everywhere in great evidence. The smashing of the old sexual taboos has not put an end to what Freud termed our "guilt culture"; rather it has merely substituted one form of guilt for another. For now people feel guilty not because they had sex outside of or before marriage, but because they have not had it, or have not had it often enough, or have not achieved enough orgasms for themselves or for their partners. Never before have so many worked so hard to achieve sexual ecstasy. Masters and Johnson are our gurus. All in all, happiness and even life itself are made contingent upon sexual fulfillment. Sex is indeed the elixir of life. No wonder our motto is Get It On! Yet one is struck by the obligatory nature of the new morality and the compulsiveness of those who adhere to it. It is nothing more nor less than inverted puritanism.

A recent study of sex manuals and textbooks concludes that these works advocate "the exaltation of sexuality." "Sex without guilt becomes the *sine qua non* of one's life. Sexual ecstasy becomes a type of spiritual ecstasy, and sexual pleasure is described as the ultimate experience." [11]

Another telling example of the sacred quality of sex is the use of subliminal messages in advertising. "Sex is the most frequently embedded word in the advertising industry," Wilson Bryan Key concluded from his extensive study of subliminal perception. He identified three ways of placing a word or picture in an advertisement so that it cannot ordinarily be seen at a conscious level but only at a subliminal or unconscious level. Virtually everything is associated with sex in media advertising, even death and violence. [12]

Bernice Martin's recent study of rock music concluded that overt sexuality was "its most precious symbol of liminality." Martin discovered that there was an "aggressive emphasis on raw sexuality," which, in turn, provided an escape from society and its conventions. [13]

Given that technology and sex are very important today, perhaps even sacred, what is the relation between them? McLuhan's book *The Mechanical Bride* broke new ground when it first appeared in 1951, for it showed both pictorially and verbally the sexualization of technical objects and the technologization of sex. He referred to the linking of technology and sex as the dominant pattern in advertising. The sexualization of technical objects reached its climax with the automobile and more recently, as Hunter Thompson has shown in *Hell's Angels*, with the motorcycle. It is not merely that voluptuous women are shown next to the automobile or motorcycle, implying that the use of the product will bring results. It goes deeper than that. The technological object is actually infused with human sexual properties: to possess this object is a sexual experience. The body of the automobile is often described in terms one would use to describe a woman—the advertisement calls attention to the car's sensuous curves, "satiny smoothness," and so on. The auto is referred to as a "date with a dream" or a "sweetheart." [14] Thus the auto becomes an attractive and desirable organism whose possession is sexual. Greeley too has pointed out the automobile-sex relationship in his analysis of the annual automobile show as a ritualized religious performance. Ernest Dichther once compared a "convertible to a mistress and a sedan to a wife." The automobile was only the first of many technical objects to become a sex symbol. Today, medical technology is often advertised in otherwise staid, medical-related journals by means of a voluptuous woman.[15]

But the opposite has occurred simultaneously. Sex has become mechanized. One obvious example is the tendency to focus on one part of the woman's body: for example, men often talk about being "leg men" or "breast men." A machine is composed of parts, some of which, when disassembled, are appreciated in themselves. Hence, the various parts of a woman's anatomy become the locus of a sexuality separated from its human context. The body comes to be seen as a love machine, all of whose parts can provide specific thrills in one way or another.

Along with the disembodied view of sex, advertising sometimes portrays the woman as an interchangeable part in an enormous machine. Commenting upon an advertisement in which four women in girdle and bra were in an assembly line, McLuhan notes that the line implies power, the power to set it in motion. Another ad begins with the question, "What makes a gal a good number?" to which McLuhan replies, "Looking like a number of other gals." Personality and attractiveness have been reduced to techniques so that "love goddesses" should all be alike. There is enormous gratification in losing oneself in a crowd, statistical or otherwise. "Telephone numbers of girls who are good numbers, smooth numbers, hot numbers, slick numbers, Maxfactorized, streamlined, synthetic blonds—these are at once abstract and exciting," McLuhan notes, before summing up, "Girls become intoxicating 'dates' when they are recognizable parts of a vast machine."[16]

Perhaps the movie *The Demon Seed* most explicitly links technology to sex by having a computer "desire" to violate a woman and have a child by her. The power of sex is transferred to technology, just as the power of technology is transferred to sex. But there are many other less explicit examples, such as the television series *Star Trek*. In numerous episodes, Captain Kirk as symbolic of good technology was threatened by a voluptuous woman, who represented bad technology.

The Nation-State/Revolution Axis

The nation and the political state (government and its bureaus) are unduly important to us today, each in a somewhat different manner. The nation is, among other things, the collective identity of a society. We think of ourselves as Americans, Frenchmen, Italians, Japanese. It is not just a matter of patriotic slogans: "America, love it or leave it"; "This is the greatest country on earth" ; "Americans are the most generous people in the world"; no, it goes beyond this. Nationalism is more than a thought—it is a romantic feeling. People actually fall in love with their nation. It is nothing less than a form of collective narcissism.

The tribe, the race, the nation, and the political state have always been considered sacred by those who shared such collective identities. Nationalism only became rife, however, in the late eighteenth and early nineteenth centuries as a consequence of the decline in the power of the local community and extended family. In the latter half of the nineteenth century, romanticism took a turn that led to its wholehearted support of the nation. Early romanticism championed the individual, especially his aesthetic endeavors. A forerunner of modern existentialism, it opposed Christian morality, industrialization, and whatever else restricted the individual. Eventually, Niebuhr argues, the romantics sought an identity more than purely individualistic. Turning away from self-apotheosis, which was pretentious and implausible to others, they found the "larger individual" in the nation. Each nation was deemed unique, a quality that was actually more important to them than individuality. "This collective individual then supplants the single individual as the centre of existence and the source of meaning."[17]

Tocqueville, who observed the growth of nationalism in America in the 1840s, saw that it was tied to the principle of popular sovereignty. Democracy and the desire for equality only add fuel to the fires of nationalism. In an apt comparison he noted that "the people reign over the American political world as God rules over the universe. It is the cause and end of all things; everything rises out of it and is absorbed back into it."[18]

The nationalism of the nineteenth century gave rise to the sacred adoration of the nation in the twentieth century.[19] Hitler's declaration that the fatherland was sacred left no room for doubt. Mussolini, Stalin, and Mao followed suit. Now the nation became the arbiter of morality: anything that furthers the cause of one's country is good; whatever hinders it is evil. Ultimately "national security" can be employed to justify any action no matter how seemingly deplorable.

Nationalism is also evident in the advertisement of consumer goods and services. Think of the countless products that are associated with America: Kinney's is the "great American shoe store"; Sears is "where America shops"; Pepsi and Coca-Cola link their products to friendship, fun, and being an American. Such ads are quite powerful, for they bring together two sacred forces—consumer goods and services and the nation.

Hand in hand with the rise of nationalism has been the growth and centralization of power in the political state. Today man expects the government to do everything for him—to maintain law and order; to provide highways, cheap food, clean water, education, and sanitary sewers; to care for the sick, the poor, and the handicapped; and to guarantee military security. He is upset about inefficiency and waste in government because it reduces his services. We desire to live in an orderly and efficient society, one that guarantees and is guaranteed. Why does man expect so much from the state and, at times, identify with it?

Ortega y Gasset suggests that mass-man (average man—a statistical concept become real), feeling anonymous, senses kinship with the anonymous power of the state and comes to believe that "he is the state."[20] And in so believing, mass-man will demand that the state's machinery be used to squelch not only rebellious acts but also creative acts—any acts that set individuals off from the majority. Nietzsche would have called it re-sentiment.

Tocqueville clearly saw how Americans were becoming increasingly attached to the state: "Our contemporaries therefore are much less divided than is commonly supposed. They do argue constantly about who should have sovereign power, but they readily agree about the duties and rights of that power. They all think of the government as a sole, simple, providential, and creative force."[21] He also states that with the "increasing love of well-being" (property, money, happiness), democratic peoples fear crime and rioting to the point of enlarging the powers of the state to insure public tranquility. Finally, he skillfully argues that equality makes men both independent and weak. Independence destroys the bonds of reciprocity, freeing one from the obligation to help others. At the same time, however, it relieves others from having to come to one's assistance. Therefore, one will turn toward the state as an outside power for help because one's peers are equally cold and impotent.

On the contemporary scene Ellul ironically asks the question, "Who really loves man?"[22] Today only he who meets the material needs of another is thought to love him. Are not our needs increasingly being met by the state? Not directly in every case, but at least indirectly. State regulations abound. And then there is the military state and the welfare state. Liberals support the latter, conservatives the former. Both groups agree about the necessity for a strong state, but they disagree about how best to spend its resources. Do we not tend to love in return him who loves and protects us? Today man's heart belongs to the state.

Nevertheless, man tends to chafe at the power behind the service and solicitousness. The reason for this is the one given earlier for man's ambivalence toward technology: the state is both security and threat. It is threat because no individual, no special interest group, no social class can control it. If it is uncontrollable, it is also unpredictable. Therefore, to a certain extent man fears the state.

In summary, the state meets man's need for identity, protection, and "love." With regard to identity there is overlap between the nation and the state. Man identifies with both. The nation needs the state, just as the state needs the nation. Inexorably linked, the nation-state is one.

Concurrent with the rise of nationalism in the nineteenth century was the growth of revolutionary fervor. Actually the two were often part of the same movement. Eric Hobsbawm notes that after 1830 the revolutionary movement in Europe divided, one segment having been transformed into "self-consciously nationalist movements."[23] Today, however, revolution is directed against the nation-state. Marx and Lenin feared the power of the state, Marx perhaps more than Lenin. Revolution has been pronounced sacred by Lenin, Mao, Castro, and countless other revolutionaries. No one is more dedicated today than the revolutionary, who often resembles the religious convert in his zeal. Whether one is a member of PLO or the IRA makes little difference. The behavior and attitudes are identical. Irrational, intransigent, willing to make any sacrifice, the revolutionary lives in a mythical universe. Even if eventually successful, the revolution could never begin to bring to fruition a fraction of the revolutionary's illusory dreams.

Noteworthy too is the gradual vulgarization of revolution.[24] The word is used to describe almost any change. For example, we hear about a "revolution in women's lingerie," "a revolution in automobile engineering," and a "revolution in taste." Revolution is further vulgarized by its constant presence in television news and in television drama. It provides vicarious enjoyment and involvement at the same time that it makes revolution comfortable. To a certain extent we all like to think of ourselves today as revolutionaries. Did not America the nation undergo a revolutionary birth? And are we not all in favor of change and progress?

At face value revolution is an attack upon and transgression of everything that the nation-state stands for. The nation-state is order; revolution is disorder. The nation-state is abstract; revolution is concrete. The superficial antagonism between the nation-state and revolution notwithstanding, there is compatibility at a deeper level. Extreme nationalism first flowered during the French Revolution. Who was more of a nationalist than Robespierre with his talk about the martyrs of the Revolution? The martyrs were not Christian but rather *French* martyrs. The French Revolution remains even today the symbol of the French nation.[25] As we have already seen, many revolutionaries of the nineteenth century were ardent nationalists. Saul Alinsky chastised American revolutionaries of the 1960s for desecrating symbols of the American nation, for example, wearing emblems of the American flag on the seats of their pants. He argued that the revolutionaries should claim such symbols for themselves because they were more representative of what America was all about than their opponents were.

Although many have asserted that everything today is profane, my argument may lead the reader to assume everything has become sacred. What escapes the two axes just described? A preliminary step in clarifying this issue involves identifying the profane. I suggest that today nature is profane—although it was sacred for primitive man. Nature has become the secular, the free zone in which man can live without great fear and reverence. Escape into a profane existence characterizes much of the current "return to nature." Nevertheless, our campers and elaborate camping gear vilify our attempt, for it seems that we cannot do anything without turning it into a technique.

At the same time there is another tendency at work: the resacralizing of nature. Surely the religious fervor of health-food advocates, conservationists, and exercise buffs is evident. There is no question that for some individuals nature has once again become sacred. Still, for the majority nature is the province of the profane, a free zone into which to escape.

The Sacred and the Profane Defined

Mircea Eliade, who has devoted much of his life to the study of comparative religion, has provided us with a sensitive understanding of primitive man's sense of the sacred.[26] For primitive man the sacred is the source of existence or reality. By living close to it and its order (rituals, taboos, laws, and so forth) man is alive to the purpose and significance of reality. The world thus becomes full of meaning and, consequently, intelligible to man.

The reason, it would seem, that the sacred is equivalent to reality is that it is experienced as power, as that which is beyond man's own power. This power induces both fear and awe in the onlooker. It is as if he is compelled to regard great manifestations of power as sacred, for his very life is at stake. The sun, lightning, rain, military weapons, and automobiles all share the power to enhance life or to kill.

The sacred, Eliade argues, manifests itself in profane or secular forms. Such a concrete manifestation is called a hierophany, the paradoxical situation of a sacred power's assuming a secular appearance. Totems and idols are different types of hierophanies. The sacred, moreover, may be either particular or general. Although the particular occurs more often, there are examples of societies for which the entire cosmos was sacred.[27]

It is often argued that the sacred is that which man esteems most highly or even worships. Sometimes it is seen as a quality of a deity. In this latter sense the sacred becomes a category of religion, whereas in actuality the reverse is true—religion is but one form the sacred may assume.[28] Perhaps religion is best regarded as a more complex expression of man's sense of the sacred.

How does man subjectively experience something as sacred? Once again Eliade has provided an answer in his discussion of primitive man's experience of the sky as sacred:

The transcendental quality of "height," or the supra-terrestrial, the infinite, is revealed to man all at once, to his intellect as to his soul as a whole. The symbolism is an immediate notion of the whole consciousness, of the man, that is, who realizes himself as a man, who recognizes his place in the universe; these primeval realizations are bound up so organically with his life that the same symbolism determines both the activity of his subconscious and the noblest expressions of his spiritual life. It really is important, therefore, this realization that though the symbolism and religious values of the sky are not deduced logically from a calm and objective observation of the heavens, neither are they exclusively the product of mythical activity and non-rational religious experience.[29]

It would appear, then, that man's subjective experience of the sacred is a dialectic of the objective qualities of certain phenomena and the human need to attribute ultimate purpose and meaning to his own life and the life of the cosmos. A theoretical question that immediately arises is whether primitive man's sense of the sacred was more conscious or unconscious. From what Eliade has written, it would seem to be less a logical construct than an immediate experience on both conscious and unconscious levels. Moreover, primitive man had no *concept* of the sacred. Modern man, on the other hand, has a concept of the sacred, but he appears to apply it only to things that *were* regarded as sacred, rather than to what is currently sacred. Hence, modern man's sense of the sacred would appear to be more unconscious, if only because his consciousness of the sacred applies only to the past. In other words, modern man thinks that he has outgrown the game of the sacred, which only a silly, superstitious people would play. Primitive man might not have had a concept of the sacred, but at least he "knew what he knew."

Without providing a once-and-for-all definition, I suggest that the following characteristics are part of the dynamics of the sacred: (1) absolute value is attributed to it; (2) it is the source of meaning; (3) myths and rituals are developed to express and live out the sacred order; (4) it is protected (sometimes by taboos) from the profane; (5) it is ambiguous in value.

There are few ideas more difficult to comprehend, I think, than the ambiguity of the sacred. The great work of Roger Caillois and of

Mircea Eliade on the subject make this point evident.[30] As a primitive experience, the sacred is a characteristic or quality that is attributed to those phenomena that appear most powerful or unusual. This is, of course, not to deny a certain objectivity (socially constructed) to it, but simply to emphasize its subjective and thus relative character.

What is sacred is simultaneously held in greatest esteem and greatest fear. It is the source of life and the power to take life away. From it man expects all rewards, success, and power; yet as a force greater than he, it might bring punishment, failure, and degradation. It is at once both desired and dreaded, attractive and repellent, respected and feared, respectful and fearful. Man is ambivalent toward the sacred: he respects that which is greater than himself, desiring to possess and control it; but, in addition, he fears it, wishing to avoid its negative powers.[31]

Man's psychological ambivalence toward the sacred is one aspect of a two-sided movement, the other being the sociological ambiguity of the sacred as expressed in its contradictory poles. Before developing this idea, let us briefly examine the concept of the profane.

The profane stands in direct opposition to the sacred—it is everything the sacred is not. It is the "world of ease and security,"[32] a neutral zone in which man can escape the power of the sacred and the heightened effect it produces. Profane actions in themselves are without meaning, for only the sacred is of absolute value.

However, the contradictory meanings the terms sacred and profane have had at any one moment is perhaps the surest sign that by themselves they are inadequate to express the complexity of the world of the sacred and profane.

The profane has had two quite different but nonetheless related meanings: it is the secular, the common, the neutral; and it is that which desecrates the holy. Historically the profane in its first sense was safe or clean for man but not for the gods, while in the second it was safe for neither. From our previous discussion we see that nature fits the first meaning and sex and revolution fit the second.

But the sacred as well has had two meanings: it is the holy, the source of positive power, and it is that which desecrates the holy, the source of negative power. The logic is that the negative power that desecrates the holy is not the holy; so it is in one sense profane or not sacred. At the same time, however, it has the power to make the holy unholy and thus it is sacred.

If we examine the definitions of the sacred and the profane together, we notice that their second meanings are identical: that which
desecrates the holy. Numerous studies have noted this ambiguity
in language in respect to the sacred and the profane.[33] In modern
English this ambiguity is preserved only in our definition of the
profane, which refers simultaneously to the safe or neutral and to the
desecrating.

All of this prompted Roger Caillois in his brilliant study *Man and the
Sacred* to suggest that rather than two terms, sacred and profane,
there are actually three terms: sacred of respect, sacred of transgression, and profane.[34] The term sacred of transgression refers to the
overlap between the definitions of sacred and profane. In this sense
Caillois's concept takes into account that the desecrating or impure is
sacred at the very moment it is profaning the holy—it is sacredly profane and profanely sacred. The power of the holy is transferred to
that which desecrates it.

The sacred, then, is the relation between the two terms or poles,
respect and transgression. But why this ambiguity of value?[35] Does it
reflect mere stupidity or a basic ambivalence toward good and evil? It
certainly is not stupidity, and ambivalence is not in itself a sufficient
answer. First of all, we should note the dialectical nature of aesthetic
and moral concepts: good is only definable in relation to evil and vice
versa. This is obvious. But, as Emile Durkheim observed, societies require that evil be committed and not just conceptualized. Second,
man's ambivalence toward evil suggests that evil is attractive and that
its expression needs to be provided for. Third, there is man's need to
control even that which is deemed most reprehensible. As Ellul puts
it, evil must be provided for in order "that the world should not be a
horrible chaos in which All and Nothing would be equally present and
equally possible."[36] Finally, evil is required so that the social order can
be renewed. This renewal took place in primitive society in the institution of the sacred festival, a time for the systematic violation of sacred
taboos.

The sacred of transgression is institutionalized to the extent that it
is set within the context of myth and ritual. Contradictions on the concrete level of the sacred (respect versus transgression) are resolved in
myth and ritual. Almost every society has possessed a myth about the
creation of the world, of the passage from chaos to cosmos.[37] The
myth of creation, a cosmogony, is sacred history, a fixed point of refer-

ence to what is "real" and "meaningful," for profane time is relative and thus meaningless. Mythical time, especially the "beginnings" or the time of creation, is that moment when the gods instituted order into the world and when the ancestors lived in relative bliss. Reality for primitive man is mythical time, a repetition and renewal of the creation of the world. For him secular history was terrifying because it was a time of becoming and thus unknown. Mythical time, on the other hand, signaled the known of being. The creation of the world, albeit perfect (or in some cases to be perfected at the end of the world), had to be repeated ritualistically in order for man to participate in it. If man refused to renew creation, he was doomed to a totally profane existence. In the primitive ontology "events were reduced to categories" and "individuals to archetypes."[38] The renewal of mythical time transported man back in time, as it were, or, in a sense, made the mythical time come to bear in the present: historical time was abolished.

Festivals, one of whose main components was the orgy, represented a return to the chaos preceding creation. Chaos was a stage in which things were undifferentiated, were formless or without order. After the festival (chaos) the taboos (creation) were reinstated. Creation, however, emerged from chaos, the source of fecundity. Hence, if creation was to be renewed, the world had to be returned to the time of chaos. (Here the ambiguity of the sacred is manifest.) Once creation was complete, chaos was once again evil. Sacredly transgressive acts were only to be performed during the festival, whereupon they signaled the return to the fertile period immediately preceding creation. At other times these same acts were subject to the most severe punishments because then they represented the chaos that threatened the new creation. For primitive man, creation, the victory over chaos, was never total or complete. During the year chaos in the forms of disease, famine, suffering, and transgression inevitably crept back in.

Chaos was a time of ecstasy that the crowd achieved through total unity and there was no greater basis for unity than wholesale transgression. Hence, it was not without a certain attraction. Eliade has pointed out that there are two distinct types of nostalgia for the "beginnings": a desire to return to the primordiality of the ancestors after creation (sacred history) and a desire to lose oneself in the primordial totality of the chaos preceding creation. For those societies in which the second type occurred, there was an inordinate emphasis on rites of transgression: orgies, violence, status reversal, and ecstasy. This sometimes, but not always, occurred in societies Eliade terms pessimistic. Victor Turner has suggested that a repressive social structure or rapid social change can create an exaggerated need for, among other things, transgression.[39]

So far we have been considering transgression or desacralization in a static way. Does the concept take an additional meaning when it is considered historically? Earlier we saw that both poles of the sacred axes are sacred, not just the holy, and that the power of the holy is transferred to that which desecrates it. Historically this is also the case, though now we are talking about one sacred *axis* desecrating another sacred *axis*.

Ellul has suggested several examples of desacralization in Western civilization.[40] For instance, Christianity succeeded in desacralizing the sacred of the Roman Empire, but then Christianity as a desacralizing force itself became sacred (holy) in the form of the medieval church. Later, Ellul argues, the Reformation desacralized the medieval church; however, the Bible, which had been relied upon to dispute absolute church authority, was made sacred. Every major desacralizing force eventually becomes holy. Historically, then, the impure becomes pure; transgression becomes respect.

For several centuries now science and its handmaiden technology have been desecrating the Christian sacred (the Bible). Although science has disputed Christian theology on an intellectual level, technology, which has absorbed science to itself, has desacralized the Christian social order. Remember that the sacred is the basis of social order, for it provides meaning. Thus the sacred order is concurrently a moral order. Technology has increasingly become the basis of morality at the expense of Christian morality. This new technological morality is based on consideration of efficiency, success, and the normal. Its modal expression is "how to," the realm of human techniques (techniques to manipulate man). Today we are attempting to regulate behavior through technology, when previously it had largely been done through ethics.[41]

The Bible has not been the only hierophany for modern Christians. Sex was considered sacred, as it has been in numerous societies throughout history. Paul Ricoeur, in his phenomenological and cross-cultural study of evil, noticed that impurity was so often *sexual* impurity. For at least this century, sex as a sacred of respect has been desecrated. All the old sexual taboos are violated. Adultery, premarital intercourse, free love, public displays of sex are all commonplace. But rising up from the ruins of the old sexual morality has been the new sexual morality. The old morality prohibited sexual behavior outside of marriage, whereas the new morality advocates, yes, even demands, sexual behavior with few restrictions as a form of "self-fulfillment." Yet the new sexual morality actually does not leave one free. One is supposed to be efficient and successful in sexual performance; therefore, we have witnessed the technologizing of sex. The new technological morality and the new sexual morality become one at this point. Gabriel Vahanian has pointed out that a "physiological technology" helped to accomplish the desacralization of the old sexual morality and the resacralization of sex. Sex is now sacred over against the technological order.[42]

What has been the major force in desacralizing the Christian social order—the technology/sex axis—has itself become resacralized. But the role of sex is complicated. Historically it has worked to desacralize sex as a sacred of respect (part of the Christian sacred order), but it has emerged now as a sacred of transgression in respect to technology. Hence, what was a sacred of transgression historically—technology—has become a sacred of respect, and what was a sacred of respect historically—sex—has become a sacred of transgression. In the old Christian sacred order, to violate a sexual taboo was a transgression. Violation did occur even on an organized basis. Geoffrey Ashe has described the various secret societies and cults devoted in part to sexual transgression over the past several centuries.[43] Gradually, however, the sexual taboos were so generally violated that it became apparent sex was no longer holy. Yet in the very act of desecrating sex as a sacred of respect it was resacralized, but now as a transgressor of the technological order. Just why sex is linked to the technological order will be explored in the next section.

The reader may wonder why the nation-state/revolution axis has not been discussed as a desacralizing force in history. Certainly it is not because it played no role. Rather it is because Christianity had accommodated itself more readily and earlier to political power than to technological consumption and to eros. Furthermore, the technology/sex axis is perhaps the stronger of the two, if only in the sense that the political state is, as José Ortega y Gasset saw in 1930, at bottom "a matter of technique." The state is organizational and political technique. Vahanian has shown that technology is man's major sense of orientation today, just as history was previously and nature before that. However, the sacred axes are inexorably intertwined so that political power (nation-state/revolution axis) did contribute to the desacralization of the Christian sacred order.[44]

Caillois's Theory of the Sacred Applied

In Caillois's theory of the sacred several things stand out: (1) the ambiguity of value; (2) the dialectical transference of power from the holy to the impure; (3) the deeper similarity of the opposite poles of the sacred. These ideas will be developed in respect to the two sacred axes previously identified. The nation-state/revolution axis will be handled first because it is less complicated.

Bertrand de Jouvenel's brilliant book *On Power* clearly demonstrates that the "true historical function of revolutions is to renovate and strengthen Power [the political state]."[45] His analysis of the French and Russian revolutions shows that the most important effect of revolution is the institutionalization of a new power even greater than its predecessor. The Russian anarchist Bakunin clearly saw that the dictatorship of the proletariat would not be temporary and would never become of the proletariat.

Ortega y Gasset observes that the state was set up to serve society, but now this relationship has been reversed. Moreover, the state has a monopoly on violence. As he puts it, "Statism is the higher form taken by violence and direct action when these are set up as standards." Ellul, following de Jouvenel, argues that the state is a "permanent aggressor" in society and that by destroying institutions such as the community and kinship that mediate between it and the people, it appears as a "permanent revolution in the eyes of society."[46]

The common denominator of the nation-state and revolution is political power. De Jouvenel has ferreted out its historical and sociological "laws." Its nature is to attack and destroy political and social authority and to manipulate the common people as a vehicle to accomplish this end. Inevitably power destroys the society and its order. As de Jouvenel puts it, "Not the form of the state but the nature of power is responsible for this tendency." Although in revolutionary societies the "state acknowledges its revolutionary function and the people accept it, only one revolution is possible because the state has acquired a monopoly of revolution and, therefore, every political power claims to be leading the political revolution to its completion." Hence, the state has become permanent revolution, and revolution is "the crisis of the development of the state."[47]

It is readily apparent that revolution is a desecration of the nation-state as holy. Revolution is self-consciously and admittedly directed against it. Less clear is the fact that political power underlies this axis and that both poles are simultaneously sacred. But the technology/sex axis presents greater problems, for sex does not appear to be a transgressor of the technological order.

Technology provokes both dread and lust; it repels and attracts. We fear technology because it might destroy us, as evidenced by the threat of nuclear war and pollution. At the same time, however, we are attracted to it, principally because of the consumer goods and services it provides. The sacred has to have its attractive and appealing side as well as its forbidding and dangerous side. Therefore, man is ambivalent toward technology, just as he is toward any sacred phenomenon.

Previously we noted that there is something strange at work in the sexualization of technical objects on the one hand and the technologization of sex on the other hand. It is the dialectical transformation of a thing into its opposite. Technology is mediated, abstract, rational, efficient, and complex; sex, on the other hand, is immediate, concrete, instinctual, inefficient, and simple. What phenomena could be more opposite? Hence, in the sexualization of technical objects we find the attributes of sex transferred to the machine so that its possession and use is an orgiastic experience. Likewise, the technologizing of sex means that the properties of technology are transferred to sex so that it becomes abstract and efficient.

Nevertheless, there is a common denominator to technology and sex—power, the spirit of conquest, the desire to possess and dominate. It is evident, I presume, that technology can be thus characterized. But sex? We have to cut through the ideological neon lights that dazzle us in order to see sex as it usually is. Freud saw sex realistically, though his insight atrophied into a metaphysical truth. Human love is eros, "an appetite, a yearning desire, which is aroused by the attractive qualities of its object."[48] Eros is not necessarily only a physical, sexual appetite. For Plato, eros included the spiritual love of the god. Over the centuries, however, it has come to be identified with physical love. Whether it is thought of as essentially spiritual or essentially physical, it remains an appetite. Our appetites lead us to attempt to possess that which we desire. Thus we often talk about lust in a way that suggests that anything can be its object. The Protestant theologian Karl Barth more than once referred to religion as a lust. Among the appetites, however, sex is one of the strongest if not actually the strongest and most devastating. More important, it is widely perceived as such. We can thus distinguish between sex and sexuality just as Kierkegaard did between the sensual and sensuality. Sensuality is an attitude toward the sensual as sexuality is an attitude toward sex. It is the collective act of sacralizing sex that produces sexuality.

The underlying basis of the nation-state/revolution axis is political power, whereas that of the technology/sex axis is possession (personal power). The former appeals to man as a member of the social group, the latter to man as an individual. Therefore the sacred axes, as the basis of social order, control man even in his most individualistic expressions and actions.

Technology provides enormous power that, although appearing to be harnessed to its uses, actually resides in the technical system. Today sex plays the role of going against the technological order, for what is less rational, calm, deliberate, and efficient than orgasm, the ultimate in the instinctual and irrational? It represents an attack upon the repression and boredom of the technical system and an attempt to become autonomous and to assert one's self in the face of necessity and collectivization. There is in sexual transgression, then, a turning against the power of the holy—technology. In the very act of transgression the attributes and powers of the holy are transferred to that which desecrates it—sex. As we have already seen, this indeed is the situation: sex is regarded as the source of power and life to the same extent as technology is. The linkage is through opposition on the manifest level but compatibility on a deeper, more hidden level. The opposition is reason, mediation, and efficiency (technology) versus instinct, spontaneity, and inefficiency (sex). The compatibility is the spirit of conquest, the eroticism, and the narcissism that underlie the technology/sex axis. Still it is more than mere compatibility that disarms sex as a revolutionary force; rather, it is its institutionalization.[49]

Perhaps a clue to why sex is the sacred of transgression today has been provided by Mary Douglas. She argues that symbolism about the individual body is largely determined by the kink of social body one is part of.[50] Technique is the basis of the social order today.[51] Sex is the primary symbol of the human body today. Both technology and sex represent power and the spirit of conquest and possession. Sex is of man's body; technology is but an extension of it. For the individual, sex is that which is most similar to his society. Moreover, by appearing dissimilar it provides a safe outlet for going against society. Hence, sex as a symbol of the individual is also symbolic of society.

Vahanian suggests that for most of Western civilization man has seen himself as spirit or soul.[52] Some Christians might object that this is a Greek concept, but it certainly has had wide acceptance in the Christian West. Now, he claims, we see ourselves in relation to our bodies. In a culture of radical immanentism (denying any transcendent reality) where would spirit or soul come from, if not from the body? Sex as man's strongest and most devastating instinct has become the chief symbol of the body.

The spirit of individual conquest, the desire to possess and dominate, is best seen and understood in consumption. Technology's overwhelming importance to the individual lies in the goods and services it provides for his consumption. These are our idols. Sex too is an object of consumption. Never before has sex been so programmed and packaged. But what does consumption really mean? Its very repetition in everyday speech almost dulls the mind to its meaning. To consume is to increase, to increase one's comfort and one's power. The power of that which is consumed is transferred to the consumer, and at the same time the consumer becomes the thing consumed.[53] Technology as the extension of man in a world of radical immanentism represents an attempt of man to make his dominion omnipresent. And while the frantic consumption of sex is quite different on one level, on another there is no difference. For compulsive consumption, whatever the object, remains compulsive consumption. Completing the dialectic, the frantic and frenzied consumption of sex has become increasingly technologized.

Previously I alluded to technological goods and services as idols. But, in another sense, they seem closer to totems. As a variant of hierophany, totemism is an expression of man's enormous dependency upon nature. Primitive man's very existence was contingent upon nature and his relationship to it. Given the domination of nature in man's everyday life, it was inevitable that nature would be regarded as sacred, just as today it is inevitable that technology and the nation-state should be so regarded. Usually, however, not nature in general but certain things in nature were regarded as sacred. A particular rock, a tree, the sun, an animal manifested the sacred, which is always embedded in something tangible. In this way the sacred keeps man on the level of the concrete, whereas myth allows him to escape it.[54] A totem animal was a certain species of animal that became symbolic of a tribe. The animal's prosperity was linked to the tribe's survival.[55] The totem animal was protected by taboos from slaughter or misuse. Of course, during the sacred festival the totem animal would be consumed, demonstrating once again the ambiguity of the sacred. Totemism demonstrates that man saw his self-increase as intimately tied to preserving the abundance of nature. Hence, many taboos were prohibitions directed against man's using up nature.

Technology's supplanting nature as sacred has meant that we live in a situation where our self-increase is not tied to conserving but to using up. For it is only through mass consumption that the economy can continue to grow. This is why many taboos have disappeared from the modern world. All our taboos are positive today—we live under an imperative to consume. Therefore, the ethic demanding consumption (which advertising promulgates) stands in the same relation to technology as taboos against consumption stand to nature. The import of this is enormous. Although primitive man saw himself as part of nature, nature was seen as much grander and more powerful. At best one could temporarily harness the forces of nature in ritual. But now with the sacred in society—in technology and the nation-state—there are no checks on human power. For technology and the nation-state are human creations, and we have linked our future to our own power. We see no need to check the growth of power, for we regard it as sacred. The result of this is the material and spiritual destruction so much in evidence everywhere unchecked human power is both a material and spiritual reality.

Interestingly, the ambiguity of the sacred is not expressed in taboo–violation of taboo but in technological consumption–sexual consumption. The nation-state/revolution axis is set up according to the taboo–violation of taboo pattern. But the technology/sex axis is more complicated. It involves two types of actions that are indirectly related. It is not a matter of consumption–nonconsumption but technological consumption–sexual consumption. The consumption is similar, whereas the content of what is consumed is manifestly dissimilar (although at a deeper level there is similarity).

The Festival and the Interrelationship
of the Sacred Axes

The sacred festival, part of which represents the institutionalization of transgression, will be dealt with at greater length in Chapter 5. However, a few preliminary remarks and examples are in order here. In primitive societies the festival was the yearly occasion for orgies, spontaneous acts of violence, and the consumption of enormous amounts of food, alcohol, and drugs. These transgressive acts represented the return to chaos, the necessary fertile period preceding creation.

Today the only yearly celebration that even remotely resembles the festival is New Year's Eve. However, Eliade has observed that religious rites need not be celebrated on an exact periodic basis; they can occur more frequently.[56] Later I will argue that although the rites of transgression and rites of expulsion appear to occur sporadically, their occurrence might be part of a cyclical pattern even if not a yearly one (see Epilogue). What then, if anything, approximates the sacred festival? I think that one would have to include rock concerts (especially the open-air variety), urban riots, the riots during and after sports events, and the rites of spring practiced on many college campuses. In addition to those festivals with more or less open membership are those that are restricted to members (secret societies such as Hell's Angels and the Manson family). Common to these events and secret societies are sex, violence, drugs, and orgiastic music.

Though not sacred in themselves, violence, drugs, and music are religious expressions, in part through their association with sex and rebellion against the technological order. Eliade observes that "whatever is not directly sacred becomes so because of its participation in a symbol."[57] There are many kinds of violence, but the religious variant is the anarchical kind pursued for its ecstatic effect. Likewise with drugs and music: they become religious when engaged in for ecstasy and communion with others.

The synthesis of sex and violence is of particular importance here. De Sade discovered that the singleminded pursuit of sexual thrills ultimately led one to sadistic or masochistic acts. He stressed what Nietzsche and Freud after him would reaffirm, namely, that pleasure and pain are dialectically related. Certainly Keats's poem "On Melancholy" makes this point at the level of imagination and reverie. But de Sade is focusing on the physical as well as the psychological. The further excursions into the realm of violent sex, especially those which receive tacit approval, for example, certain forms of kinky sex, are simply an intensified protest.

Sex, whatever its form, symbolically expresses man's rebellion against the technological order; so do violence, drugs, and popular music, though to a lesser extent. This is why they occur together not only in festivallike rituals today but also in the media. As a transgressive value and act, revolution likewise has strong media representation. One might even make a case for the media's being the main source or the perpetrator of the festival today! Let us briefly look at examples of transgressive acts both in and out of the media with special attention given to the interrelations of the sacred axes.

An extremely important example of normalized transgression is "disco." The atmosphere of the discotheque is erotic—the clothes, make-up, music, visual images, and the dancing. Some of the dance steps and movements simulate sexual intercourse, others a more violent sexuality. In one of the most famous discotheques, Club 54, the use of alcohol and drugs was reportedly very extensive. Ecstasy derives from the rhythmic beat of the music, the alcohol and drugs, and the repetition of the dance movements.

The Jim Jones cult almost perfectly exemplifies the dialectical relationship of the sacred axes. Sex, violence, drugs, and revolution were all in evidence and, especially for Jones, increasingly a preoccupation. Jones saw his cult as a revolutionary movement, but, interestingly, his own behavior seemed to point more and more toward a nonpolitical fascination with sex, violence, and drugs.

Of course sex and revolution are inexorably linked in the public imagination in the commonplace slogan "sexual revolution." Some see sex as a revolutionary force, revolution from "below the waist," whereas others see revolution as an erotic and festivallike activity.

The movie *Star Wars* brings together technology and revolution. The entire movie is a paean to technology, punctuated with the theme of revolution. Even the Force is largely presented as a technique, albeit a mystical one. The real content of the movie is its special effects.

Occasionally a movie or television program will capture the true function of ritualized transgression. For instance, the movie *Rollerball*, while certainly not artistically memorable, did illustrate the technology/sex-violence axis. In the totalitarian, technologized, futuristic society, violence was institutionalized in the form of a spectator sport called rollerball, a singularly brutal sport. The movie showed that this ritualized violence was only a safety valve, an outlet, and not a decisive going against the social order. It was a case of ordered disorder. *Rollerball* is a poor man's version of *Brave New World*. In Huxley's great novel the totalitarian but benevolent society encouraged, actually demanded, free sexuality and drug use, while violence was replete in the movies everyone attended. As Huxley noted, the people had the illusion of freedom, in part a result of their dubious freedom to transgress.

Sex and violence are major themes of novels, television programs, and the movies. Revolution is sometimes thrown in for good measure. These ingredients almost guarantee success. The soap operas permit the vicarious enjoyment of sex and violence for otherwise conservative and puritanical individuals. Truly it is the media that permit us all to partake of the festival.

The intertwining of the sacred axes in the media and in commonplace expressions only demonstrates that these axes are not independent. Rather they are complementary to one another. Technique and the nation-state are the twin bases of the social order today. As we have already seen, the state is increasingly technical in orientation, just as technology is increasingly financed and controlled by the state. Perhaps the complementarity of axes can best be illustrated by examining the kind of "religion" each axis gives rise to.

Political Religion versus Private Religion

Earlier it was noted that religion is one form that the sacred may assume. The two sacred axes form the basis for divergent but related religions. The technology/sex axis gives rise to a plethora of "personal religions," whereas the nation-state/revolution axis is the source of political religions.

Will Herberg was one of the first to talk about personal or private religion in the sense it is to be employed here. In his classic work *Prot-*

estant Catholic Jew, Herberg argued that the American Way of Life had to a great extent supplanted the traditional theological content of Protestantism, Catholicism, and Judaism. The American Way of Life has its civic and personal sides. Its civic aspect is concerned with democracy and free enterprise. The personal side, on the other hand, has to do with "'peace of mind,' happiness, and success in worldly achievement." But "peace of mind" is actually what we most desire. Here religion becomes a kind of drug, a "spiritual anodyne," that leads to adjustment and a sense of being normal. The faith of this religion, Herberg argued, is a "faith in faith."[58] Herberg, of course, was only confirming what Ernst Troeltsch had forecast decades earlier— that modern religion would turn individualistic and mystical. The American Way of Life, then, in its personal side centers on consumption, which is in part mystical. Does not consumption as a spiritual value necessarily lead to mysticism? What else is the nonrational identification with and adulation of goods and services if not mystical in the Jamesian sense of the term? Ultimately religion itself becomes an object of consumption, not unlike any other good or service in our society.

Luckmann has likewise emphasized the personalizing of religion as a consumer choice. He argues that the sacred cosmos is dependent on the "private sphere" and is finally heterogeneous.[59] In so arguing, Luckmann fails to take into account that the heterogeneity of personal religions centers about the technology/sex axis, whose underlying basis is possession and consumption. Thus there is an order to the plethora of personal religions. Because, however, the two poles of the sacred axes are manifestly contradictory, the covert unity is difficult to ascertain. What could share less in common than the cults and therapies that range from the Jim Jones cult through encounter groups and group sex clubs to Christian Science?

Personal religion does not always lead one to join a cult, sect, or therapeutic group. At times it is only expressed in religious attitudes.[60] For instance, the keen interest in the occult, astrology, parapsychology, and flying saucers today is essentially religious. So too is the extraordinary devotion to popular music and its "gods." Certain aspects of the counterculture, on the other hand, such as open sexuality and drug use, are religious in nature. One can pick up these religious attitudes through the media without ever having to join a group. Rather than being integral members of communities and ex-

tended families today, we are organized into "consumption communities."[61] Today everyone is "into" something: jogging, wines, health
foods, gourmet cooking, antiques, sex, gardening, meditation, to
name a few. Together the host of personal religions and religious attitudes either support or attack the technological order. Yet at the same
time both types are centered on the personal attempt to be happy, feel
good, and "get high" through consumption. On a recent Christian
television program, a singer proclaimed to a rock beat that Jesus
drove her "higher and higher." The moral is, I suppose, that there is
no better "high" than Jesus.

There is another side to religion that Luckmann's otherwise sensitive analysis omitted: political religion. Personal religion cannot provide a sense of communal purpose, for it leads us to look only within
ourselves for meaning. Political religion attempts to provide the collective meaning that personal religion denies. The great political religions of this century include Nazism, fascism, Marxist communism,
and American democracy. It can have either a conservative emphasis
on the nation-state or a revolutionary thrust, in keeping with the ambiguity of the sacred axis. Simondon has developed a hypothesis that
politics has largely supplanted what we have traditionally called religion as a spiritual unifying force.[62]

He argues that at first primitive man possessed a global relationship
to nature and to society through magic. Eventually, however, technology, in superseding certain magical techniques, destroyed man's
global relationship to nature. At this point religion developed to provide once again a global outlook. Now technique and religion together
provide what magic previously did by itself: both a technology and an
ideology. The final stage is the development of human techniques
(technology for the control of man), which invade and permeate religion, leaving it unable to provide an acceptable world-view. Science
and technology, we must remember, eventually destroyed the transcendental assumptions of Western civilization, replacing them with
an immanentist outlook. In a world perceived as self-contained and
relative, politics has had to create order, for now order is seen to be
man-made. Thereupon politics takes up the slack and provides this
global outlook and relationship. There seems to be little question that
traditional religion has been politicized today and that the serious
questions are thought to be political in nature.[63] Political ideologies
have supplanted religious theologies.

The point of this is that the sacred axes give rise to two different but complementary types of religion: personal and political. Complementary, because from the late eighteenth century onward, politics and political religions have been promising their believers happiness defined in terms of consumption. Therefore, political religion ultimately promises the very thing personal religion seeks. It would appear that personal religion is stronger in advanced capitalist societies, whereas political religion is stronger in less developed societies. Political ideologies weaken somewhat in a society whose members have achieved the good life, the goal of all modern ideologies. In societies whose members have less, the political ideology is much more important, since it is the vehicle by which everyone will be transported to the good life. Personal religions are but denominations within the larger political religion. Political religions attempt to supply the collective meaning and spiritual unity that personal religion never can.

CHAPTER THREE

Sociological Symbols of Evil:
Social Problem as Prototype

*By thus identifying social reality with its own
analytic devices, sociology does what it can to alleviate
the shortage of symbols that has impoverished American
culture since the passing of the age of doctrine.*

PHILIP RIEFF
Introduction to Cooley's *Social Organization*

Why is this chapter called "Sociological Symbols of Evil" and not "Social Symbols of Evil"? By using the term sociological do we restrict ourselves to symbols of evil that appear in academic sociology? The word sociological is being used to point to the fact that, on the one hand, mythical discourse is institutional (in this case the institution of sociology) and, on the other hand, some sociological writing does influence the larger society. Of course, the opposite is true as well: society influences sociology. The relationship is dialectical, for at the very least the institution of sociology is part of society and society is conceptually part of sociology. That is why the issue of whether sociology leads society or vice versa is a false one. One plausible theory has it that a writer's ideas are slowly disseminated to the general public in something like the following manner: academicians write about the "great man's" ideas and teach students about them, whereupon journalists and others help popularize them in newspapers and magazines until ultimately the theorist's concepts become part of common parlance.[1] An apt example is the thought of Freud. Many people are familiar with terms like unconscious, Oedipal complex, sublimation, and especially ego, super-ego, and id. Scant few of these people, however, have ever read any of Freud's works. At best some have read commentaries on him.

But that is only one part of the movement. The great writer too, it seems, has been influenced by his culture, especially at the level of irrational belief. At times he is among the first to sniff out the scent of cultural change. Nietzsche, for instance, could simultaneously attack so much of modern culture (social Darwinism, nationalism, and science, for instance) but still be swept up in the current of the immanent and immediate and the cult of the self.

It would seem that society exudes certain cherished beliefs and assumptions that most of us are only dimly aware of, that certain great writers and other artists assimilate some of these beliefs to a greater or lesser extent, and that they are then passed on in an organized way, that is, in the form of a theory, a poem, a scientific treatise. Thus the cherished assumption exists in both inchoate and polished forms. (Later we will see that this is true of myth as well.)

It should be noted that the term sociological will not be restricted to academic sociology. Instead it will refer to all the social sciences at the collective level of analysis. Still, most of my examples will be drawn from academic sociology, if only because it is here one finds most of the discussion of evil in modern societies. Historically academic sociology has been bequeathed what the other social sciences did not wish to claim for themselves. Evil in the form of social problems has always been more the province of sociology than of the other social sciences. Many early (1900–1930) textbooks on social problems discussed the relationship of sociology to ethics, and some authors even suggested that sociology would eventually supplant ethics.[2] Sociology is the main province of symbols of evil today, reflecting those in society and giving them expression.

The symbiotic relationship between academic sociology and social reform has been noted by countless writers. Some of the best accounts of this merger have traced the development back to Auguste Comte and Henri de Saint-Simon.[3] The key to understanding this link between sociology and reform is the term positivism. For Comte positive referred not only to the positive rebuilding of society but also to the positive methods by which sociologists would formulate scientific laws. But one does not even have to restrict oneself to instances when the term positive occurs, for the rhetoric of Comte and most social scientists since his time contains, in Richard Weaver's words, a "melioristic bias." Even our concepts reflect this. Pointing out social scientists' propensity for a Latinate vocabulary, Weaver goes on to observe that "the diction of Latin derivation tends to be euphemistic." The significance of our optimistically covering over reality is as follows:

> It seems beyond dispute that all social science rests upon the assumption that man and society are improvable. That is its origin and its guiding impulse. The man who does not feel that social behavior and social institutions can be bettered through the application of scientific laws, or through some philosophy finding its basic support in them, is surely out of place in sociology. . . . The very profession which the true social scientist adopts compels him to be a kind of a priori optimist. This is why a large part of social science writing displays a *melioristic bias*. It is under compulsion, often unconsciously felt, I am sure, to picture things a little better than they are. Such expression provides a kind of proof that its theories are working.[4]

The most extreme statement of the moral and religious aim of sociology was made by its founding father, Auguste Comte. Sociology, according to Comte, would eventually formulate two kinds of scientific laws—those of social statics and those of social dynamics. Social statics would tell us the lawful relations among people at any one moment, whereas social dynamics would inform us about the laws by which we passed from one form of organization to the next. And sociologists as the discoverers of such laws would rightfully be the spiritual and moral guides of society. Sociology as religion would tell us what to do in order to make progress. Evil would be those forms of behavior that interfered with the evolution of society toward its utopian perfection. Herbert Spencer and Marx and many more were imbued with this hope in varying degrees. Hence, sociology has always been concerned with the analysis of evil and, wittingly or unwittingly, with its control. Now it is one thing to claim that sociology studies evil or what the people in a society regard as evil, for certainly one can regard values as facts to be interpreted, but it is quite another to suggest that unintentionally and unknowingly (after Comte) sociology has both reflected and helped articulate society's deepest religious beliefs in its theory and research, even when it has claimed to be value-free. This, however, I maintain.

The Relationship of Symbol to Myth

Following Ricoeur, we distinguish between metaphor and symbol on the one hand and between symbol and myth on the other hand. Symbol is defined and used differently in psychoanalysis, poetics, and the history of comparative religion. For our purposes symbol will refer to *religious* symbol.[5]

Metaphor involves the use of a single sign to point to two different qualities. Metaphors create a tension between the literal and figurative meanings of a word. They are creative because they force us to see things in a new way. "All the world's a stage," wrote Shakespeare, "and all the men and women merely players." The literal meaning of world was its physical properties as common sense and science could elaborate. But Shakespeare gave world a dramaturgical meaning, implying that life is a drama, humans are actors, and the world that we walk upon is truly the setting or stage for this drama. The world and a stage are similar in that both are things we walk upon, but different in their meanings.

Metaphors remain on the semantic level, Ricoeur argues, whereas symbols have a nonsemantic dimension. That is, the figurative meaning of a religious symbol transports us into the realm of the sacred, of what we experience as sacred. It is in this sense that Ricoeur talks about religious symbols being "bound." They are bound to the cosmos and man's experience of it as sacred. For instance, Eliade has noted that water is an almost universal religious symbol.[6] One of its figurative meanings is rebirth. In this context, however, rebirth is not primarily semantic; it is less an idea than the experience of a believer, which is nonsemantic. As Kierkegaard once said, "Faith begins where reason leaves off." Therefore, one can say that metaphors, which operate on a semantic level, permit a higher degree of logical precision than do symbols, which point to a realm about which humans have but approximate knowledge.

Symbols are more primitive than myths because their larger context or fuller story is only implied; myths, on the other hand, are explicit—they articulate the symbol by providing a narration of sacred time and sacred space. The myth is more than implied by the symbol; it is, as it were, condensed into it.

It appears that myth and symbol defy once-and-for-all definition. Myth can be defined, but one must guard against excessive abstraction.[7] If myth is in part a reflection of man's coming to grips with a specific, concrete reality, then it must change, as man's reality (which is in part socially constructed) changes. For instance, to see an appeal to a deity as an invariant structure of myth is a mistake; for religious feeling can affix itself to something besides a god. This is certainly the case today: modern culture is atheistic but nevertheless deeply religious.

Myth expresses belief, religious yearning, and man's irrational desires. It directs our spiritual needs to something more than man, and in the case of those myths dealing with evil, with the origin and elimination of evil—with man's salvation. Myth is explanatory and provides a raison d'être for existence that instrumental reason cannot. Contrary to what Marx said, myth is not superstructure only; rather, it can be the motivating factor in the development of material structures. Material structures such as the economy *mean* nothing in and of themselves but only in man's consciousness of them. There is no point in denying that material structures can take on historical necessity, but it is because of the meaning man attributes to them that he attempts to foresee their future course and direct their evolution. While still keeping a dialectical perspective, perhaps we can say that myth is the "condition of loyalty of the mass of the people to a certain civilization." Besides securing man's loyalty it motivates him to action with its images of reality. Ultimately myth is total or global in outlook, providing man with anchor points—it is the absolute synthesis by which everything fits together and makes sense. Furthermore, myth may be either conservative or revolutionary, securing man's conformity or inspiring his resistance. Finally, myth is an "anonymous discourse" in that it appears not to (and does not) have an author. This is why primitive man thought it to be supernatural.[8]

Some writers distinguish between etiological and ontological myths. An etiological myth explains the origin of a civilization, an institution, or some such phenomenon, whereas an ontological myth makes once-and-for-all pronouncements about the nature of man. Etiological myth is analogous to what today we call a philosophy of history and ontological myth to a metaphysical anthropology.

Our main concern is with myths of evil. Although by no means restricting himself to sociological analysis, Ricoeur has outlined three principal functions of the myth of evil. First, it envelops mankind in a single history with the protagonist of the myth standing for all the rest of us. Second, it gives movement and meaning to history by providing a beginning and an end to human existence. Third, by means of a story it accounts for the paradox of man's good fundamental or ontological being over against his actual evil condition in history.[9] Or, in other words, the myth of evil is a narration about the origin and eventual demise of evil, man's salvation, and the hero or heroes who accomplish it. The myth of evil contains both etiological and ontological presuppositions. The etiological here refers to that part of the narrative which explains the origin of evil and the movement of history to its denouement, whereas the ontological refers to statements about man's nature.

Although the symbols of evil in their most explicit usage have certain historical and cultural boundaries, they are all interrelated, mutually implicative, and even dependent upon one another for their full meaning.[10] There is a sort of cumulative movement to the symbols and myths of evil. One could locate and date a symbol or myth according to its accidental form (unique cultural and historical context), but not the symbol or myth *type*.

Let us draw upon Ricoeur's book *The Symbolism of Evil* to illustrate our discussion of symbols and myths of evil.[11] Three symbols of evil have been predominant in the history of culture: defilement, sin, and guilt. The first symbol, defilement, is linked to a ritualistic world-view in which some things, persons, and actions are pure, some impure, and some secular (profane). Evil is external and enters one like a stain or an infection. Yet the representation of defilement never became a literal physical stain, for it always connoted a spiritual blameworthiness. Defilement is rarely concerned with the individual's intentions because, as in modern criminal law, it assumes strict liability. Therefore the objective occurrence is more important than the motive. Cultures in which evil is primarily symbolized as defilement have not separated moral violations from misfortune and suffering. Human evil as well as physical calamities are both punishments. As Hans Kelsen has masterfully demonstrated, the primitive world held that among those facts that most affected the interests of the community, the harmful occurrences were interpreted as punishment from the gods and the beneficial ones as rewards. Hence, man's subjective state was one of dread or ethical terror when he had violated the taboos, for he knew that punishment was inevitable.[12]

The concept of sin does not totally break with that of defilement.

Certainly the Christian concept of possession by the devil as a special case of sin is very similar to defilement with respect to the externality of evil. Nonetheless, there are more dissimilarities than similarities between the two symbols. The first idea represented in sin is that of being "before God" or in his presence. The major theme of the Book of Job is that even a morally correct person like Job is, compared to God, sinful. Man is imperfect because only God is perfect. The next idea is the paradoxical one of the infinite demand of God on the one hand and the finite commandment on the other hand. The infinite demand is made known through the prophet who tells the people the perfection that God demands. The commandment is to all appearances a compromise or a diminution of the infinite demand—it is, in Ricoeur's words, the ethical moment of prophecy. The commandment gives man directives that, while difficult, seem more possible than the demand of God-like perfection.

The subjective dimension of sin seems closer to defilement than to guilt. Because of the infinite demand of God as expressed through the prophets, man experiences terror as the "wrath of God." In God's presence man is blinded, even smitten and destroyed. Sin conjures up a sense of the awfulness of God. The symbol of sin is not so much a personalization of sin; for all men, no matter what their station or lot in life, are nothing when compared to God.

Ultimately sin is a broken relationship with God as well as a power that can lay hold of man. The former idea is to the myth of the fall of Adam as the latter is to the myth of the fall of Satan to earth.

Guilt differs from sin principally in that it represents the individualization and internalization of sin. Now it is "I" who am the sinner and not the collective "we." The internalization results in a conscience that ascertains degrees of sinfulness in a quantitative sense where before there was only the presence or absence of sin. Scrupulosity is the logical conclusion of guilt. It is a form of alienation in which one becomes one's own judge and jury. Scrupulosity is an attempt to fulfill the infinite demand of God implicit in the finite commandment. Guilt is to reparation as sin is to repentance. To repent is to return to God, to have one's broken relationship with God repaired, but not through one's effort; to make reparation is to compensate for the degrees of sinfulness by the quantity of one's penance—the greater the sin the greater the reparation. With guilt the ideas of "before God" and the power of sin are lost, for now it is the solitary "I" who sins by himself and must make amends on his own.

The first myth type that Ricoeur identifies is the drama of creation. In this myth the genesis of evil is concurrent with the beginning of the world. Evil is chaos, against which the good god or gods fight. Creation represents the triumph of good over evil; consequently, salvation is synonymous with creation—it is implied in it. However, because chaos always threatens to rear up its ugly head and because the struggle against chaos was the time of renewal, ritualistic reenactment of the creation of the world becomes necessary to preserve the social order.

The second myth is that of the fall, sometimes referred to as the Adamic myth. In this myth too creation is good. But then there is an unexplainable evil act on the part of man's representative which is not precipitated just by human weakness: tempting man is another power, Satan the fallen angel (or some other figure, depending on the culture). As a consequence, man is forced to leave Paradise and inhabit a world of evil and suffering. Ultimately God forgives man and comes again to restore creation. Salvation then is linked to an eschaton.

The third myth, which reached its greatest artistic expression in Greek culture, is called the tragic myth. Here the gods tempt and provoke a man of unusual gifts whose fault (if it is really a fault) is to strive too much, to place himself outside the cosmic order in his struggle for greatness. Man is guilty and his eventual demise is inevitable. Salvation is aesthetic and issues from viewing the spectacle of the performed tragedy. In this view freedom becomes the aesthetic experiencing of man's necessary failure in rebelling against fate.

The fourth myth is that of the exiled soul. It appears at face value to be little related to the others, though like the tragic myth it was highly developed in Greek culture. Sometimes called the Orphic myth, is has nourished Platonic philosophy and Neoplatonism ever since. It assumes a dualism of body and soul. It is only indirectly and through subtle reasoning that the myth eventually defines the body as evil and the soul as good. The soul comes to the body to expiate the evil it had previously been associated with. The body is both a hell-like place of expiation and the source of new temptations. For the evil committed in a life anterior to this one, the soul is punished by becoming imprisoned in a body, and for the subsequent evil committed while in the body, retribution is exacted in Hades. Thus the themes of reincarnation and the transmigration of souls were integrated into the myth. Death expiates evil in this life, while life expiates the evil of the prior life. Salvation is achieved through knowledge or gnosis: that the body is desire and leads to evil. This knowledge enables the soul to control and overcome the body. Withdrawal from bodily desire leads to reunion with the divine.

If the reader is a speculative sort and unfamiliar with Ricoeur's work, he is probably already attempting to sort out which symbol goes with which myth. It seems that the symbol of defilement and the myth of the drama of creation go together, and the related symbols of sin and guilt with the myth of the fall (especially in Hebraic and Christian culture). This leaves us with the Greek myths of tragedy and of the exiled soul. Ricoeur does not deal with the symbolism of evil in these myths in great detail, for they never became the exclusive religious world-view of any society. They were invariably syncretized with other myths.

Sociological Concepts of Evil

If one examines textbooks and monographs in the social sciences over the past eighty years or so, one discovers a bewildering array of terms for evil: social pathology, social problem, social disorganization, social maladjustment, cultural lag, value conflict, social dysfunction, social deviance, and most recently, social concern. Not fully recognizing these terms as *symbols* of evil, the authors often refer to them as concepts, paradigms, definitions, models, perspectives, approaches, and even theories. In an effort to sort them out and reduce their number, sociologists have begun to type them.

In one of the most popular recent attempts at synthesis, Earl Rubington and Martin Weinberg identify five "perspectives" on social problems: social pathology, social disorganization, value conflict, deviant behavior, and labeling. Note that the perspectives were about "social problems," which thus escape explication. Another writer identifies four "attitudes" or "concepts": social problems, social pathology, social disorganization, and social deviance. Still another author reduced the "paradigms" to three: deviant behavior, social and cultural disorganization, and functionalism. Finally, a most recent work reduces the "definitions" to two: functional and normative (although a combined approach is possible).[13] Not to be outdone, I have taken it as my task to reduce the "symbols of evil" to one.

There is considerable agreement that this field of sociology has been and perhaps continues to be among the most bankrupt in all of sociology. Over the past forty years the attack on one or another of the "perspectives" has been relentless.[14] Much of the criticism boils down to exposing the values implicit in an author's perspective. If one were to summarize the criticisms repeated most often, the following would be included: (1) the concepts are too vague and general; (2) the theory is at a low level of abstraction; (3) the concepts express the bias of the writer, which is usually that he implicitly accepts the prevailing mores (for example, the small-town, middle-class, Protestant bias of social pathologists in Mill's critique); (4) the analysis is at an individual and not a social level; (5) the writer confuses fact and value; (6) the concept assumes consensus in society when in fact dissension prevails; (7) the concepts are reified or tautological or both (this is related to the first criticism). If, as critics have pointed out, the "concepts" of social pathology, social disorganization, social problem, and the like are devoid of content, being too vague and too general, this suggests then that their purpose may be other than rational and scientific. Could it be that their true purpose is as symbols that are the precursors and summaries of myths embodied in sociological theories?

The quotation from Rieff at the beginning of the chapter suggests that reified concepts serve as symbols. While in agreement, I would like to further assert that the tautological nature of such concepts can likewise provide a clue to their symbolic status. First a few words about reification and tautology, then some illustrations.

Reification is one of the most important concepts for social scientists to grasp. Unfortunately there is widespread disagreement about its definition. Certainly Marx made a brilliant contribution to the understanding of reification in his critique of idealism and capitalism. One form of reification is the mistaking of the concept for its referent in reality so that one believes that concepts have a life of their own apart from their human creation.

For instance, Thomas Szasz once remarked that he begrudged no one the use of the term mental illness as long as he remembered its metaphorical quality—that it was a theory, not a fact. It goes something like this: people are sick in their minds or emotions as people

are sick in their bodies. Mental illness as a concept is a way of organiz-
ing and thus explaining why certain people behave in odd ways or adhere to strange attitudes. But, as Szasz went on to observe, after a
while many began to believe that people had mental illnesses within
themselves as someone might be possessed by a devil. Therefore, the
mental illness (an explanation for the unusual behavior and attitudes)
became a distinct entity along with the unusual behavior and attitudes.[15] It is only one more step to tautology at this point, as we shall
see later.

Another example is offered by Carl Becker in his analysis of the
French philosophes. Through the Middle Ages up until the late eighteenth century, Western Christian thought had a religious conception
of nature: the natural world operated according to laws established by
God. Nature was a "logical construction dwelling in the mind of God
and dimly reflected in the minds of philosophers." Hence, there was
little chance that man's concept of nature would be mistaken for physical nature. The crucial point is that nature as God's creation was kept
distinct from God's laws, by which it operated, and from man's feeble
attempt to formulate these laws. In the eighteenth century, however, the
rationalists had more or less pushed God out of the picture by making
him the architect and engineer who conceived of and created the universe but then left it on its own. Thereupon nature and its laws were
identified with the observable behavior of nature. Instead of regarding the descriptive laws of nature's workings as heuristic theory, they
mistook the laws for nature itself and actually felt they had done away
with the concept of nature. For the philosophes descriptive laws of nature became knowledge of things as they were in themselves. They
did not recognize that their conviction about the immanent nature of
things was just as much a belief as their predecessors' belief in the
transcendental nature of things.[16]

Reification is a continual problem in the social sciences and in social
life. Man tends to forget that social reality is a human construction,
and he is inclined to perceive existing cultural categories as absolute,
having a life of their own apart from man.[17]

Reification is a sure indicator that man is operating on the symbolic
level. The example of mental illness will be dealt with later, so we will
concentrate on the example of nature. As Becker shows, eventually
the reification of nature reached the point that nature had become
deified. Nature was an entity that people addressed, appealed to, yes,

even prayed to. Nature and its laws had truly replaced God as the center of the universe. To what myths was the symbol of nature related? Science and history! These two myths will be analyzed later but, suffice it to say, their combination led to the view that a future utopia would be created through science and technology and implemented by politics.

Although the problem of tautology is not necessarily linked to that of reification, the two sometimes appear together in the social sciences. Tautological thinking is circular reasoning in which one substitutes for a term a synonym of it and then relates the two (the term and its synonym) in a causal or some other logical manner. Earlier, in giving the example of mental illness, I mentioned that it is but one step from reification to tautology. Again with mental illness, using the unusual behavior and attitudes that mental illness explains as indicators of mental illness produces a circular chain of reasoning. Mental illness causes the unusual behavior and attitudes but it also *is* the unusual behavior and attitudes insofar as the unusual behavior and attitudes are the only or at least the major indicators of mental illness. Thus it is being said that unusual behavior and attitudes cause unusual behavior and attitudes.

Barbara Wootton provides several examples of tautological thinking in psychology and sociology. About psychopathy she concluded: "For to say that a persistently anti-social person behaves as he does because he is a psychopath, when psychopathy is defined as persistently anti-social behavior, is indeed on the same level as saying that what puts people to sleep puts people to sleep, or that the room is cold because the temperature is low." [18]

Another of her examples is a scale developed by Sheldon Glueck and Eleanor Glueck for distinguishing neurotic delinquents from nonneurotic delinquents. Neurotic delinquents can be detected by having a low score on common sense and a high score on feelings of insecurity and anxiety, feelings of helplessness and powerlessness, fear of failure and defeat, and defensiveness of attitude. The "normal" delinquent scored higher on common sense and lower on the last four items. However, as Wootton points out, nowhere is there a substantive definition of neurosis; moreover, the snatches of definition scattered in Glueck and Glueck's other writings come dangerously close to the items on the scale. This is tantamount to defining neurosis by the attitudes and feelings they wish to explain by neurosis.

The rationale for the scale is that it is needed because we do not know what forms the attitudes of neurotic delinquents assume, but if we already know this by definition, where is the need for the scale?

A cogent nineteenth-century example of the processes of reification and tautological thinking resulting in a symbol of evil is provided by David Rothman in his brilliant analysis of the creation of asylums in America.[19] Prior to the 1820s Americans had never conceptualized crime, delinquency, insanity, and poverty as social problems or social disorder. Rather they were regarded as spiritual failings of the individual or, at most, of his immediate family. In this earlier period a belief in predestination existed, and one of the signs of one's predestination to hell was a serious deviant act. But with increased social mobility, the desire to get ahead, and the breakdown of the old class hierarchy with industrialization and modernization, the same deviant acts began to be understood as failings of social order, as social disorder. Titillated by the hope of striking it rich or making it on one's own, but uneasy about the influx of immigrants and the increased geographical mobility at all levels of society, Americans were still ambivalent about industrialization. Looking nostalgically to the closed communities of the seventeenth and eighteenth centuries, they anticipated re-creating these in the asylums they built. Seeing social disorder extant in all social institutions, they attempted to provide order in the lives of the inmates through a regimentation of work, exercise, meditation, and moral advice. Some of the reformers went so far as to suggest that the asylum would act as a model for the rest of society and would even rub off upon families in need of guidance about child-rearing practices.

Social disorder became reified when Americans began to see it everywhere and to talk about it abstractly. One could use the term social disorder and everyone knew what he meant. Paradoxically, it also became tautological, for social disorder was then used to explain all the forms of deviant behavior, which were themselves taken as the indicators of social disorder. The circle was now complete. Crime, delinquency, poverty cause crime, delinquency, poverty. Social disorder causes social disorder.

Mere tautology is no sign that a concept is actually a symbol on a different level; reification is a much better indicator. But when the two occur together, one can be sure that one is involved on the level of mythical discourse. Rothman has suggested that the reified and tautological concept of social disorder existed among social reformers and the public in the nineteenth century; let us briefly look at it among sociologists.

In one of the most thorough critiques of rudimentary sociological thought, Albert H. Hobbs summarized eighty-three textbooks written between 1926 and 1945 about concepts such as social disorganization.[20] He examined what were thought to be the causes of social disorganization (Hobbs noted that social pathology and social problems are synonymous terms), its indices, its effects, and what it is in itself. No single textbook was guilty of the following array of logical atrocities, but even only in a collective sense the findings are damning.

Almost without exception he found no serious attempt to define social organization or social disorganization. Instead the writers usually identified social organization in a vague and abstract manner with consensus, inferring of course that social disorganization was the lack of consensus. Social disorganization and its synonyms were being used in an intuitive and nonrational manner. The writers assumed everyone knew what the concepts meant. As was mentioned earlier, the relation between the primary and secondary meanings of a symbol cannot be objectified; it must be lived and experienced. So too with social disorganization. But just as important is the great emphasis on the description of the various forms of social disorganization almost as if they existed factually as social disorganization. When we put the two together—the lack of a precise definition of social disorganization and the overemphasis on description and the factual—it becomes evident social disorganization was being used in a reified manner.

The major causes and indices of social disorganization were seen to be economic factors like poverty and unemployment. Other indices of social disorganization included forms of deviant behavior such as crime and delinquency. Numbered among the effects of social disorganization were crime, delinquency, and so on. Here then is a hopeless quagmire. Social disorganization has the same causes as indicators and the same effects as indicators. The script for social disorganization goes something like this: economic factors (poverty, unemployment) are both causes of and indicators of social disorganization, which is itself indicated by economic factors and forms of deviant behavior and which in turn causes forms of deviant behavior, which are also indicators of social disorganization. Social disorganization is social disorganization is social disorganization. Social disorganization is social disorganization by any other name. It should begin to be evident that the writing about social pathology is not basically rational and scientific discourse. Its reified and tautological forms make us suspect that we are dealing with myth.

Rubington and Weinberg have attempted to date the rise and fall within American sociology of certain conceptions of evil. Social pathology had its heyday in the first two decades of the twentieth century; social disorganization supplanted it and remained dominant until the 1960s, when social deviance (labeling) became the fashion. However, Rubington and Weinberg did not seriously consider social problem as a conception. Perhaps there is good reason for this. Social problem as a conception of evil is as old as sociology, and it is the one conception that has resisted having its assumptions exposed, though it has not been without its critics.[21] Social problem is without question the most popular of such concepts among the public.

From Sociological Concepts to Sociological Symbols of Evil

Problem is ultimately derived from the Greek verb *proballein*, "to throw before." In tracing the usage of the word, the *Oxford English Dictionary* suggests that from at least the fourteenth century on, problem meant a "difficult or puzzling question proposed for solution," even a riddle. By the sixteenth century it meant a "question proposed for academic discussion," and by the eighteenth century problem had come to include among its meanings those puzzles, riddles, and obstacles in the material world to be solved. By then it had even broadened its definition to take in social issues. In 1795 Edmund Burke used the word in the context of what the political state should direct or leave alone in the lives of its citizens. In the nineteenth and twentieth centuries "social problems" became common parlance.

But what are the full implications of regarding other people and their behavior and attitudes as social problems? No one has better addressed this question than Gabriel Marcel in *Man against Mass Society*. When I regard human evil as problematic, I am assuming that it is *external* to me, something outside of and in front of me, an obstacle to be overcome. Moreover, the problematic view of evil assumes evil is *objective*, but this too implies that I (the problem solver) am not volved in it and also that it can be engineered away. This view actual. destroys responsibility in that it allows us to wash our hands of evil, to see it always in others, never to see our complicity in it. For as Marcel notes, the problem solver "remains in a non-problematic sphere." In short, this view is nondialectical, refusing to recognize the incredibly complex results of every action one person performs in relation to others. Finally, this view assumes a collectivistic or holistic orientation, for as Marcel puts it, "I make evil problematical when I treat it as a kind of breakdown that might happen in a piece of machinery, or as something lacking, or a functional failure."[22] There is a revealing contradiction in the problematic view of evil: my own involvement and responsibility in evil is denied, for evil is external and objective; but at the same time other people's responsibility for evil is affirmed, insofar as their evil disrupts the efficient functioning of the larger collectivity. This is a total substitution of social responsibility (making one responsible only to the group) for individual responsibility. Consequently I am not responsible for evil, but neither are others except insofar as their behavior (and implicitly mine as well) upsets the smooth functioning of the collectivity. The motto is, Everyone and no one is responsible for evil. That is, no one is responsible to himself for evil, but everyone is responsible to the collectivity for evil.

The world of problems and solutions is a world in which means have been given preeminence at the expense of ends. Everything is problematic and must remain so in order that even more effective solutions can be generated. This is the realm of the technological. A solution is technical efficacy—success. To solve a problem is to be successful. Essentially then a social problem is failure cast in technological terms.

If evil is problematic, what does it mean to demand a solution? A solution eliminates the problem, removes it as an obstacle. The realm of politics is the clash of opposing beliefs, interests, and needs where the most that can be expected is compromise. Now a compromise is no solution, for in a compromise both sides lose something and thus are dissatisfied to some degree. As de Jouvenel points out, "What makes a problem political is precisely that its terms admit no solution properly so-called."[23] That there be a solution to political (social) problems is a plea for the end of politics, at least of a minimally free and open politics. A solution can be applied only in a totalitarian and dictatorial manner, and in truth, under such circumstances the problems are not political but merely technical.

Our great commitment to instrumental rationality prevents our seeing that the solving of social problems demands a fund of knowledge that an elite would administer much in the manner of Plato's republic or, better yet, Comte's positivistic society. A society that "solves" its "social problems" is a consciously directed and controlled society. Usually a society's morality and politics are in part spontaneous, unconscious, and unpredictable phenomena, but social planning (engineering a solution to present and future problems) would leave a society a mass society whose members' behavior is predictable and controllable.[24]

As astute a critic as Irving Horowitz fails to perceive this when, in an otherwise excellent essay, he contrasts a problems approach with a systems approach. He correctly perceives that solutions to social problems in the real world bring subsequent problems demanding still further solutions. It is likewise true that social workers and others applying social-science theory to the solution of social problems do so in a less than systematic way. The systems approach, on the other hand, assumes a totally organized universe, not a gallimaufry of problems.[25]

But here is the rub. The two approaches are different sides of the same coin: to see the world in terms of problems and solutions is to take a systems approach. Horowitz is really saying that at this moment we are unable and perhaps unwilling to implement a totally planned society (systems approach); as a consequence, our solutions to social problems are piecemeal and self-defeating.

Social pathology as a concept is usually thought to be a biological metaphor in which society is likened to an organism. Actually the concept owes more to medicine than biology. Before the end of the eighteenth century, pathology or morbidity was contrasted with health, which was, in fact, defined in terms of precise qualities of an organism that were lost in illness. But thereafter the bipolarity was the normal and the pathological. Normality replaced health or, we should say, became the new concept of health. Now health referred to the regular functioning of the organism and pathology to that which deviated from it. Of special importance is the role that the concept of epidemic played. In the eighteenth century an epidemic became a pathology that afflicted a large number of people. As Foucault notes, "There is no difference in nature or species, therefore, between an individual disease and an epidemic phenomenon."[26] Both suggested that pathology was a deviation from regular or normal functioning. And as it turned out, the concept of social pathology in sociology referred to the deviant functioning of either individuals or collectivities, although more often than not it was used in its individualistic sense. After an exhaustive review of the sociological literature, one writer concluded that social pathology did not refer to a sick society but only to certain deviant individuals. Hence the prevailing social order was not questioned.[27]

Yet the issue of sick society versus social pathology is in large measure a false one, as Foucault has already suggested.[28] The concept of normal is inherently statistical. The normal or average functioning of an individual is determined by finding out how much the individual deviates from others—in other words, from the average, a statistical norm. A sick or pathological society, on the other hand, could only be determined by statistical comparison with other societies at the same stage of development. Hence the norm was set in the former case by a single society and in the latter case by several societies. The medical conception of pathology assumed then, in both its individualistic and collectivistic manifestations, the normal, regular, efficient functioning of the larger organism. The normal is, in an evolutionary framework, that which survives.

Still we must admit that biological concepts, including the notion of social pathology, had considerable influence on sociology. The influence, however, was mutual. Apparently biology in its theory of the organism borrowed the concept of the division of labor from economics and sociology; social Darwinism, in turn, borrowed it back from biology. Adam Smith had earlier explained how the increased specialization of work functions would make a society more productive. Hegel and Comte attempted to demonstrate how an increased division of labor would not threaten but aid social unity, thereby anticipating Durkheim's organic solidarity. De Jouvenel explains how biology made use of the concept of the division of labor:

> Biology made a decisive advance when it came to see every living organism as a structure of cells; these cells show, it is true, an almost infinite diversity as between one organism and another, and even within the same organism; and the higher the

form of life, the greater is the variety of cells which make it up. The loan from political economy of the concept of division of labor then brought forth the idea that all these cells had, by a process of functional differentiation, evolved from a primitive cell which was relatively simple. And the successive stages in the perfection of organisms corresponded to stages in the progress of the "natural" division of labor. So that in the end organisms came to be regarded as higher and higher forms of one and the same process—that of cellular cooperation, by way of division of labor—or else as "societies of cells" of an ever growing complexity.[29]

The end result is that social Darwinism made use of a social-science concept enriched by biology. Spencer's "The Social Organism" in 1860 completed the analogy between biological and social organisms. One of the essay's ideas has sustained sociology in its major theory types—social Darwinism, functionalism, and Marxism—to the present: "The life of a society, as of an organism, is independent of the lives of any of its component units, who are severally born, grow, work, reproduce, and die, while the whole body survives, increasing in mass, in completeness of structure, and in functional activity."[30]

De Jouvenel has argued that until the early nineteenth century a nominalistic or atomistic view of society prevailed in the West, although there were sprinkled throughout history metaphorical allusions to society as a totality. But with the rise of nationalism as a political religion, people began to identify themselves more as members of a nation and less as members of a community. The nation became reified so that it was regarded as a superorganism over and above its citizens. It appears that until people could have the spiritual experience and political experience of being part of a nation, it was difficult to conceptualize society as an organism.[31] The implications seem clear enough: social pathology is symbolic of a deviation from the normal, evolutionary course of one's nation. As organisms, nations win or lose, succeed or fail, survive or die. To deviate from a normal, evolutionary course is ultimately to perish.

The modern meaning of organization derives from the meaning of organ as instrument or agency. Raymond Williams notes that it is an "especially difficult word, and its history is in any case exceptionally complicated."[32] There is a relationship between organism and organization that is quite important for purposes of exegesis. As we have already seen, organism as a concept embodied the idea of a division of labor originally derived from political economy. Durkheim's concept of organic solidarity is an apt illustration, for with it he tried to show the superiority of a technical organization or a society organized around specialized work function over a natural or mechanical society in which the members are but little differentiated.

While romantics of the nineteenth century railed against the evils of technology, industrialization, and instrumental rationality in favor of nature, social scientists more often than not attempted to show the compatibility between technology and nature. Organic for the scientists implied a high level of technical organization, whereas for the poet and painter it meant natural simplicity. Therefore, organization as instrument or agency and organism involving the division of labor are highly compatible. For just as the members of an organism arranged in a hierarchical order function to maintain homeostasis, so too is organization today essentially bureaucratic, featuring both a hierarchy of authority and efficiency. This being the case, we should expect to find a certain compatibility between the concepts of social disorganization and social pathology. If something is to be considered organized, it must be efficient. Thus social disorganization is at bottom inefficiency.

Historically the social disorganization concept, although present in one form in the work of Charles Cooley, received its biggest boost from *The Polish Peasant* by William Thomas and Florian Znaniecki. The authors dismissed social pathology as a value-laden concept, which was only a substitute for "morally abnormal." But they suggested instead that "abnormality is mainly, if not exclusively, a matter of deficient social organization. . . . And from this standpoint, the question of the antisocial individual assumes no longer the form of the right of society to protection, but that of the right of the antisocial individual to be made useful."[33] Thus the antisocial (abnormal) individual needs only to be made efficient or useful, not as an entity in himself but in relation to the larger society. Over the years critics have maintained that the concept of social disorganization was actually applied to the same violations of middle-class morality as the concept of social pathology before it. This issue will be discussed later in the chapter.

Rubington and Weinberg suggest that the deviant-behavior perspective held sway over academic sociology in the 1950s and into the 1960s. They identify it with the work of Robert Merton and Edwin Sutherland, among others. Deviant behavior is behavior that deviates from or violates a norm. Merton once distinguished between the social disorganization concept and the deviant behavior concept as follows: social disorganization refers to organizational inefficiency, whereas deviant behavior refers to the individual violation of a moral norm. A rather neat distinction. According to Merton's scheme social disorganization has nothing to do with morality and its violation, but only with questions of organizational adequacy. Deviant behavior, on the other hand, refers precisely to immorality.[34]

Unfortunately Merton's distinction does not reflect social reality. By this I mean that organizational efficiency is a moral value in our society, as Max Weber clearly saw in his theory of bureaucracy. Furthermore, it is impossible to exclude the moral from human organization. To proclaim that the concept of social disorganization refers *only* to a scientific or technological assessment of a particular form of organization is to gloss over this. How people organize themselves, even to pursue practical interests, is part of their larger morality.

Then too his emphasis on deviant behavior as a violation of a *moral* norm fails to recognize to what extent our morality has become a factual morality—concerned with the normal, the successful, and the efficient. Daniel Boorstin's chapter "Statistical Morality" in *The Americans: The Democratic Experience* is excellent here. He argues that increasingly the norms of public opinion, what most people do and what most people think, the statistical average, are moral norms. In short, the normal has replaced the moral or, more precisely, become the moral. And insofar as the successful or the efficient in the form of technique becomes the standard, it tends to merge with the statistically normal. Ultimately the concept of deviant behavior is symbolic of the statistically abnormal.

Therefore the concept of deviant behavior is quite similar to the concept of social pathology, but with one important difference. The concept of social pathology, as we have already seen, is symbolic of a deviation from the normal evolutionary course of a society, something which, while statistical, can only be measured historically and comparatively. The concept of deviant behavior, on the other hand, is symbolic of a statistical abnormality within a society at a particular moment. It is an individual deviation from statistical norms formulated in a static way, that is, without historical and comparative coordinates. Social pathology is to social Darwinism as deviant behavior is to functionalism. But perhaps this distinction is less crucial than it first appears to be.

The social-deviance, labeling, or societal-reaction approach, while it has roots in the value-conflict approach of the 1940s, only took hold in the early 1960s.[35] The distinction between deviation and deviance, according to its proponents, lies in the subjective nature of evil. Rejecting the natural-law theory that certain acts are inherently evil, the social-deviance writers stress the relative and subjective qualities of what eventually comes to be regarded as deviant. Evil is in the eye of the beholder. Morality becomes a matter of public opinion when society is broken into conflicting groups; consequently, it is politicized as well. Hence, when it comes to accounting for the labeling of certain acts and people as deviant, the answer is invariably cast in political terms. The assumption is that society is composed of either competing social classes (a Marxist variant) or competing interest groups (more a Hobbesian "war of all against all" approach). Those individuals, groups, or classes who are powerful establish a morality that favors their material interests at the expense of their opponents' interests. The powerful, then, use this morality to judge the less powerful and to keep them in place. All of this was said in the nineteenth century by Nietzsche in his discussion of "master morality."[36]

Deviance, then, is a quality that the powerful have attributed to the powerless. Deviance is symbolic of powerlessness or a failure to control public opinion. There is a certain similarity among the social-problems, social-pathology, social-disorganization, and deviant-behavior perspectives in that they all assume the unity of society. The social-deviance approach stands alone in denying the unity of society and, in exposing the powerful, *appears* to be taking the side of the powerless. How does one explain this difference between the social-deviance approach and the others? The answer lies in the paradoxical nature of modern societies, in the dialectic of the static and dynamic, and the necessary and the ephemeral.

At the level of structure and options, modern societies are static; at the level of events they are dynamic. An excellent analogy provided by Ellul is the relation of a wheel to its axle. Although a wheel turns thousands of times, its distance from the axle remains the same. The wheel is dynamic (it turns), but it is static in relation to the axle. The twentieth century has witnessed the accretion of techniques into a technical system. Technique by its very nature rules out options (true alternatives) in providing the single best method. But it is continually shifting events that give the appearance of vast change and make us feel "future shock." Technique spawns new techniques and moves into areas previously untouched. It allows for an enormous and be-wildering number of superficial differences, for example, all the "op-tions" on an automobile. Therefore, technique as the structure of modern society makes possible the almost infinite variety of sizes, shapes, colors, and accessories of consumer goods and the great di-versity of consumer services that together so bedazzle us.[37]

But how does this affect politics and the labeling of others as de-viant? This question leads us to consider the necessary and ephem-eral. Political decisions today are for the most part necessary deci-sions; that is, they are the result of a technological logic and the demand for efficiency. If a country is to survive, let alone succeed, it must develop technologically, and its politics too must become bu-reaucratized (a technique of organization) and propagandized (a technique of human persuasion). One has little choice but to engage in power politics in its almost exclusively technologized form.

The ephemeral side of politics is the world of current events and political image making. There is no continuity to the news, but only a random presentation of "serious," shocking, or interesting stories and facts. It is our preoccupation with current events and being well in-formed that actually prevents us from grasping the necessary side of politics. Public opinion, a normative attitude toward something about which most often we know very little and which is usually based on an irrational emotion, is part of the ephemeral side of politics:

> If everybody is in agreement that nowadays the exercise of au-thority is solely based on public opinion; if the ruling powers draw their splendid existence from public opinion; if, on the other hand, it is true that opinion must come from outside, never being self-generated; if finally, this opinion exists except in connection with a new event—then we will understand both the influence of the news phenomenon and the ephemeral char-acter that it necessarily imposes on political affairs.[38]

The necessary and ephemeral often interact in the same political decision so that a decision necessarily arrived at because of technical considerations—for example, dropping the atomic bomb on Japan to end the war sooner, to test our nuclear sophistication, and to demonstrate our preeminence—has only momentary impact: the destruction of Hiroshima and Nagasaki was considered a step toward freedom and soon forgotten (it was only later the political left focused on this act for propaganda purposes).

Public opinion, as Ellul suggests in the above quotation, comes from the outside, from propaganda. Propaganda both depends on public opinion and creates it. This is why no government, no party, no political organization can be without it. Fueled by ideology and myth, propaganda integrates the in-group, agitates against the out-group, and incites both groups to action. Yet propaganda must be sensitive to public opinion, curry its favor, and unlock its secrets. The link between the propagandist and the propagandee is shared ideological beliefs. Hence, with the diversity of competing political groups and political ideologies, there is bound to be conflict. But at a deeper more unconscious level, myth unites the very groups that ideology sets at odds. It is apparent that at the level of ideology and public opinion each group will have its own definitions of deviance corresponding to its particular interests. Hence, deviance becomes a matter of politics. Horowitz and Martin Liebowitz have pointed out the merger of social deviance and political marginality.[39] The socially deviant are those relatively powerless individuals and groups unable to get their moral definitions accepted by the majority and by those in power.

However, the conflict of ideologies and public opinions is but part of the dynamic and ephemeral side of modern society. The necessary and static side is technique and its symbols and myths. Now we can bring together the five symbols of evil. Social problem, social disorganization, deviant behavior, and social pathology are symbols of evil cast in technological terms: failure, inefficiency, statistical abnormality, and nonsurvival are expressive of that which is harmful to the necessary, static, and unifying side of modern society. Social deviance, on the other hand, is a symbol of evil signifying the ephemeral and dynamic side of modern politics (morality): powerlessness as a lack of public opinion. But just as the necessary and the ephemeral and the static and the dynamic are dialectically and inexorably related, so too are the first four symbols related to the fifth.

Notwithstanding the difference between the first four symbols and social deviance, there is an obvious similarity. Insofar as failure, inefficiency, statistical abnormality, and nonsurvival are all manifestations of powerlessness, social deviance as powerlessness in public opinion is similar. Therefore, social problem, social disorganization, deviant behavior, social pathology, and social deviance are all symbols of powerlessness in a society where technology and the nation-state are considered sacred. In the next chapter we will see that all five symbols are tied to the myth of progress and technological utopianism.

The remaining four concepts are synonymous with one or more of those already considered. It is surprising that social maladjustment never caught on in sociology, for it was perhaps a somewhat more popular term in common usage. Certainly there were complete textbooks on social adjustment and discussion of the subject in other texts. One of the persistent themes coming out of "scientific" and evolutionary sociology was man's need to adjust to his environment, not just for survival but also to insure progress. Social maladjustment was just a synonym for social pathology. Both concepts assumed the theory of evolutionary progress.

Social dysfunction would appear to be synonymous with social disorganization. Dysfunctions are the negative consequences for the social organization of an event or an act. A dysfunction is something that is inefficient in regard to some organization or system.

Cultural lag is sometimes regarded as a variant of social disorganization, other times as a separate perspective. It was implicit in Thomas and Znaniecki's concept of social disorganization. They regarded abnormal behavior as sometimes the result of transition from one form of organization to another, which might indicate that the abnormality represented a failure of a new form of social organization to "take" soon enough. More precisely, cultural lag expressed better than any other concept save that of social problem our worship of technology. Evil was the failure of man's modest creation—culture—to keep up with his stupendous creation—technology. A corollary was that man should use technology to "solve his problems."

The concept of value conflict is similar to that of social deviance. Like the social-deviance approach, it focused on the subjective side of social problems: (1) that they have to be defined as such to be problems; (2) that there is widespread disagreement about values; and

(3) that some groups or classes are more powerful than others.[40] The main difference between the value-conflict and social-deviance approaches appears to be the level of analysis: the former at the collective level is concerned with collective definitions of social problems, while the latter at the individual level focuses on how individuals come to be defined as deviant.

It may not be readily apparent what relation, if any, exists between symbols of evil and the sacred of transgression. Or more concretely, what is the relation between social problem and sex, violence, and revolution? The symbolism of evil has to do, in the first instance, with the *form* of evil: defilement, sin, guilt, social problem. The forms of evil all imply theories or myths of how evil came to be and to assume the form it has. The sacred of transgression, by contrast, specifies exactly what within that theory and form is *most* defiling, sinful, guilt-provoking, or problematic. Or, in other words, the sacred of transgression defines the *content* of evil.

We will use the technology/sex axis as an example. Technology represents instrumental rationality, the mediated, and the efficient; sex, on the other hand, represents the instinctual, the immediate, and the inefficient. On one level sex is everything technology is not. Now as we have just seen, social problem and other modern symbols of evil all figuratively point to the opposite of the good (technology), that is, to the inefficient. If social problem is the form and theory of evil in a technological society, sex is the content that most threatens that order. Remember that the sacred keeps us at the level of the concrete, whereas symbol and myth convey us to an imaginary, abstract realm. Symbols of evil, then, are of the sacred of transgression, expressing it indirectly as form and theory.

There are two additional issues concerning the symbols of evil we need to discuss before moving to the realm of myth. The first is the relation of the social to the moral. Hayek once noted that there has been a gradual substitution of the word social for the word moral.[41] Thus when the term social conscience appears, it usually refers to a taking into account of the consequences of one's actions as a criterion of good and evil—the end justifies the means—as opposed to examining whether one has violated moral principles. But to know what the total consequences of an action are, a full knowledge of the functioning of the system would be required. And yet this knowledge is not within the purview of the layman but of the expert. Ordinarily morality is a creation not of one mind but of many, not totally planned but spontaneous, not totally rational in a utilitarian sense but rational with respect to some transcendent beliefs. But the knowledge of all consequences can only be the knowledge of an intellectual elite. And it is illusory to boot, for who can know *all* the consequences ahead of time unless behavior is totally predictable and controlled, or, in other words, repeated? In this sense social implies social planning in which the future is but a repetition of the past. Social planning, in turn, expresses a technological utopianism, an idyllic steady-state condition in which nothing changes but is only infinitely repeated. Repetition, as we see later, is a principle both of science and of myth. The social has gradually replaced the moral, and the meaning of the social is the technological. And because social substitutes for moral, it follows that technological substitutes for social. On the semantic level the full meaning of the prefix social with the words pathology, disorganization, problem and deviance becomes clear: it is symbolic of technology and the nation-state as sacred.

The second question is, Why have sociological symbols vacillated between seeing evil in the individual and in society? If one takes an atomistic view (society as a collection of individuals), evil is always and only in the individual. But if one regards society as a totality, for example, the nation-state as a superorganism above and beyond the individuals who compose it, then evil resides in the organism or system as a failure of function. Here the individual is reduced to a social cipher.

But why, if the sociological symbols of evil are collectivistic in their mythical manifestations, did many social scientists use them to refer to individual deviations? The inconsistency is explained in part by the fact that most nineteenth- and early twentieth-century sociologists were either romantic or Christian individualists. The collectivistic implications of sociological theory had not supplanted these contrary beliefs but simply lay side by side with them. Later, as more sociologists came to use a particular sociological theory as a world-view, much of their individualism was cast off.

Therefore I am suggesting that social Darwinism, Marxism, and functionalism as representative of sociological theory were all collectivistic in their mythical implications. In the following chapter we will examine how evil is explained by each of these three theories. The sociological symbols of evil that have been discussed are not necessarily explicit in the major sociological theories. However, as we will soon see, either the myth of progress or the myth of technological utopianism, which are directly related to these symbols of evil, was present in the major sociological theories.

CHAPTER FOUR

From the Myth of Progress to Technological Utopianism

The principle of immanence, the explanation
of every event as repetition, that the Enlightenment
upholds against mythic imagination, is the
principle of myth itself.
MAX HORKHEIMER and THEODOR ADORNO
Dialectic of Enlightenment

Daniel Bell has suggested that functionalism and Marxism are the two major paradigms of modern sociology. To these will be added social Darwinism, the major paradigm of American sociology in the nineteenth century. We shall examine the thought of Spencer as representative of social Darwinism, Marx as representative of Marxism, and Durkheim as representative of functionalism. We shall also consider the myths from which these theories draw sustenance.

Spencer, not unlike Dewey and the other pragmatists, was preoccupied with finding a scientific basis for right and wrong, which ultimately became the principle of evolutionary progress.[1] The cause of evil was the organism's failure to adapt to his environment. Life in this narrative is a struggle for survival with the gradual elimination of the less fit members of the species. The idea of evolutionary progress suggested a cumulative improvement shared by the most fit individuals: phylogeny is recapitulated in ontogeny. The progress the species has made is repeated in the individual. Now Spencer believed that evolutionary progress was not just biological but mental and moral as well.

This is the key. For the belief in spiritual and not merely material progress implicitly linked power and good, might and right.

Good for Spencer was the perfect adaptation of the organism to its environment or, in other words, survival. William James observed that in Spencer's thought the survival of the body, whether individual or social, was an "absolute end." Because the process of adaptation is always at work, over time evil tends to disappear. Spencer provided for an "unknowable" who might have originated the evolutionary process, but it was, in all actuality, a mere afterthought. There is not here as with the myth of the Fall any dramatic loss of innocence, any sudden shift from good to evil. Good and evil in this scheme are relative. In evolutionary thought previous adaptations make possible new adaptations. What exists is better than what was yesterday but worse than what will be tomorrow. However, because the evolutionary process is continuous, the relative evil of today's good in comparison with tomorrow's good is minimized. The normal or the average is good, for it makes possible future perfection. Today's relative evil is rationalized away as necessary for the utopian future.

Spencer's view of society as an organism conflicted with his extreme individualism in politics. To take this metaphor seriously is to reduce man to a mere functionary. For if the individual is but a member of the larger organism, which inevitably works toward homeostasis, then he loses his right or, better yet, his ability to dissent from the larger organism's spiritual unity. Of course, Spencer was unaware of the contradiction between the logical implications of regarding society as an organism and political individualism. Ironically, man's condition in modern technological societies increasingly resembles that of a member encapsulated by his organism, making Spencer's metaphor prophetic.

Spencer saw the evolution of the social organism in two stages: the military and the industrial. In the military stage, societies are geared toward survival. Those individuals who are most powerful will rule over others despotically, and similarly those societies that possess military traits and virtues to the highest degree will conquer their rivals. Conflict is everywhere—it is the war of all against all both within society and between societies. But as the conquest continues and societies come into greater contact with one another, there are fewer and fewer territorial units, until there is but one society.

And this is industrial society. Suddenly, as if by magic, peace and tranquility reign. Cooperation in the form of the division of labor of industrialization holds sway. World-wide society has nothing left to conquer outside of itself so it turns its attention to the industrial arts. In this utopia the individual will be respected, will be free, and will work in harmony with others. Hofstadter concludes that for Spencer industrial society brought nothing less than a "new human nature . . . peaceful, independent, kindly, and honest." With this new man ethical problems disappear. Not all social Darwinists agreed with him. Some, like William Graham Sumner, did not think the utopia as such would ever be realized in this world and believed that progress would be much slower than Spencer anticipated.

History, for Spencer, led to a secular utopia. It was this end point or culmination that gave history meaning. But short of the utopia, history was evolutionary progress. A question, seemingly vital at the time, was the relation of man to evolution. Lester Ward and later the pragmatists objected to what in effect was Spencer's reified concept of evolution. Spencer saw the role of sociology not as providing direction to evolution but only as warning people what not to do so as not to interfere with it. He had mistaken the concept and theory of evolution for its referent in the world outside and had made man a pawn of his own creation—evolution. But, as we shall see later, in discovering a scientific basis for ethics it made little difference whether one saw man as the manager and director of evolution or its servant. Spencer unwittingly had made science a tool of history (something Marx did as well); science was the handmaiden of history conceived of as evolutionary progress. Yet science was the most important force of history because ultimately it was to be the source of man's greater adaptability and eventual perfection. Spencer just could not see that if science, sociology in this instance, was telling us what not to do in order not to interfere with evolution, it was also telling us what to do. For one has to have some positive norm from which to gauge the negative. In this sense science was directing the course of history. Therefore, what Spencer was actually preaching was submission to science and its handmaiden, technology.

The writing of Karl Marx is sometimes divided between that of the young Marx and that of the old Marx. It is in the earlier writings, especially the *Economic and Philosophic Manuscripts of 1844*, that his idealism most stands out.

For Marx private property and the division of labor that made it possible were at once the content and cause of all evil. Marx's theory divided history into stages characterized by the form of ownership of the means of production.[2] Development in the forms of production results in a more complex division of labor and a greater discrepancy between rulers and the ruled. Beginning with the tribal ownership of private property (for example, slaves), history has demonstrated a progressive growth in the kinds of property and the relative proportion of private to public property, especially individual private property. Marx believed in technological progress but not in moral progress. For in Marx's scheme exploitation grew with increases in the ownership of private property and the division of labor. Exploitation, however, was to end with the emergence of a world-wide classless or communist society. In that utopia there would be no private property, no division of labor. There is no elaboration of this utopia but only glimpses. The oft-quoted thought in *The German Ideology* alludes to man's freedom to create himself, that is, to work without constraint and restraint:

> While in communist society, where nobody has one exclusive sphere of activity but each can become accomplished in any branch he wishes, society regulates the general production and thus makes it possible for me to do one thing today, and another tomorrow, to hunt in the morning, rear cattle in the evening, criticize after dinner, just as I have a mind, without ever becoming hunter, fisherman, shepherd or critic.[3]

An earlier (by two years), more subjective version comes at the end of his essay "The Power of Money in Bourgeois Society":

> Assume *man* to be *man* and his relationship to the world to be a human one: then you can exchange love only for love, trust for trust, etc. If you want to enjoy art, you must be an artistically cultivated person; if you want to exercise influence over other people, you must be a person with a stimulating and encouraging effect on other people. Every one of your relations to man and to nature must be a *specific expression*, corresponding to the object of your will, of your *real individual* life.[4]

In the earlier writings the emphasis is on the individual self, freedom, and nature, whereas in the later writings the emphasis is on society (social self), necessity, and history. The earlier writings spell out Marx's ethical ideal; the later writings attempt to demonstrate the inevitability of this ideal in history. His materialism is, after all, only a concealed idealism.

The champion or hero in this myth is the proletariat, which struggles and eventually overcomes the bourgeoisie.[5] As exploitation becomes unbearable, as wealth concentrates in fewer and fewer hands, the proletariat cannot help but see through the dominant ideology and perceive correctly their true enemies.

The dynamics of the struggle between oppressor and oppressed center about the means or forces of production. What man does and what he produces is what he is. There is no fixed or constant human nature, but rather a nature relative to production in history and society. As Eric Voegelin has pointed out, nature is a "god-term" in the earlier writings (just as history is in the later): man is part of nature, a species being whose alienated condition will be alleviated in the future when he is free to work, that is, to create himself by fulfilling his innate potentiality. In nondialectical fashion and by a verbal sleight of hand, Marx has man both subject to and dominant over nature, both part of nature and a separate and distinct entity. All in all he uses nature and man interchangeably.[6] But later references to history substitute for earlier ones to nature. If human nature is relative, then it is subject to the forces of history. Nature was used symbolically to theorize about man's ideal condition, whereas history was used symbolically to theorize about the material process through which that condition was to be realized. History, as a record of what has been, was reified and eventually deified in the later Marx and became, like nature before, a virtual synonym for man. For if the ideal is embedded in the material, is inevitable, derives from what is, why talk about it at all?

Marx was no less enchanted with science than his contemporaries. He considered himself a scientist and his philosophy of history scientific. Scientific socialism would eventually triumph. Marx's theory, with its great emphasis on the forces of production, was close to being one of technological determinism. The evolution of the forces of production to the point of their necessary control by the entire society would bring about the classless society. And what else would enable man to hunt, fish, criticize, and raise cattle at will but a technological cornucopia?

A number of writers have analyzed the mythical dimension of Marxism. Eliade has suggested that the Marxian myth is akin to the age-old tradition of the Golden Age that both precedes and follows history and to the Judaic-Christian belief in the coming of the Messiah or the second coming of Christ. Karl Lowith, in perhaps the most brilliant interpretation, has suggested that Marxism and, for that matter, other modern philosophies of history derive a sense of absolute meaning—an end or culmination to history—from Christianity. However, they secularize and vulgarize this belief by making the end of history immanent and to be realized by man's own actions. Robert Tucker, in his excellent critique, has referred to Marx's and Hegel's view of history as "God's self-realization" or the process of man's deification. Marxism, like social Darwinism, met people's need to hope at a time when Christian religion was on the wane.[7]

It is doubtful that Marx ever used, at least with any frequency, the symbols social pathology, social disorganization, or social problem in his writing. Yet they were certainly implied.[8] Marx's philosophy of history, which asserts technological but not moral progress, assumes the concept of social pathology. Insofar as Marx's utopian ideal was a united, even uniform and static society, the concepts of social problem and social disorganization were suggested.

Functionalism, the third major paradigm of modern sociology, is sometimes traced back to Durkheim, although one could push its origins back to Spencer. When Spencer used function as "any process which is essential to the maintenance of a living system," he was using it in a more abstract and general way than his predecessors, anticipating its modern usage.[9] The term function was borrowed from biology and assumes an organic analogy, but not in a totally literal way, as evidenced by Spencer's definition. Society is viewed as an organism or a system. Those activities that contribute to the sustenance and growth of the system are functions and those that are harmful are dysfunctions.

Richard H. Tawney has traced changes in the meaning of function. As early as the seventeenth century and certainly by the eighteenth century, function "as an activity which embodies and expresses the idea of social purpose" was being supplanted by a mechanistic view— a function was a consequence. This mechanistic view coincides with the scientific view of the universe as a great machine. Machine, system, or organism—that is not the point, however. The important thing is the fact that men stopped defining purpose in transcendental terms and made it immanent; that is, purpose was inherent in the nature of things and as such could only be gauged scientifically. And because, as Ernst Cassirer has noted, science necessarily imposes order on that which it studies, purpose was embodied in a larger unit, a system, organism, or machine. This new immanentist and collectivist view saw purpose as the larger system's ability to maintain itself and survive. Stanislav Andreski has shrewdly noted that functionalism as well as social Darwinism assumes natural selection and survival of the fittest. Any organism or system that consists of parts more or less integrated and "whose functions are not adjusted to each other or to the demands of the environment will be destroyed by its competitors." This is the assumption of functionalism, for why does a system strive to maintain equilibrium or homeostasis except to survive? [10]

One might almost conclude that functionalism is to Comte's social statics as social Darwinism (evolutionism) is to his social dynamics. Social Darwinism and Marxism are theories of history, of the laws of social change, whereas functionalism is a method of interpreting human actions outside of time. Still, like social Darwinism and Marxism functionalism employs a systems approach.

Functionalism *judges* human actions by what contributions—positive or negative—they make to the larger system.[11] In this sense functionalism is an expression of a technological "psychosis"[12] (which has both bourgeois and socialist expressions) that wants people rewarded only for their technical contributions and not for what they are. Once again the theme of survival of the fittest. Power is glorified, right and might are equated; the end justifies the means. But now the end is immanent and is survival/success.

Let us examine *The Rules of Sociological Method* by Emile Durkheim; Durkheim was the first functionalist, and he did not completely give up his interest in evolution. One of his chapters, "The Normal and the Pathological," is a gold mine of information about the functionalist view of evil. In this well-written and well-reasoned essay, Durkheim laid down three rules for distinguishing between the concepts of the normal and the pathological when applied to social phenomena:

1. A social fact is normal in relation to a given phase of its development, when it is present in the average society of that species at the corresponding phase of its evolution.

2. One can verify the results of the preceding method by show-
ing that the generality of the phenomenon is bound up with
the general conditions of collective life of the social type
considered.

3. This verification is necessary when the fact in question occurs
in a social species which has not yet reached the full course of
its evolution.[13]

To arrive at these rules Durkheim rejects other, more simplistic
methods. He begins by asking the reader whether he is willing to define health (the normal) as the "perfect adaptation of the organism to
its environment." Almost before we can answer he rejects that definition because it does not deal with degrees of adaptation and because it
assumes that "every organism corresponds to some external state of
the environment," which, he asserts, is unproven. The next definition
of health he attacks is "that which maximizes our probabilities for survival." But would you then call reproduction, which entails a risk for
the woman, and old age and youth, stages of life in which one is susceptible to disease, pathological? Obviously not. Those who use this
definition, he argues, assume that each characteristic, each internal
state, corresponds to some external state that works either to ward off
or to contribute to disease and death. But this is not so, for some states
are general or accidental conditions not crucial to the survival of the
organism. And not all diseases are fatal—some can be controlled or
eliminated. An otherwise healthy person can suffer from a variety of
illnesses that do not threaten his longevity. Yet if we could use mor-
tality rates as an indicator, we could distinguish between healthy and
morbid conditions. But how does one establish even approximately
the times of birth and death for a *social* organism?

Durkheim was saying, in effect, that one's definition of health must
take into account individual differences, changes in the species over
time, and differences between species. In other words, a relative, not
an absolute standard, must be sought, at least at this stage of the social
sciences.

The sociological phenomena most widely distributed in the entire
species and useful to the survival of the species (or at least natural to
it) are normal or healthy. But the normal here is not the average in
Adolphe Quetelet's sense of the term. The Belgian statistician conceived of the average as those characteristics most widespread among

individuals in a society. Quetelet often talked about the "average type," an arithmetic mean of individual characteristics. This individualistic and atomistic attitude, of course, irritated Durkheim, who was a staunch proponent of the primacy of the objective and collective over the subjective and individual. Individuals were of societies and not vice versa. Therefore it is not surprising that Durkheim's criticism of Quetelet in *Suicide* suggested that while a phenomenon like suicide might not be an average or normal phenomenon within a society, when examined historically and cross-culturally it might be average.[14] If all successful societies have suicides occurring at about the same rate in the course of their evolutionary development, then suicide is a normal phenomenon. The question is not the relative frequency of suicide within a society but rather the comparative rate of suicide, that is, one society's rate versus that of another. Only on this basis could one compute an average rate of suicide.

In taking this position Durkheim was exhibiting a full-blown functionalism. For in arguing that crime and suicide were normal phenomena, he was also, according to his second criterion, suggesting that they had beneficial consequences for the integration and stability of society. But this functionality needed to be empirically tested in those societies whose evolutionary culmination had not been reached, because during a period of transition certain social phenomena may perhaps remain widespread without really being functional to the newly emerging order.

Yet this objection was raised in a perfunctory manner, for he argued, "It would be incomprehensible if the most widespread forms of organization would not at the same time be, *at least in their aggregate*, the most advantageous."[15] Advantageous to survival, that is. That the general would not survive is inconceivable if one accepts the idea of evolution.

But, as Steven Lukes points out, Durkheim in practice did contradict himself by regarding certain general conditions as dysfunctional. Although labor conflicts and anomie were widespread in industrial societies, he still regarded them as pathological, perhaps because they did not fit his view of the future integrated state of industrial society[16] or because he did not see how they could contribute to "the general conditions of collective life" in the present. Or perhaps the first view colored the second.

Ultimately, then, the normal is that which is general or average in a cross-cultural sense while remaining functional to the survival of the society. Durkheim cleverly combined the conception of the statistical average with that of success/survival, and at the same time he synthesized functionalism and evolutionism.

But what about modern functionalism? It makes no overtures to evolutionism, though this is still implied, as Andreski noted. William Goode, a proponent of functionalism, suggests that functionalism has tended to neglect social change not because of any inherent weakness but because the high-powered tools of sociology are more readily applied to *modern* society.[17] This linkage of functionalism to technology (tools of science) is crucial, as I will attempt to show.

In place of Durkheim's conception of the pathological, modern functionalists substitute the concept of social dysfunction. Shorn of its historical and cross-cultural referents, it means very simply, as Merton indicates, behavior or events that have consequences detrimental to the maintenance of the extant social order. Social disorganization, Merton claims, is a neutral and not a moral concept that refers to multiple social dysfunctions. Moreover, social disorganization refers to how efficacious and efficient something is in an organizational sense. The norm against which the concept of social disorganization is dialectically formulated is social organization, a perfectly functioning, efficient totality, or, in other words, a utopia.

Except for the early romanticists, from Comte onward utopian thinkers have pinned their hopes on technology to create a perfectly ordered, smoothly functioning society. Comte knew very well that to achieve this utopian state no aspect of life could be spared scientific scrutiny. Morality too would have to become "scientific." This is the full meaning of an absolute functionalism: the reduction of an act's meaning exclusively to its consequences. No one would reasonably object to a limited functional analysis; it is when consequence becomes meaning that one must object. The preoccupation with consequence and not human purpose secretly yearns for a technological utopia in which human purpose (the ends of an action) has become automatic. In this situation an action would be reduced to its means.

It is in the technological utopia that the normal in Durkheim's sense and the average in Quetelet's sense would become one. There would then be nothing deviant, nothing normal, but only an efficient totality. The technological utopia is a static society. Durkheim's evolutionary conception of the normal would then be meaningless. The average would be universally present because everyone would think alike and behave alike. How else could it be in a totally controlled environment?

It has not been my intention to suggest that these theories *are* myths. Rather they contain mythical elements. Following Ricoeur, symbol is a first-level myth, whereas etiological and ontological myths are second-level myths. The theories we have briefly examined— social Darwinism, Marxism, and functionalism—contain either explicitly or implicitly both levels of myth. Before proceeding to a discussion of the second-level myths, let us examine what these three theories share in common.

First, all three imply the concept of social pathology or the other related concepts (social disorganization, deviant behavior, social problem, deviance). Second, all imply the theory of progress. The sociological symbols of evil represent nonprogress. The theory of evolution applied to society, social Darwinism, assumes that each subsequent form of society is more complex or more perfect. This assertion about evolutionism is so often stated that it has become commonplace. More rarely is Marxism accused of a belief in progress.

Marx's belief in progress was concealed beneath a vicious attack upon ruling-class institutions, private property, and money. Much of what others saw as progress, Marx saw as retrogression. Charles Van Doren has pointed out, however, that not all who have held to the theory of progress have done so in a total way.[18] Marx was one of those who believe in material, technological progress but not in social progress. That is, Marx believed that the forces of production were the driving force of history. Each major technological change necessitated an alteration in the relations of production (division of labor, class relations, and the like) until both were in harmony in the communist utopia. But until that final state, social relationships deteriorated— were marked by greater exploitation—because with each increase in the forces of production there was a corresponding increase in private property and concentration of power in the hands of the ruling class. There was a perfect inverse relationship between technological progress and social retrogression.

Finally in late capitalism came the apocalypse: the proletariat would rise up and smash the bourgeoisie—no more exploitation. But it was not until the forces of production had spent themselves or worked themselves out, which is to say that a condition of abundance had been achieved, that social relationships would be healed. After the apocalypse came the golden age, an aesthetic utopia in which everyone has opportunity to fulfill his potentiality, to create himself.

Several things stand out in this narrative. First, social relations are completely dependent upon technological developments. Second, because each stage, according to Marx's theory, is a necessary condition for the next, there is a sense in which his criticism of exploitation is blunted. For if capitalism is necessary for communism to emerge, how can it be wrong? Thus the forces of production progress toward a utopian outcome. One could expect technological progress, but one would have to wait for social or moral progress until the "end." It had to be so, as sensitive and perceptive as he was about the exploitation and misery of his times. Others had to close their eyes to it in order to suggest that universal progress was at hand. Marx's philosophy of history was an ingenious solution to the paradox of technological progress and moral retrogression.

The Etiological Myth of Progress

A distinction can be made between an etiological or explanatory myth and an ontological myth, which is concerned with some permanent quality of human nature. The explanatory myth is a narrative about the beginning of a civilization or tribe or about its future state. In the myth of progress the narrative is essentially about the future.

The modern myth of progress is so well known and has been so roundly criticized that it needs scant introduction. There were other periods in the West when the experience of progress was idealized. In classical Greece, for instance, it was only among the educated classes and for but a short period in the fifth century B.C. that this belief was widespread.[19] And certainly the Judaic-Christian conception of the irreversibility of history can hardly be thought of as progressive, for there is no assurance here that man is becoming better or that what he does necessarily leads to the Eschaton. The modern theory is unique in the intensity and exclusiveness of its commitment to progress.

The modern theory of progress began to flower in late-eighteenth-century France.[20] Disillusioned by political and religious corruption and enamored with science and reason, the philosophes set out to discover the laws of history and "man in general," the essence of humanity. Regarding nature as still something to be perfected, they saw man in the same light—humanity would eventually be perfected at some future time. Man's reason would allow him to perfect his institutions through political and social reform. The philosophes looked to posterity to justify their attack on faith as superstition. At this time progress was not thought to be necessary and inevitable, but it was fully anticipated. Because of their emphasis on freedom, but especially because of their disdain for the present political and religious arrangements, the philosophes were unwilling to see historical progress as an inexorable process, at least up until their entry into history. From now on, they reasoned, there would be no stopping a progressive movement toward a "heavenly city" of man's doing.

By the middle of the nineteenth century progress was becoming a household word. And when progress was wedded to evolution, the results were nothing short of stupefying. Who could doubt it? But now progress was the unilinear movement of history toward a future state of utopia. This movement was both necessary and continuous. Spencer, Hegel, Comte, and others believed that industrial society was the incipient phase of that anticipated utopia. Evolution had been reified; it was no longer regarded as theory. It was fact, and so was the future it projected.

As a myth, progress helps to solve the relativity of good and evil implicit in an immanentist conception of the world. In this theory evil is gradually eliminated: today is better than yesterday, tomorrow better than today. All events and actions short of the utopia are both good and bad; they are better than those which came before, but worse than those which will follow. Nevertheless, even in this ambiguous theory of evil, the actions of today, even when compared to the future in an absolute way, are good in that they are necessary. That is, the myth of progress assumes necessary continuity to history. The past was necessary for the present; the present is likewise necessary for the future. This suggests that the normal replaces the moral, or more precisely, becomes the moral. This belief represents the ethicization of power in all its forms: success, efficiency, survival, the normal, and control of public opinion.

Levi-Strauss maintains that myth serves to bridge contradictions within a society. Is this applicable to the myth of progress? Progress eventually solves the relativity of evil by making the relative evil of today necessary to achieve the ultimate good of tomorrow. In the nineteenth century this myth made class conflict and economic exploitation palatable, for in the future we would all be successful. In the twentieth century it has been used to justify the growth of the political state, which alone can guarantee technological utopianism.

This myth met man's need to hope at a time when Judaic-Christian hope was on the wane. It was a response to what Eliade has called the "terror of history." It justified and gave meaning to the suffering of the moment. Unlike many other etiological myths, the golden age of this myth lay only in the future. Meaning lay at the end rather than the beginning of history.

The myth of progress was not experienced in a vague and abstract way, however. Technology and its hierophanies, consumer goods and services, had not yet made great inroads. But still progress could be rooted in one's country. Social Darwinists, positivists, and Hegelians all saw progress occurring in the West. As Hegel said, "Europe is the goal of history." Progress was reified as technological progress and national progress.

Progress did not supplant Christianity's eschatological hope all at once. Ernest Tuveson has demonstrated how Christians in America came to see their country in salvation terms.[21] Nationalism was amalgamated to a Christian framework. Eventually, however, nationalism became independent of Christianity as it more truly became the American religion. At this point progress provided nationalism with hope for the future.

In order to understand better the myth of progress, it is necessary to explore its assumptions. Consciously or unconsciously its proponents were atheists. Even those who still claimed to believe in God had reduced him to a mere abstraction (the Prime Mover, the Great Architect), at the same time making nature autonomous. Nature's laws replaced the personal God of Jews and Christians. However, they believed that through science man could perfectly apprehend these laws, and to this extent they reified nature. Nature was what science said it was. The distinction between the facts and their explanation was blurred. Wittingly or unwittingly they became immanentists. Immanentism might be defined as a belief that the world is only what it appears to be, a belief in brute facts, a belief that meaning and purpose are self-contained. Immanentism, the polar opposite of transcendentalism, is the deification of matter and the immediate. It raises scientific observation to the status of absolute. This implies a deification of the scientist, for if his apprehension of nature provides perfect knowledge, he is "above" nature in the same way God used to be. Vahanian duly noted this in his depiction of modern culture when he said, "To kill God is to become god oneself; this is the meaning of the transition from radical monotheism to radical immanentism which has taken place in Western culture."[22] Science itself is not responsible for the absolute immanentism; the cause lies in something one can rightfully call the myth of science, which goes hand in hand with the myth of history.

The Ontological Myths of History and Science

While history has always been the narrative part of etiological myths, today history has itself become a myth. History as the totality of objective facts about the past has been elevated to the status of the absolute. Virtually everything today is put into its historical context. We think we know something when we know its history. Robert Maynard Hutchins once remarked that much of teaching in the humanities and social sciences had fallen into the rut of just giving the background, that is, the history, of a topic. The media use history as a way of getting perspective on the news. History is seen as all-encompassing— nothing is outside its purview. Now this reified and deified view of history is precisely what is mythical. It has been reified to the extent that it has become a thing in itself (its conceptual status has disappeared) and deified because if it is all-encompassing and nothing escapes its vision, it is divine.

This myth of history assumes two forms. The first is history as a mass of brute facts without a thread holding them together. The world is viewed as "something in the making, something which can at best be only tentatively understood since it is not yet finished."[23] This is historical relativism or historicism as Eliade defines it. In this view history has no beginning or no end and thus no ultimate meaning. The second is history as the structure of past facts. This is an immanentist philosophy of history. The events of history are both necessary and continuous. History is a material process that unfolds in accord with certain laws. History here becomes the "scientific" theory of history.

Now it is my contention that the history-as-structure form of the myth is present in the etiological myth of progress and historical relativism in what we refer to as technological utopianism. History is ascendant over science in the myth of progress, whereas in technological utopianism science is dominant.

The myth of science would seem to possess at least four components of belief: (1) that the scientific method guarantees complete objectivity; (2) that science can discover ultimate truth (a knowledge of things as they are in themselves); (3) that science is universal in its capacity and applicability; and (4) that science can provide a basis for ethics. All four work to create the grand illusion that science can save us.

Perhaps Theodore Roszak was the first to discuss the objective state of consciousness as mythical.[24] This objectivity may take one or more of several forms. It is sometimes argued that if one pursues research with precise and rigorous use of the scientific method, one's original presuppositions, moral choices, sentiments, and beliefs will be negated or at least neutralized. Or at times it may involve the denial that science has philosophical assumptions (for example, B. F. Skinner's past defense of behaviorism) and the denial that science is at bottom a world-view and lifestyle. But this is exactly where the myth resides— one abandons oneself to the "pure" method. It is almost as if one's assumptions and choices were sins that the magic or grace of the method washes away, leaving the researcher clean and spotless, or at least leaving the finished piece of research immaculately conceived.

Of course if one attains perfect objectivity then one should discover truth, that is, knowledge of things as they are in themselves and not merely as they appear to us. Most scientists do not hold this view today. (But remember that we are talking about myths that operate on a society-wide level.) Earlier in this century science began to give up the philosophical theory of causality for that of probability. As Hans Kelsen has so brilliantly noted, the original theory of causality assumed a total and perfect knowledge of everything simultaneously, which prior to the seventeenth century was attributed only to God.[25] Eventually this perfect knowledge, or at least its potentiality, was transferred to science.

The universality of science is related to the belief that all science is numerical and that everything can be quantified.[26] The method as practiced is essentially mathematical, involving an attempt to quantify what is essentially (at least in human affairs) qualitative. But what if the qualitative defies quantification and can only be grasped dialectically? If the scientific method is objective and if everything can be quantified, then science can be applied to all phenomena and is infinite in its potentiality.

Science as a foundation for ethics has been entertained for several centuries. This notion follows logically from the view that society is no different from nature.[27] If society as nature operates according to certain laws (either strict causal or probabilistic), then they can be discovered. This was Comte's dream and the social Darwinists', and it was implicit in Marx's work (despite his disavowal) and even in that of the functionalists. However, every attempt to discover this scientific basis has had to assume some universal value, whether survival, happiness, or success, which upon closer scrutiny turns out not to be universal at all. The English empiricist David Hume discovered long ago that reason alone cannot lead one to distinguish good from evil.[28] The very attempt to discover a scientific basis for ethics can lead to skepticism and even to a kind of fatalism.

The question arises: If society operates according to certain laws, what difference does it make whether we discover them and publicize them? Are we not bound by them no matter what? The obvious retort is that although this might be true for strict causal laws, it is not true for probabilistic laws, which are less iron-clad. Still, if we discover probabilistic laws of society and make them mandatory, do we not in a sense turn them into causal laws? At the root of this desire to supply a scientific basis for ethics is the immanentist assumption that the only world we have is the world of facts, of what is; consequently, the world is a phenomenon to be adjusted to. What ought to be is derived from, even is, after all, only what is. This is one reason for the almost frenzied preoccupation today with exposing other people's beliefs as ideological. In a world of facts, people's beliefs only conceal and rationalize what their interests are. Today every belief and morality is seen as ideological. Therefore the quest for a scientific basis for ethics ultimately ends up in an abandonment of ethics.

From Progress to Technological Utopianism

Many of us have written and continue to write about progress as if it were still a living myth.[29] Actually the exposure of progress as ideology is in itself a sure sign that it no longer functions as a myth. When Carl Becker wrote *The Heavenly City of the Eighteenth Century Philosophers* in 1932, he recognized that the belief in progress was no longer able to inspire people to action. It has taken a long time for most of us, who prefer to think that progress was still alive in the heart of man if only to make our criticism of it seem more daring and brilliant, to catch up with him.

What often happens in this endeavor, however, is that the ideal that has been exposed as ideology is, in the act of exposure, once again restored to a position of prominence. By this I mean that the concept of ideology refers to an ideal that has not been acted upon in a universal way. For instance, in the Marxian concept ideology concealed ruling-class interests; in other words, it was specific to one class over against another class. Since ideals are almost always presented in universalistic terms, an ideal that is only partially acted upon is destroyed in the process. When Marx exposed justice, freedom, and the like as ideology he was inadvertently restoring them to their "true" status as universal human ideals. It was not that Marx objected to justice and freedom: he objected to the bourgeoisie's hoarding them to itself.

This is precisely what happened to the myth of progress. It was exposed as ideological when it became apparent that the ideal of progress—technological utopianism—was not being realized. World War I, the Great Depression, and poverty, among other things, worked to make progress appear incredulous. World War II, the Cold War, inflation, and continued poverty rang the death knell of progress. But social scientists continued to write of progress as if it were alive and well, and in so doing they kept it alive, at least its ideal—technological utopianism. And it is technological utopianism that today meets the same need the myth of progress met previously. Rather than their being in competition, however, technological utopianism is only the fulfillment of the myth of progress. Let me explain.

Vahanian suggests that man has defined himself (human nature) in relationship to three concepts: nature, history, and technology. Eliade has shown that it was only with the emergence of Jewish and Christian faiths that man began to see history as irreversible.[30] Until that time in both East and West man attempted to control secular history by periodically returning to the time of creation, sacred history. Just as nature periodically regenerated itself, so also did society. History was cyclical. The more often man felt he could ritualistically return to the beginning, the better he could eliminate the "terror of history," that is, suffering.

For the Jew and the Christian, man was not primarily part of nature but the new man of the Eschaton. The future coming of the Messiah or the second coming of Christ gave history meaning. Moreover, because this personal God intervened in human history, especially insofar as men live out their eschatological expectations in the present, history was something to be embraced, not to be avoided. Man's history and divine history intersected, then, at various points.

Lowith has demonstrated that the theory of progress represents a secularization of the Christian Eschaton.[31] Here too history takes on meaning because of a future ending of history. But in this version there was no transcendent God remaking human creation into the heavenly Jerusalem, rather it was a utopia constructed by man himself through scientific and technological advances.

The myth of progress was in one sense more about history than it was about science. When the myth came alive science and technology were in their infancy. Hence the utopia was still in the future. It was necessary then to see scientific and technological breakthroughs as immanent in history and to be realized in the future. Insofar as history is a human creation, the myth of progress is a wager about man's capabilities to "effect all things possible." But there were two major setbacks. The first has already been discussed: the moral atrocities of the twentieth century. The second, which is to be understood in relation to the first, is the very success of technology itself. The more technological progress continued unabated, the worse our "social problems" seemed. Our very successes in the nonhuman area make our failures in the human area that much more difficult to bear.

Increasingly unable to accept progress, modern man has had to face the "terror of history" symbolically disarmed. Consequently, there have been at least three distinct responses to the apparently meaningless suffering of life. The first is the return to nature, more specifically to the primordial beginnings as reflected in the sacred festival and ecstasy. All the attempts to find communion with others, whether in drugs or sex or even in mysticism, whether verbalized in myth or not, represent a return to nature. The second is the great increase in apocalyptic yearnings. Edward Tiryakian and Jurgen Moltmann have recently called attention to the proliferation of "end of the world" scenarios. Moltmann points out that this perspective is not pessimistic but optimistic, insofar as most who hold to such a belief are convinced that they are among the elect who will be saved. This second reaction to the terror of history defines salvation in relation to history rather than to nature as the first does. The third reaction is what Vahanian calls technological utopianism. It is a demand for the utopia right now. Technological utopianism is oriented to the present, the myth of progress to the future, and the myth of the eternal return (drama of creation) to the past.[32]

Utopianism has returned in full force; its strength is as great as it was in the nineteenth century. But now it is called for immediately. Books on the subject proliferate. Buckminster Fuller's *Utopia or Oblivion* frankly poses the issue: our "social problems" and environmental problems are so great that we have no other choice but to effect the utopia. This theme is echoed by B. F. Skinner, who in *Beyond Freedom and Dignity* urges the implementation of a technology of behavior control. In *The Coming of the Golden Age*, Gunther Stent takes somewhat a different tack. Arguing the well-known idea of an outer limit beyond which evolution cannot proceed, he ignores major world problems in order to forecast that progress will end with the appearance of a Golden Age. Stent is fully aware of the Golden Age's history as a myth but anticipates that we in the modern world can pull it off.

There are many more indicators of the current fever for utopia than books. The preoccupation with health reflects this desire for utopia. What else is it but a quest for earthly immortality? Some even suggest that death can be overcome. But first disease must be eliminated. Physical fitness, nutrition, preventive medicine, beauty aids—all are part of the utopian quest. Christopher Lasch has called health a religion, but this is only so in a very general way. Still, he is correct about its importance as a spiritual value. Vahanian has suggested that the Greek concept of soul, often identified with reason, dominated man's conception of himself in the West until fairly recently, when it was replaced by the concept of the body. This is in keeping with the radical immanentism of the modern world. Advertising, which is perhaps the best indicator of modern society's most cherished beliefs, has expressed the desire for utopia. Alcoa tells us, "We can't wait for tomorrow." The emphasis is on the "can't wait," not the "tomorrow." Another ad suggests that "the future is now."

Then there is the desire for security—retirement annuities, insurance, social security, and so on. We demand to be taken care of and provided for. This represents a desire to render the future safe, to eliminate or at least control the unexpected. A corollary of the desire for security is the demand for total liability. No disaster or misfortune can just happen anymore. Politicians and the public alike demand that we place the blame on somebody. That there be somebody liable for every occurrence, that nothing happen by chance, suggests a totally planned and totally regulated society—a utopia.

Less evident as a sign of utopian desire is our inability to accept inefficiency. Much of what we call inefficient is really only inefficient from an individual point of view (efficiency is gauged from the collective point of view). Often our criticism of bureaucracy or of having to wait for something is based on a standard of *absolute* efficiency. Absolute efficiency is the attribute of the utopia.

A final indicator of the utopian quest is social planning. Both public and private sectors feels compelled to plan for the future. The assumption, of course, is that to some extent the future can be predicted and that we can control our physical and social environments so well that what will happen can be allowed to happen.[33] Conferences on the future, economic and urban planning, long range planning, futurism—it all comes to the same thing: an attempt to put an end to history.

Technological Utopianism versus the Drama of Creation

As we have previously seen the major difference between the etiological myth of progress and technological utopianism (in its full-blown form) is the respective roles allotted to the ontological myths of history and science. In the myth of progress history is, as it were, ascendant over science. Although science is the main propellent of history in this myth, it is history that has been reified, almost deified. History here is at bottom man's technological accomplishments and, in respect to the future, his scientific potentiality. In the myth of progress there is hope for the future; history can be trusted.

In technological utopianism, on the other hand, history ceases to be a structure and becomes only a mass of facts for science to manipulate in the here and now. Previously history as structure was to be adjusted to while one waited and hoped for the future utopia. Now science puts an end to history as structure because through its ally, technology, it can accomplish the utopia now.

Insofar as both progress and technological utopianism are oriented toward the utopia, they can be considered together in comparison with the drama of creation myth (myth of eternal return). Eliade has repeatedly demonstrated that primitive man lived as closely as possible in correspondence to the archetypes—those primordial events and personages that occurred concurrently with the creation of the world.[34] Primitive man's sacred existence was a ritualistic repetition of the archetypes sanctioned through a creation myth. By repeating these original gestures, primitive man could return to his origins and in so doing abolish history, which is only profane time. As was mentioned earlier, it was first with the Jews that a conception of history's irreversibility emerged. With it, of course, came related concepts that are identified with Western civilization: faith, individuality, the dignity of the person, and human freedom.

Seemingly the myth of progress had aped the Judaic-Christian conception of history with its sense of the future giving meaning to history. This similarity notwithstanding, the myth of progress only shows its deeper attitude toward history in technological utopianism. History's repetition is what it assumes. The modern attempt to control and predict the future assumes repetition, as Kelsen has so brilliantly noted:

> Predictability is a criterion, though by no means the only criterion, of causality; but it is not causality itself. The presence of a causal nexus is proved not only by the fact that, as in an experiment, a predicted effect actually occurs, but also by the fact that the past existence of a fact assumed to be the cause of a given event can be demonstrated. The application of the law of causality to future events, an application which originated in practical necessity, is a secondary function resulting from the fact that cognition, although independent of volition and action, is placed at their service. Prophecy is no longer pure cognition but knowledge applied to technique. The future can be surmised from the present only on the assumption that the past, by which the present is explained, repeats itself in the future. Whatever is grasped of the future by means of knowledge is, at bottom, merely the past.[35]

The implication is clear: the application of science to the future confines us to a repetition of past and present. In this sense there is no difference between the myth of the eternal return and technological utopianism—both limit history to a repetition of the past. Social planning, then, is a ritual to the myth of technological utopianism.

According to Ricoeur, the two most essential characteristics of the myth of creation are its propositions that evil is chaos and that salvation is coeval with creation. The good gods (order) triumph over the bad gods (chaos), and thus salvation accrues to the maintenance of order (creation). Since this triumph is not total and permanent, it needs to be periodically repeated.

So it is with technological utopianism. As Cassirer has pointed out, the epistemology underlying science assumes "that the first data of human experience are in an entirely chaotic state."[36] Science represents the imposition of order upon chaos (meaningless historical data). Remember that in technological utopianism history is devalued to meaningless brute facts. Moreover, most of the data science deals with are historical. Salvation, which is coterminous with order, resides, then, in science. George Lundberg was not being facetious with his title *Can Science Save Us?* Technique becomes the ritual which allows the good order of science (probabilistic or causal laws, not ethical laws) to be repeated endlessly. Just as science imposes an intellectual order on the chaos of history, technique imposes a social order on it. Technique, whose only principle is efficient ordering, is the infrastructure of modern society. Technique is to ritual as science is to myth.

One implication of this discussion is that if the myth of progress and technological utopianism are comparable to the drama of creation myth, then social problem is comparable to defilement as a symbol of evil. Strictly speaking, the concepts of social problem, social disorganization, and deviant behavior as reflections of technological utopianism are most similar to defilement.[37] Because of its evolutionary implications, social pathology is more related to the myth of progress. Still, ultimately there is no difference between progress and technological utopianism. What do social problem and defilement have in common?

For the symbol of defilement, fault is an external happening or occurrence almost to the exclusion of individual intentionality. In the ritualistic world-view, individuals are rewarded for their good acts and punished for their evil ones by gods and without fail. Of related importance in this view is the failure to distinguish evil from misfortune. Each and every negative occurrence is a punishment. In large part this follows from interpreting nature as no different from society. What happens both in nature and in society is a consequence of the law of retribution. When good and evil are synonymous with social order and disorder respectively, it follows that the objective happening and its consequences will be emphasized at the expense of subjective motives.

So too with the concept of social problem. The distinction between evil and misfortune is not made. Everything that occurs operates here not according to the law of retribution but according to the principle of causality. In masterful fashion Kelsen has demonstrated that the philosophical principle of causality derived from and, indeed, is a secularization of the law of retribution. Every cause has an effect, much as every evil act is punished and every good act rewarded. Society and nature are similar concepts in the technological view just as they were in the ritualistic view. The concept of society and nature were rent apart most forcefully with the concept of Christian freedom. Here nature acted in perfect accord with God's will, but society did not, because individuals were free to disregard it. With Hume's critique of causality (it assumed a perfect knowledge of every relation at once) and modern findings in physics, the law of causality was supplanted to a great extent by that of statistical probability. As a "secularization" of the law of retribution, the principle of causality assumed a transcendental referent. Only a Supreme Being could have a complete knowledge of all past, present, and future relations in order to rule the world by retribution or by causality. Thus the law of probability lends itself better to modern, immanentist assumptions, for it does not assume an overall design or Providence at work. Moreover, with the scientific world-view being applied to man and society, the laws of statistical probability were deemed to be at work in society no less than in nature. Once again the two concepts are merged, but this time instead of nature's being read through society (law of retribution), society is read through nature (law of probability). Human evil and natural misfortune are of the same ilk—they both follow the laws of probability.

There is no room for intentionality and for individuality in this view. Evil once again has been made external. Accidents and illnesses are just as much social problems as are crime and delinquency; all are a consequence of the "violation" of probabilistic laws.

In several important ways the symbols, social problem and defilement, and the myths, technological utopianism and the drama of creation, are similar: both involve a view of history as repetition and a view of evil as external and socially determined. However, there is one crucial difference. Insofar as technology provides man with a way of really acting upon nature, it is more nearly possible for man to create the total order (technological utopia) he desires. Primitive man could live according to the archetypes, but physical suffering and misfortune were a constant threat. Modern man is able to control even suffering and misfortune to a great extent.

Nevertheless, the application of technique to man's spiritual life is much different from technique applied to his material existence. At this stage the human techniques applied to man's psychological state resemble magic more than technology.

CHAPTER FIVE

The Magical and Ritualistic Control of Deviant Behavior

*We are unaware even today, as we study technique—
the techniques that relate to men—that we are drawing
on the great stream of magical techniques.*
JACQUES ELLUL
The Technological Society

We must begin by defining ritual, magic, and technique, if only in a preliminary way. Following Eliade, Wendell Beane and William Doty have defined rituals as "symbols in acted reality; they function to make concrete and experiential the mythic values of a society, and they can therefore provide clues to the mythic values themselves. Hence rituals *act*, they perform, modulate, transform. . . . Rituals are also significant as a means of maintaining a sense of the sacred, as a means of sustaining religious devotion and ecstasy for the individual."[1]

Now the relationship of myth to ritual is hotly contested in anthropology, the history of comparative religion, and literature. Geoffrey S. Kirk, based upon his study of Greek mythology, suggests that they are not necessarily related. On the other hand, Clyde Kluckhohn, in his seminal article published in the 1940s, suggested that myth and ritual are usually found in tandem. He defined ritual as "an obsessive repetitive activity—often a symbolic dramatization of the fundamental 'needs' of the society, whether 'economic,' 'biological,' 'social,' or 'sexual.'" Myth, on the other hand, is "the rationalization of these same needs, whether they are all expressed in overt ceremonial or not."[2] Even among writers who agree that myth and ritual are necessarily related, there is disagreement about which came first, myth or ritual. But whether one preceded the other or both occurred simultaneously, the basic idea is that there is a homologous relation between the two. Levi-Strauss, while accepting the idea of a relationship between myth and ritual, denies that it must be homologous. He provides the example of the Pawnee myth of the pregnant boy, for which there is no corresponding Pawnee ritual. However, there was a ritual in a neighboring tribe whose values were the inverse of those in the Pawnee myth but whose underlying structure was the same. Levi-Strauss suggests that myth and ritual of different tribes can stand in dialectical relationship when the system of which they are part includes both tribes. For instance, before the eighteenth century both the Pawnees and their neighboring tribes were part of a larger tribal organization.[3]

Following the lead of Ricoeur, Eliade, and Ellul, I wish not only to regard myth and ritual as related but also to see myth and ritual as part of a larger cultural pattern that includes symbol and the sacred. In Chapter 3 we suggested a relationship between symbol and myth. Now a relationship between myth and ritual, whether direct or indirect, overt or covert, has been established. But where does the sacred fit into the picture? Beane and Doty's definition suggested that rituals help "maintain a sense of the sacred." The sacred is the "order of the world," an order, however, that has to be lived out.

The sacred or, more precisely, its hierophanies keep man on the level of the concrete, whereas myth places man in a fictive, abstract universe.[4] Ritual becomes a way of enacting a myth and thus moving back to the concrete. Myth and ritual center about sacred relations. Myth tells us directly or indirectly how the sacred affects man, enabling man to get his bearings in the sacral universe. Ritual becomes a vehicle for bringing to fruition mythical values and goals or acknowledging their presence.

I think some of the disagreement about the relation between myth and ritual can be accounted for by confusion over the sacred and the profane. Some writers consider any sign that communicates meaning a symbol, whereas Ricoeur defines symbol as a sacred sign with double intentionality (see Chapter 3). Not all of what passes for myth and ritual is related to what is *currently* sacred. As we have already seen, sacred relations (sacred axis) are not static—they change historically. But previous mythical and ritualistic expressions of the sacred do not immediately die: they live on as vestiges of the past. This is especially true of mythology, which often attains the status of literature when it has become secularized. It is not surprising that within a society there would be a gallimaufry of myths and rituals, the secular coexisting with their sacred counterparts. Nothing short of an exhaustive sociological and historical analysis of the society in question would enable the researcher to sort out the living myths and rituals from the decadent ones.

Eventually, then, the rituals to be discussed in this chapter will be related to myths and sacred relations so that the larger cultural pattern can be clearly apprehended. Before examining certain rituals we will examine one of their components—magic—and distinguish it from technique.

Magic versus Technique

In our discussion of modern technique, we are referring to means and the ensemble of means whose sole rationale is efficiency. It is customary to distinguish between material techniques and spiritual techniques.[5] Material techniques involve physical means of acting upon the world, whereas spiritual techniques refer principally to the practice of magic. It would appear that historically magic was the first set of techniques to develop.

Now, some object to the designation of magic as technique, but consider the following: (1) magic mediates between man and the gods in the same manner material technique mediates between man and nature; (2) magic and technique both aim for efficiency; that is, when the precise formula, rite, chant, or invocation has been discovered, it is not changed; (3) both are pragmatic; (4) both are effective. After a thorough study of the phenomenon, Masson-Oursel has termed magic a "scholasticism of efficiency."[6]

Nonetheless, there are some important distinctions to be made between spiritual and material techniques. Magical rites are limited to a particular civilization with no apparent diffusion occurring. Societies resist foreign magic because the magic is intimately tied up with the entire web of rites, myths, symbols, and the sacred. To accept someone else's magic is tantamount to accepting his entire way of life. Material technique, on the other hand, has been readily diffused. But more important, there has been no real progress in the practice of magic. It has always worked because people desired it to work, believed in it, only took into account its efficacious "results," or restricted its measure of success to the spiritual. Material technique, in contrast, has made indisputable progress in many civilizations. For these reasons we tend to downplay, if not ignore, the spiritual techniques, even those in our midst today—many of the so-called human techniques such as therapy, propaganda, and advertising. And if magic's usual setting was ritual, is it possible this is the setting today for the practice of certain human, spiritual techniques?

The Ritual Cycle

One of the earliest systematic studies of ritual was made by Arnold van Gennep. Although his work by no means spanned the entire range of ritual, it did deal exhaustively with what he came to call "rites of passage," the ceremonious movement from one status to another. Included in his catalogue were rites of separation, transition rites, and rites of incorporation. Not all three, however, are of equal importance or as fully developed in a particular culture.

Rites of incorporation are the ceremonies involving the practice of magic by which an individual is brought into a group and made to possess what the group already has. Rites of separation are the inverse of these in that through their performance an individual is physically and spiritually separated from his group. Van Gennep pointed out that the two sets of rites are founded on the same idea, "the setting apart of a given object or person."[7]

In the rites of separation the individual is separated from his status and group only to be initiated later into a different status and group; for example, before a boy becomes a man he must be taken from his mother and youthful peers. The third type of ritual is that of transition or margin. The individual's situation is ambiguous—he is neither where he was nor where he is headed. It is a rite of preparation for incorporation. At this stage there is a suspension of the rules, and the individual is often impelled to do what is forbidden.

Rites of incorporation, separation, and transition together form a pattern; they derive meaning and purpose only in relation to one another. Thus van Gennep terms the rites of separation "preliminal," the transitional rites "liminal," and the rites of incorporation "post liminal." Liminal refers to threshold in both spatial and temporal senses and in either physical or spiritual terms. It was the genius of Eliade to perceive that individual rites of passage recapitulate the collective rites of chaos and creation. Just as one's community returns to the time of origins, the time of the creation of the cosmos out of chaos, so too the individual must die to his old status and ways in order to be born to his new status. Eliade suggests that the collective rites of expulsion and transgression symbolize chaos or death, whereas rites of creation symbolize order and life. For the individual the rites of separation and transition symbolize death and the rite of incorporation symbolizes life. Therefore, both the individual rites of passage and collective of rites creation form a similar pattern.[8]

Like Eliade, Turner has attempted to extend van Gennep's theory so that rites of passage refer to rites involving a change in "any type of stable or recurrent condition that is culturally recognized" as opposed to only a change in status or office.[9] In effect Turner has broadened the concept to take into account all culturally sanctioned change of a ritualistic character. The implications are far reaching. It now becomes possible to see all rituals of change, collective or individual, as forming an overall system.

Rites of Order

For a long time now observers have been duly noting the secularization of traditional holy days such as Christmas and Easter. The commercialization of the holy days militates against their proper observance. What were once holy days are now secular holidays, the argument goes. Missed in the discussion, however, is the fact that these holidays have been resacralized as holy days of consumption. Boorstin's brief history of the American celebration of Christmas is apt.

In 1867 Macy's department store stayed open until midnight on Christmas Eve to accommodate shoppers and to increase profits. By 1870 December had supplanted May as the retailers' best month. Within the decade of the 1880s one store increased its wholesale purchase of Christmas tree ornaments from twenty-five dollars' worth to over eight hundred thousand. Slowly but surely the Christmas "gift which first had the force of good manners actually acquired the force of law." Witness the proliferation of Christmas bonuses and gifts to paper boys, postmen, and milkmen, for example. A most revealing indication of the transformation of Christmas and other holidays into "festivals of consumption" was a proclamation Franklin Roosevelt made at the behest of a leading businessman: it moved Thanksgiving from the last Thursday of November to the fourth Thursday, thereby adding a week to Christmas shopping that year. Greeting cards have their origin in the exchange of Christmas cards. Actually all our holidays have become holidays of consumption, as Boorstin has observed, but especially the nonpolitical ones. For instance, in 1935 a member of the National Father's Day Committee queried: "After all, why should the greatest giver of gifts not be on the receiving end at least once a year?" "The gift idea, Mrs. Dodd explained, was a sacred part of the holiday, as the giver is spiritually enriched with the tribute paid his father."[10] In the context of the argument of this book, her statement can be reinterpreted: the gift is not sacred because it is a symbol of love and appreciation but because it is a hierophany, more specifically a totem. The gift becomes the manifestation of technology. Actually, in our example, love and appreciation are a consequence of the gift and not vice versa.

But it is Christmas that is the main festival of consumption, a veritable cornucopia of goods and services. Today people spend months getting ready for it. No one can afford to wait until Thanksgiving to purchase gifts today, for they are all picked over by then. If once Christmas shopping officially began immediately after Thanksgiving, today there are no such restraints. To capture the essence of Christmas today one need only observe the opening of Christmas presents. In many families, individuals open presents in order so that everyone can enjoy what each has received; however, often the tempo gradually increases so that by the end all are opening their presents simultaneously. The psychological frenzy thus displayed culminates in collective ecstasy: the Christmas wrappings are attacked in a delicious assault on what stands between one's self and communion with one's totem (the present). When the ritual is finally completed, there is a great sense of relief—relief that the momentary satisfaction of a desire brings and relief that the work of shopping is over. The latter is evidence of man's ambivalence toward the sacred: man is both attracted to and repelled by it. Many people today complain about the onus of shopping and purchasing gifts for so many people, and in this respect Christmas is dreaded. This is nothing more than a chafing against a sacred imperative.

There is another set of rites that are related more to the nation-state. This would include the Fourth of July, Memorial Day, Veteran's Day, and Thanksgiving. Lloyd Warner has provided a detailed analysis of the ritualistic quality of these holidays and of how they express the deepest political-religious beliefs of the community.[11] The ritualistic nature of Memorial Day celebrations received special attention. Memorial Day can be seen as a sacred rite that unites all the living and the living to the dead. It is a celebration of American freedoms, democracy, and God's special favorite—America.

Certainly the Fourth of July is the main rite in relation to the nation-state, as Christmas is in relation to technology. The Bicentennial celebration of 1976 was a celebration of America's origins, a year-long Fourth of July. Thanksgiving would seem to be as much a celebration of the technological order (for example, note the emphasis on the consumption of food) as a celebration of the nation-state order. Actually all the rites participate in both sacred axes, though some less obviously so. Insofar as all the rites of order involve the consumption of prodigious amounts of food and drink, the exchange of greeting cards, and sometimes even the exchange of gifts, they are a celebration of the technological order. And even in those rites that are ostensibly nonpolitical, we must remember that America is thought of as the most advanced technological society and is the world's pacesetter in a consumption-oriented lifestyle. Therefore, a celebration of technology is indirectly a celebration of America.

The idea that the Fourth of July and other nationalistic holidays are rituals of order is certainly not new. It has often been written about in the context of civic or civil religion. But that Christmas, Easter, Halloween, Mother's Day, and Father's Day are rites of consumption and order is not as widely accepted. Boorstin is one of the few to interpret them so. The rites of consumption are part of what was identified in Chapter 2 as personal religion; the other rites of order are part of what was termed political religion.

Anticipating criticism that today most Americans participate in the political festivities in a lukewarm manner, I shall simply respond by pointing out that religions eventually lose the zeal of their believers and settle down to becoming moralities.[12] Obviously we are much more exuberant about the rites of consumption and their attending personal religions.

Although the rites of order have received attention from social scientists, rites of transgression and rites of expulsion, at least as they appear in modern societies, have received next to none.

Rites of Transgression

Rituals of transgression are part of the larger group of transition rites in which the condition of liminality prevails. The rituals of transgression, then, are related to several other types identified by anthropologists: rituals of status reversal and rituals of rebellion. Let us briefly examine them.

Edward Norbeck has pointed out that anthropologists have largely ignored the possibility that ritualistically mediated conflict makes a positive contribution to a society. Until the 1960s Max Gluckman had published the only major writings on this theme. Many of his examples were drawn from politics and involved situations where authority was momentarily suspended or authority relationships were reversed.[13]

One of his examples, drawn from a Zulu tribe, was a three-day ritual performed each year in which the king's subjects were allowed to challenge his authority. The king was denounced and verbally abused, obliged to explain his previous decisions and behavior, and eventually threatened. Of course, these transgressions would hardly have been permitted the rest of the year. Gluckman's major hypothesis was that rituals of conflict perform a cathartic role in society by relieving or symbolically resolving conflict without threatening the social order. However, these rituals, he argued, would occur only in societies whose order is actually unchallenged.[14] Caillois's ideas about the sacred of transgression would suggest that while Gluckman saw certain sociopsychological functions of the ritualized rebellion, he failed to see its larger symbolic meaning (the basic ambiguity of the sacred).

Turner has made a contribution to the study of transition rites in his research on status elevation and reversal (fraternity and sorority "turn-about days," in which members and pledges exchange roles and members are harassed, are examples of status reversal). He has observed the "dialectic of developmental cycle" in which respect and transgression, elevation and degradation, inequality and equality, structure and communitas are inexorably linked. Communitas for Turner is the communion of equals shorn of their actual structured relationships and free to treat one another as concrete, integral human beings. Now this temporary mood of communitas is just what occurs in the festival, in rites of status reversal, and in all rites of transition. Structure, on the other hand, refers to the full range of institutions, statuses, and roles in a society. Together the two form a dialectic of structure and antistructure (communitas). Turner comments on these dynamics:

> As a matter of fact, in the liminal phases of ritual, one often finds a simplification, even elimination, of social structure in the British sense and an amplification in Levi-Strauss's sense. We find social relationships simplified, while myth and ritual are elaborated. That this is so is really quite simple to understand: if liminality is regarded as a time and place of withdrawal from normal modes of social action, it can be seen as potentially a period of scrutinization of the central values and axioms of the culture in which it occurs.[15]

Not all transition rituals pertain to conflict, as evidenced by the vast number of rituals of status elevation; nevertheless, the number of those centering on conflict is vast indeed. Norbeck's analysis led him beyond rituals expressing political conflict to include, as similar, those involving the transgression of societal rules. He concluded that both types were "part of a still larger order of institutionalized practices . . . [that] provide controlled, periodic relaxation of many other rules." However, it is curious that Caillois's study of the sacred and his concept of the sacred transgression have been so routinely ignored. Eliade as well has dealt with the basic ambiguity of the sacred. Turner was very close to Caillois's and Eliade's insight when he concluded that communitas is invariably considered to be sacred because it "transgresses or dissolves the norms that govern structured and institutionalized relationships and is accompanied by experiences of unprecedented potency."[16]

Before discussing transgressive rituals of sex, violence, drugs, and revolution several observations are in order. First, the groups, cults, or secret societies engaging in these transgressive acts often have initiation rites that may or may not involve transgressions and may or may not involve all three stages of passage—preliminality, liminality, and postliminality. Second, some of the rituals involve prearranged procedures; others appear spontaneous. Third, the myths related to these rites are the inverse of the myth of progress and technological utopianism.

Where does one begin to describe the plethora of sexual rituals? The easiest and most obvious place is with the secret societies and cults whose preoccupation is sex. The group-sex phenomenon is of special interest because perhaps nowhere else is sex and sex alone the object of such adulation. Participant observers and just plain observers seem in perfect agreement about these rites—there are even guide books on the subject. One is struck after a "perusal of literature" by the number of rules governing group sex: for example, there are rules about how to find interested people, how to create a sensuous atmosphere, how to initiate a new couple, and how to maximize sexual satisfaction. There are do's and don't's on virtually everything. Perhaps the most stringent regulations deal with avoiding emotional involvements, which would threaten one's marriage. One observer claimed there were three principal ways of avoiding this: (1) swing with another couple only one time; (2) no intramarital dating; (3) encourage the bisexuality of females.[17] Another writer listed the ten commandments for swingers:

1. Thou shalt be prompt.
2. Thou shalt not bring another couple.
3. Thou shalt be lean and clean.
4. Thou shalt stay as clean as thou starts.
5. Thou shalt not pry.
6. Thou shalt never engage in sexual activity with thy own spouse to the exclusion of others.
7. Thou shalt not fight or be jealous of thy spouse.
8. Thou shalt never force thyself upon someone else.
9. Thou shalt never say "I love you."
10. Thou shalt remember there is a time and a place for everything.[18]

Most of the ritual centers on the physical appearance of the house and behavior leading up to sexual activity. There are guidelines about how to arrange beds, what to provide in the bedrooms, what to serve as refreshments, what to offer as entertainment (stag movies), when to undress, what to say as a cue to others that the festivities should begin, and what sexual games ought to be played. Open group sex (sex in public with several couples) even more than closed group sex (in private, often with only one other couple) has all the appearances of a festival. Everything here is concentrated on sustaining people's sexual interest and maximizing pleasure as long as possible.

Less formalized but ritualistic nonetheless are the sexual activities of certain groups not totally devoted to the pursuit of sex. The Manson family's ritualized sexual acts are infamous. Almost as notorious are those of Hell's Angels and other outlaw clubs. Hunter Thompson's description of a gang rape (an act in which sex and violence intersect) centers upon its ritualistic quality:

> A girl who squeals on one of the outlaws or who deserts him for somebody wrong can expect to be "turned out," as they say, to "pull the Angel train." Some of the boys will pick her up one night and take her to a house where the others are sitting around with not much else to do. It is a definite ceremony like the purging of a witch: the girl is stripped, held down on the floor and mounted by whoever has seniority. The punishment is administered in a place where everyone can watch, including the mamas and old ladies, although most of the Angel women are careful to avoid these shows.[19]

Less explicitly violent are many of their public sexual performances with willing victims. Whether on a pool table or in the town square, club members give vent to their sexual urges.

But it is not only outlaw clubs and swap clubs that are making a cult of sex. It is more widespread than that. Open-air rock concerts and collegiate rites of spring are often the occasion for public sex. The open-air rock concert with its open sexuality, widespread use of drugs, and orgiastic music often spills over into violence as well. Setting a time for the concert, obtaining financial backing, partitioning off an area, isolating the participants—what else can this be but institutionalization? And what can the collective chanting and synchronized movements, the mandatory smoking of marijuana, the ecstatic dancing, and the "free time" for sex be but ritualization?

The rites of spring provide an example of even more complete institutionalization. These annual rites, openly sanctioned by university officials at many schools, receive an enormous amount of planning and preparation: tickets, refuse baskets, first-aid stations, guards at every point of entry to the campus, and entertainment are all provided for ahead of time. Typically the scene involves thousands of students jammed together on the grass in the center of campus with various rock groups entertaining. Beer, wine, and marijuana are everywhere in evidence. At first, activity is restricted to rhythmic movement to the music, dancing where possible, smoking, and drinking. As the day wears into the evening, sexual intercourse and other forms of sexuality become more frequent. Toward the end of the festivities violence in the forms of insult, fighting, rock-throwing, and property destruction takes over. Campus and city police wait like vultures on the outskirts of the campus to make sure the delirium and mayhem do not spill over into the surrounding town.

The open-air rock concert, collegiate rites of spring, and rioting after sports events illustrate the coming together of sex, violence, drugs, and music, although not all four activities are present in any one festival. It appears that there is less awareness of the symbolic meaning of sex as one moves from the more formalized (swap club) to the less formalized (rites of spring where sex is a spontaneous part of the festivities). The implications of this will be discussed later.

Ritualized violence, like ritualized sex, is prevalent today. Richard Cloward and Lloyd Ohlin developed an ideal type—conflict subculture—about urban gangs whose central activity is violence. While admitting that most gangs are diversified in their avocations, they suggest that there are gangs that approximate this "pure" type. These gangs devoted to violence are secret societies in the same sense the group sex clubs are. Whatever the case, there is a vast literature describing the ritualistic violence of such groups. One account of a youthful street gang suggested, "We were almost bred for fighting . . . we enjoyed parties, swimming pools, going to movies, and collecting girls, but fighting was the name of the game." [20] After some of these younger gangs graduated to the older groups, the ritualistic character of the violence is more evident. The following is a description of a gang fight:

> Once everyone was together, they would march to meet the other gang. On the way they would discuss what they were going to use—knife, brass knuckles, whatever—and they're hollering, cussing, tellin' folks they got to get out of the way and

screamin' Vice Lawd' because they want everybody to know who
they are. The other gang does the same thing. . . . Everybody
has something to identify them. The Cobras had a big sweater
with a Cobra snake on it, and the Lords had capes like Batman,
an earring, and sometimes black scarves. . . . During the fight,
the baddest guys in the Vice Lords meet the baddest guys in the
Cobras. . . . The next day everybody recuperated, but fighting
goes on until one group wins.[21]

Ritualistic gang rapes are both sexual and violent, and in some cases
the violence is clearly the primary factor. In a description of one such
instance, Thompson observes, that "It was not a particularly sexual
scene. The impression I had at the time was one of vengeance. The
atmosphere in the room was harsh and brittle, almost hysterical."[22]

Less formalized is the violence that erupts during or after certain
sports events, urban riots, and the like. Robert Conat, in his sympathetic portrait of the Watts riot, provides one glimpse of the festival
quality of violence, as rioters destroyed a car: "The kids, jumping on
it, beat an ear-busting tattoo against its sides, danced on the roof, and
waved their hands in the three fingered *W* sign that was blossoming
everywhere. The *W* of the Watts gang. The mob was molding an identity for itself."[23] On the more spontaneous end of the ritual con-
tinuum is the following scene reported in the press:

DOWNTOWN PITTSBURGH TORN INTO SHAMBLES
    A massive World Series victory celebration exploded Sunday
night into a rampage of destruction, looting and sex-in-the-
streets.
    Newsmen reported two apparent assaults—some of them in
full view of hundreds who cheered the assailants—displays of
public lovemaking, nudity and drinking.
    At the height of the melee a police desk sergeant said he had
calls reporting about a dozen rapes. . . .
    The disturbance left the downtown area in shambles.[24]

Once again we see different levels of awareness of the symbolic
meaning of violence as one moves from secret societies of violence to
spontaneous eruptions of violence. We should also note the coming
together of sex, violence, and drugs.
Drug usage is perhaps the most readily apparent and ritualized of

these religious activities. Howard Becker identified three steps in becoming a regular marijuana user: learning the technique, learning to
perceive the effects, and learning to enjoy the effects.[25] The group
teaches the initiate how to smoke, how to recognize its effects on others and himself, and how to enjoy what is not inherently pleasurable
in a psychological sense. Along the way there is a whole etiquette of
do's and don't's about using marijuana. Almost commonplace is the
observation that passing the cigarette in a circle of users is a ritual of
communion or integration. One observer (but nonparticipant) at a
middle-class pill party was conscious of the ritualism involved: "A
large part of the attractiveness may be the ritual associated with this
kind of group abuse: the PDR [a holy book], the Source [the medicine
man whose preparations promise a polychromatic world of sensory
and mystical experiences], the sharing of prescribed materials in a
closed community, the sawing and grinding [of pills], the being privy
to the Pythian secrets of colors and milligrams and trade names and
contraindications and optimum dosages."[26]

Today there is widespread use of drugs even among individuals
who are not members of groups primarily devoted to drug usage. But
here as with sex and violence there seems to be variation in users' understanding of the symbolism connected with its use: the drug dev-
otee and the occasional user comprehend it quite differently.

One must be careful in discussing the ritualistic quality of revolution. Revolution does not take place in the festival, but then the festival is but one expression of the sacred of transgression. As we have
seen previously, the very word revolution has been so vulgarized it can
refer to almost any occurrence. It is within the broad ideology of revolution that sporadic rebellions take place. Caillois has observed that
war in the twentieth century shares much in common with the sacred
festival: both are paroxysms that interrupt the calm routine of everyday life; both create great tension in social life; both snatch people
from their occupations and avocations; and both effect a period of ecstasy, of communitas.[27] Revolution no less than war has all the characteristics of the festival. J. Bowyer Bell has provided an interesting
comparative study of recent revolts (for example, Northern Ireland
and Palestine) in which he discovers great similarities among the participants in the revolt. Ideologically committed and driven by a sense
of urgency, the new rebel becomes part of a new "world of unusual

values and strange disciplines, and pursues a life of hardship and risk." [28]

Harold L. Nieburg, who has clearly seen the ritualistic nature of the student "revolution" of the 1960s, provides some insights: "The festivals of radical militancy became *de rigueur* in the late 1960s and developed a pantheon of ritual figures and slogans. Blood-tingling verbs like *smash* and *rip off* and phrases like 'Up against the wall, Mother Fucker!' were combined with ceremonial profanations of all kinds, including the strongest obscenities available." Furthermore, he points out the transitory nature of such rituals, citing research that indicates that student rebellions typically lasted about two weeks; then "fatigue, boredom, and the call of private values and life-situations reassert themselves." [29] The point is undeniable that the sacred of transgression takes place within not outside the extant social order.

As we move from the political revolutions in Northern Ireland and Palestine to the student rebellions of the 1960s and 1970s, we notice a decrease in symbolic awareness and greater spontaneity, just as was the case with groups devoted to sex, violence, and drug use.

Let us turn our attention to several unresolved issues concerning rituals of transgression. One is how conscious participants are of the symbolic character of their transgression. This might imply that there are myths of sex, violence, drugs, and revolution that inspire transgressions with or without the full awareness of the participants. Norbeck has raised the question of awareness in his discussion of transition rites in Africa. Some of the research indicates that participants were aware of the symbolic meaning of their actions; in other research the data were insufficient to be able to determine one way or the other. [30] From our brief and sketchy analysis of rituals of transgression, it seems plausible that there are different levels of awareness or consciousness of symbolism as one moves from the level of those fully committed to the transgressive act (for example, secret societies such as swap clubs, drug groups, violent gangs, and revolutionary movements) to those only incidentally and sporadically involved (those drawn in by "contagion" to spontaneous celebrations of sports events, for instance).

Ricoeur is helpful here. As we have already seen, a symbol is a first-level myth. At this level the myth has not been fully articulated and developed. Those who believe in the symbol, without the aid of further mythical elaboration, may not even be consciously aware of it. Their commitment to the symbol would be largely unconscious. Hence those members of secret societies devoted to transgressive acts are conscious of their symbolic commitments, whereas those who occasionally are swept up into collective transgressive acts are perhaps only unconsciously committed.

The verbal defense of sex, violence, drugs, and revolution is perhaps best referred to as "antimyth." That is, it represents a going against the dominant myths of progress or technological utopianism. These antimyths are quite similar to what Eliade has termed the myth of the eternal return. In this myth man ritualistically returned to the time of origins, either to the chaos immediately preceding the creation of the world or to the Golden Age of creation. In commenting upon the cosmogonic myth of the Ngadju Dayak of Borneo, Eliade interprets the meaning of the orgy: "The orgy takes place in accordance with the divine commandments, and those who participate in it recover in themselves the total godhead. As is well known, in many other religions, primitive as well as historical, the periodical orgy is considered to be the instrument *par excellence* to achieve the perfect totality. It is from such a totality that a new creation will take place."[31] The fuller significance of Eliade's observations will have to wait to be drawn until the next chapter. Suffice it to say that the need for communitas, for total communion with others, can be greatly intensified in periods of perceived hopelessness and meaninglessness.

The commonality of the antimyths of sex, violence, drugs, and revolution is their desire for communitas and total renewal. The myths of progress and technological utopianism, on the other hand, promise only a continuation and perfection of the technological order. I should point out that just as the sacred of respect and sacred of transgression have a common underlying basis, technology/sex as possession and nation-state/revolution as power, so too do the antimyths and myths share the utopian desire for perfection and happiness. The antimyths complement the myths by providing immediate communitas, whereas the myth of progress or technological utopianism can only provide mediated experiences. Thus we are stressing the complementarity of the antimyths and not merely their surface opposition to the myths.

The antimyth of sex is almost omnipresent. Sex therapists and the media proclaim its (magical) powers. Correctly performed (via technique) it makes us happy, healthy, and successful; in short, it totally renews our lives. We even wonder, Is there sex after death? However, the antimyth of sex actually is a paroxysm against the technological order, an ecstatic outburst that is still tied into that order (the emphasis on a good sex life as a prerequisite for success and its reduction to a technique). Maurice North's analysis of the meaning of sex and its relationship to therapy seems to me among the very best to come along. Short of calling it sacred (this is implied), North accurately perceives how overemphasized it is, how extravagant its claims are, and, most important, how tied in it is to the technological order.[32]

The antimyth of violence contends that violence will renew either the social order (in this instance it merges with the antimyth of revolution) or the individual. Violence is seen as having a purifying effect. Georges Sorel's book *Reflections on Violence* remains a classic, but in his attempt to work out an ethic of violence he eventually fell prey to its spell. As if violence could be shackled with limits and boundaries! Perhaps the most influential mythical statement about violence has been that of Franz Fanon. In a curious contradiction he berates (and rightly so) the colonizers for their exploitation of colonized peoples. He brilliantly demonstrates how the violence of the colonizers degrades and dehumanizes them even more than the objects of their violence. Eventually, however, he suggests that one's manhood or the manhood of one's people is contingent upon doing violence to (even killing) the colonizers. In the former case violence degrades, in the latter case it renews and purifies. Here is the myth in a nutshell.[33]

Mythology about drug use sometimes draws upon Eastern philosophy. Western intellectuals such as Timothy Leary (*The Politics of Ecstasy* and *Psychedelic Prayers*) and Aldous Huxley (*The Doors of Perception* and *Island*) have drawn upon Eastern sources and were among those most commonly cited in underground drug publications. Here drugs are defined as the source of true religious experiences, ecstatic and mystical. The drug user is portrayed as one reborn into a new reality in which not only his perceptions but also his relations with others are purified and intensified.

The antimyth of revolution tends to blend together with that of violence insofar as violence is a component of revolution as conceptualized today. Revolution is thought to accomplish the establishment of a totally new social order, one in which justice, equality, and freedom will reign. But in all the utopian theories of revolution a "leap of faith" is necessary in order to arrive at the utopia. That is, it is never adequately explained just how man's nature will be so transformed (and history of man's inhumanity to man be abolished) that the bright and glorious new order will not have to be totalitarian in order to secure peace and tranquility.

It is interesting how the antimyths of sex, violence, drugs, and revolution become amalgamated in theory and in practice. Thus one speaks of a sexual revolution or the revolutionary potential of drugs. Revolution itself is sometimes portrayed as erotic or sensual (Herbert Marcuse). In practice sex, violence, and drugs form the trinity of the festival; moreover, some of those most involved were also revolutionaries, although, to be fair, it appears that some of the most zealous revolutionaries were puritanical about drugs and less than enthusiastic about a purely sexual revolution.

I do not wish to give the reader the impression that only those who commit transgressive acts participate in the festival. Quite the contrary: on account of the media everyone can take part in these activities. One can get his fill of all of these activities merely by watching television, going to movies, listening to popular music, or watching the news. If the effect of the media were largely rational and if people simply watched the sex and violence to have their views against them confirmed, I might accept the view that the media's presentation of these themes had little effect on those who consciously opposed them. But the enormous popularity of soap operas cannot be totally explained by the fact that bored and lonely people need to see interesting people whose lives they can share. Viewers seem at least as interested in vile characters as in the more or less decent ones.

As for sexual behavior, there has been even more of a change in what can be publicly represented, Nigel Kneale argues, than in the behavior itself. In his view this is where the sexual "revolution" is truly located. Yet this is not as comforting as it might be to the opponents of the revolution, for the media permit a kind of voyeurism on our part. The media's impact includes a blurring of the distinction between fact and fiction: everything is transformed into image. The media, especially television and the movies, permit a mythical escape into chaos (transgression) and into the Golden Age (the technological cornucopia of advertising) that comes after it. Therefore, everyone, young and old, consciously supportive of and consciously opposed to the sexual revolution, can participate in rituals of transgression. The sex, violence, drug use, and revolution of the media can be vicariously experienced by everyone, thus permitting mass ecstatic transgression of the technological order.[34]

Rites of Expulsion

In many societies mass transgression of sacred taboos was preceded or followed by ritualistic scapegoating, which involves the transfer of evil onto some other thing, animal, or person, who bears the collective evil of the community. He may be a willing or, more usually, an unwilling victim; and the evil he bears may be either invisible or visible, that is, embodied in something material. Originally the victim was regarded as divine, which would explain his power to expiate sins. Sir James G. Frazer explained that in the beginning the dying god was not a scapegoat; rather he was killed in order to protect divine life from the decay of old age. In the same society there would also be a ritual for the elimination of sins. Eventually, he hypothesized, the two ceremonies were combined so that the dying god now could take the community's evil with him to the "unknown world beyond the grave." As Frazer observes, however, the divine status of the victim is quickly forgotten. Moreover, today the victim often becomes the precise opposite of divine, "for when a nation becomes civilized, if it does not drop human sacrifices altogether, it at least selects as victims only such wretches as would be put to death at any rate. Thus the killing of a god may sometimes come to be confounded with the execution of a criminal."[35]

Perhaps no one has called more attention to the ritualistic scapegoating of deviants in modern society than Thomas Szasz, who has focused most of his research on the mentally ill. Recently, however, he has researched the "ritual persecution" of drug users and pushers.[36] As brilliant as much of his work on the subject of scapegoating is, it fails to make an important distinction for our purposes: the distinction between day-to-day social-control procedures and sporadic movements of great intensity to eradicate some form of evil. The modern rites that most approximate primitive rites for the expulsion of evil are neither our criminal justice system nor our civil commitment proceedings for the mentally ill, but instead are the irrational purges (such as the McCarthy Communist "witch-hunting" of the 1950s) that to some extent work outside of and go beyond ordinary social-control practices.[37]

Kai Erikson has called attention to this phenomenon in his analysis of three "crime waves" in seventeenth-century America: the Antinomian controversy involving the harassment of Anne Hutchison and her followers, the persecution of English Quakers, and the hunting down and eventual burning of witches at Salem.[38] In each of these instances the societal response to the offensive action appeared all out of proportion to its seriousness. In perceiving the Puritans' muscular reaction to the offensive acts as an attempt to define the cultural boundaries of their community, Erikson stresses the symbolic meaning of each form of deviance. Nevertheless, he does not proceed far enough in his symbolic analysis. He perceives the theological controversies largely in political terms: the dissidents represented a threat to the political power that the Puritan elite enjoyed. At times, especially in regard to the Antinomian controversy, he pokes fun at their theological hair-splitting, as if it were slightly ridiculous.

But Erikson fails to take into account that for seventeenth-century Puritans the Bible had become sacred.[39] Thus Anne Hutchison, the Quakers, and witches represented for the Puritans an attack upon the Bible as the *objective*, revealed word of God. In the Puritan scheme the political and economic orders were to be biblically based; consequently, an attack upon the social order was also an attack upon the Bible. Therefore, the persecution of Anne Hutchison, Quakers, and witches can be interpreted as acts of ritualistic scapegoating. Evil as an attack upon the Bible was expelled in the three "crime waves." With the expulsion of evil once again the biblical order could be reinstated.

Other sociologists have analyzed various crime waves, purges, witch-hunts, and so on in the manner of Erikson. Often they have been less interested in the symbolic meaning of these movements. For instance, Walter Connor, in a study of Stalin's purge of political dissidents, claims that he was more interested in Erikson's argument about the relatively constant volume of those processed by social control agencies than in the boundary issue.[40] In so focusing his study he misses the symbolic meaning of the Stalinist purges as a way of keeping communism holy. The expulsion of political dissidents was an attempt to renew the sacred Communist order.

If there is anything that qualifies as the ritualistic expulsion of evil in the late 1960s and early 1970s, certainly it is the attempt to suppress illicit drug use. It seems beyond question that there was a "dramatic increase in drug use," especially among the young, but even more important for our purposes was the increase in opposition to drugs, an opposition Norman Zinberg and John Robertson call "hysterical." In 1968 thirty-four thousand adults and fifteen thousand juveniles in California were arrested for marijuana offenses, a figure ten times greater than that of 1962. It is impossible, of course, to determine which factor, the increase in drug use or the increase in opposition to it, better accounts for this statistical increase. But this is not crucial to my argument. A 1969 Harris poll found over 90 percent of those interviewed thought illicit drug use to be a chief factor in the moral decline of America. Likewise a *Boston Globe* poll of the same year found that 83 percent of the interviewed named nonmedical drug use as the greatest problem of the country in general and of young people in particular. In a perusal of three major newspapers on a day on which there was no spectacular drug news to report, Zinberg and Robertson found the *Boston Globe* devoted eleven columns, the *Washington Post*, sixteen columns, and the *New York Times*, nineteen columns to the drug problem. The historian William O'Neill suggests in his portrait of the period that drugs induced "panic" in the old.[41]

Previously I have argued that drug use represented a religious attack upon the technological order, especially in conjunction with sex as a sacred of transgression. The sociologist Orrin Klapp suggests that the public began to sense that the drug problem was a "challenge to the very foundations of modern social order."[42] This is correct; yet without further theoretical development it remains, like the public's reaction itself, too vague. We must probe a bit deeper.

John Helmer recently suggested that the public's reaction to drugs showed the "ideological and political character of the drug danger." His empirical investigation of drug use among soldiers in Vietnam demonstrated that the antiwar soldiers regularly used marijuana, opium, and heroin, whereas the prowar personnel used only alcoholic beverages. It would appear, then, that drug use had become symbolic of revolution, at least for the public, if not for the users. Interestingly, many drug users were not politically involved; moreover, some political radicals were critical of those whose revolution was but a personal one of sex and drugs.[43]

I think the key to understanding the public's translation of drug use into political revolution is the relationship between the two sacred axes. The sacred axes are ineluctably intertwined; the technological order is necessarily today also the order of the nation-state. Thus drug use as a going against the technological order is concurrently a protest against the nation-state. Furthermore, politics has supplanted religion as a spiritual world-view, as a means of establishing a global relationship to the world. The technology/sex axis can only lead to individual religious attitudes and not to religion in the strict sense of the term. Therefore, for the purposes of collective scapegoating, the ritualistic expulsion of evil on a societal level, it is necessary to translate even those actions transgressive of the technological order (including violence and drugs) into political acts. But the question still remains: Why drugs and not sex, violence, or revolution? One can only speculate, but it seems to be a matter of convenience. That is, actual revolution was too rare. Violence was too pervasive; much of it was of a nonreligious nature. Then too, few groups were devoted to it. Sex was sacred, albeit in a transgressive way. To have centered ritualistic scapegoating on sexual offenses would have made sense if sex were a sacred of respect. But given that it represents a transgression of the *technological order*, sex does not appear as threatening as it otherwise would if it were a direct transgression of sexual taboos. And finally, nonmedical drug use was already illegal.

The ritual expulsion of the evil of drug use was an attempt to renew the American social and political order. Drug use was symbolic of political revolution and, in this regard, was no different from the communism of the 1950s that Joseph McCarthy and his supporters attacked.

A Note on Transgression and Expulsion

Up to this point rituals of transgression and rituals of expulsion have been considered as distinct rituals when in fact they are closely related. In his classic work *The Golden Bough*, Frazer observed that the "public and periodic expulsion of devils is commonly preceded or followed by a period of general license, during which the ordinary restraints of society are thrown aside, and all offenses, short of the gravest, are allowed to pass unpunished." Eliade suggests that these two types of rites are to some extent interchangeable in that both symbolize chaos. It is not necessary that both rituals be enacted. Eliade has repeatedly shown that no society has institutionalized the full spectrum of rituals.[44]

It is interesting that sometimes the rites of expulsion precede those of transgression, while other times the reverse occurs. Caillois has suggested that the rites of expulsion (in those instances where they precede the festival) are by themselves insufficient because "they only serve to bury a dying and sullied past, *which has had its day,* and which must give way to a virgin world whose festival is destined to hasten its arrival."[45] On the other hand, when the rites of expulsion follow those of transgression or when they stand alone, perhaps they represent a return to chaos for the year ahead by way of its expulsion, which is, of course, the first moment in the renewal and restoration of order.

Rituals of expulsion, then, are not merely functional to the extant order in helping to unite the community against the deviant and to reinforce communal values. They are much more than this, for in themselves they have the magical power to create order. The logic is not "scapegoating *reinforces* the social order" but rather "scapegoating *brings about* this order" by banishing evil (chaos). For the functionalist order exists first, and then comes scapegoating. But in the mythical world scapegoating occurs first and order follows.

Therapy as Technique and as a Rite of Healing

Strictly speaking, a rite of healing is not a rite of initiation, though the two can merge as in shamanic initiations. Therapy has often been compared to a healing rite. Is it possible, however, that much of modern therapy functions as much as a rite of initiation as it does as a healing rite? Briefly stated, a rite of healing involves certain magical practices by which a patient is brought back into and joined together with the community through participation in collectively held myths.

Levi-Strauss's brilliant essay "The Sorcerer and His Magic" provides an excellent point of departure on this theme. He interprets the autobiography of a Kwakiutl Indian from Vancouver, which Franz Boas had obtained and used in the 1920s. Quesalid began as a skeptic about sorcerers and their magic but eventually became one himself, losing his earlier detachment from what he was doing. The particular technique of healing Quesalid became adept at involved sucking on the patient in an attempt to extract the foreign body believed to be the cause of the illness. At the right moment the sorcerer throws up the small piece of down he has hidden in his mouth and shows to patient and onlookers alike the down covered with blood, which the sorcerer has obtained by biting his own tongue or pricking his gums. Sorcerers in other villages regarded illness as spiritual and not physical, so that they had nothing convincing to show the patient and community. Levi-Strauss notes that many if not most illnesses cured are of the psychosomatic type (as indeed all illness would seem to be) so that Quesalid's cures were first psychological and then physiological. Quesalid was apparently the most successful sorcerer around; he had won the confidence of the entire community.

At this point Levi-Strauss's analysis of the dynamics of healing begins. He demonstrates linguistically that the sorcerer's spiritual crisis and resulting healing powers are thought to be a divine gift. This cultural definition precedes the sorcerer's success at healing. Now the healing process involves a triad relationship of healer, patient, and community. As it turns out, the first and third terms—healer and community—are the most important. When the community accepts the healer's story about his calling to be a healer, it believes in him, and this belief is the source of the healing. As Levi-Strauss notes, "Quesalid did not become a great shaman because he cured his patients; he cured his patients because he had become a great shaman."[46] After Quesalid had cured patients other sorcerers could not, his rivals were disconsolate because they realized at this point that the community had lost faith in them. And with that their already-limited healing power would be diminished if not lost altogether.

But it should not be thought that the healer's role in the drama of healing is completely subordinate to that of the community. On the contrary. In order to lend credence to his claim to be a healer, the sorcerer must be skilled at "abreaction," in this case, the ability to recreate vividly the occasion of his calling. He must convince his audience that he truly has had a calling, whereupon their trust is bestowed upon him.

What role does the patient play in all this? By believing that he is cured if and when the sorcerer is convincing, he can aid the community in believing in both the patient's cure and the sorcerer's power to heal. Levi-Strauss hypothesizes that it is not just the convincing performance of the healer in extracting the source of the disease but also the healer's ability to bring about a similar ecstatic experience in his patient, a sense of a calling and being divinely guided, that convinces the community. Hence there exists a close affinity between patient and sorcerer. Both are abnormal in the sense that they have psychological experiences foreign to the rest of the community. It is no wonder that so many former patients became sorcerers, for both roles are on the fringes of society. Yet the community must view and accept the abreactions or ecstatic states so that what cannot be fully understood because it has not been experienced can at least be integrated into a structure—healing—that the community sanctions.

Turner has vividly described how a Ndembu doctor practiced his craft.[47] Like Levi-Strauss's sorcerer, Turner's doctor ("ritual specialist") performed a variety of rites and involved the community in the cure. But there are differences between the two healers. In Turner's example the doctor defined his professional role as a mediator of community conflicts. The patient's disease is interpreted as evidence of dissension in the community. Public confession of the patient's conflicts with others and their antagonism toward him was used to bring the disease to a dramatic denouement. Thus the doctor's job was to restore good will among neighbors. Differences notwithstanding, the most important similarity for our purposes is the involvement of the community in the cure.

Does psychotherapy function in the same way that primitive healing did? Yes and no. Yes, when it works, in the sense that the patient undergoes an abreaction or conversion, that the patient's expectation that he will be cured allays anxiety, and that the patient is provided hope in the form of mythical beliefs. No, in the sense that the very meaning of therapy is different from what it was in the past.

There have been numerous studies on the placebo effect in medical and psychological treatment. Jerome Frank summarizes his excellent discussion of the topic by stating that successful cases involved patients predisposed to trust others, who readily accepted "symbols of healing" and who received the enthusiastic concern of the therapist. It is the group therapies, however, that are most similar to primitive healing, principally because they sometimes supply the necessary ingredient of community that is missing from other forms of therapy. The group's approval of its leader is the source of his effectiveness with the patient, and the group's approval is contingent upon the leader's ability to live out and exemplify the commonly held myth: happiness is the discovery of the "true self." North's admirable analysis of psychotherapy demonstrates that the quest for the true self is both central and religious to that enterprise. The false self is the self that others have made of one, whereas the true self is what one wishes to be and makes of oneself. The techniques for achieving this true self and happiness involve a renunciation of one's old beliefs and, at times, one's statuses and a concerted effort to achieve mystical and ecstatic states. In line with Levi-Struass's analysis, the group therapist attempts to create the ecstatic state in his patients, a state in which the true self emerges.[48]

It would seem that the more traditional forms of psychotherapy are less successful initially than the group therapies because they cannot supply the missing term—community—in the structure of healing. Yet the group therapies are not especially successful in the long run unless they can provide clients with a permanent group. Transitory groups represent the destruction of that more permanent community upon which healing is dependent.

It would seem that the magic of primitive healing is still present in the many forms of modern therapy that are verbal in nature. Among those who have boldly voiced the view are Szasz, Andrew Malcolm, and North. Others, such as Frank and Ari Kiev, while comparing psychotherapy to primitive healing rituals, have been more reluctant to assert that there is no essential difference between the two. Perhaps the firmest evidence of the magical practices of modern therapy is provided by Richard D. Rosen in his aptly titled book *Psychobabble*. Much of his analysis centers on the empty verbiage, on the jargon with its lack of specific, concrete referents, and on the new therapies, most of which are group therapies. Collectively they represent an attack upon language and reason in the name of ecstasy, ultimately becoming vulgar forms of mysticism. For the repetition of empty words, psychological clichés, and commonplaces produces nothing other than an altered state of consciousness not unlike hypnosis. It is akin to the repetition of all propaganda, including advertising. By learning certain key phrases and repeating them in a group context, the client hypnotizes himself and helps hypnotize others. Rather than trying to change one's environment, one's behavior, or one's moral convictions, one attempts to change reality through make-believe and fantasy.[49]

Just as pervasive as spiritual technique (magic) in modern therapy is material technique, which acts directly upon man's behavior and body. In the eye-opening book *Behavior Control*, Perry London identifies three major categories of human control: (1) control by information: psychotherapy; (2) control by information: hypnosis, conditioning, and electronic tools; (3) control by coercion: assault (punishment), drugs, and surgery. London hypothesizes that psychotherapy was the first technique of control to develop (primitive healing rituals) because in part it is technologically the least sophisticated of the three. It is, after all, *only* verbal. Our previous discussion has indicated the extent to which group therapy has graduated from the first level of control to the second. Malcolm's *The Tyranny of the Group* demonstrates this conclusively. Not only mass hypnosis but also other conditioning methods are the order of the day. Both the understimulation (deprivation) and overstimulation of the senses work to reduce the individual's reason and make him more susceptible to group commands.[50] Some of the groups have moved into the third stage of control—coercion. Punishment, especially the psychological variety, is common in some of the group therapies, as Malcolm has carefully documented.

In respect to healing, modern therapy appears to have gone beyond primitive healing rites in the degree of control exerted over the patient. As we continue to experiment with drugs (to control depression, for example) and with our ability to control bodily processes (for instance, biofeedback), it is evident our quest is for the perfect technique—the perfect material technique. In light of the relative ineffectiveness of "insight therapies" and other verbal techniques, there is a growing movement for truly effective control, which means control of bodily processes such as the brain and the central nervous system. Joel Kovel attributes the great popularity of therapy in America to "our undying faith in technique and meliorism."[51] This says it all: the essence of therapy is technique. Our faith in therapy is a by-product of our faith in technology.

Anticipating later discussion of the topic, I will simply point out here that technique is pure form without moral content. London has seen this perfectly in his remark that therapy whose sole aim is to alter behavior (action therapy) "sees its methods as instruments rather than objectives and makes use of whatever comes to hand to change behavior—like hypnosis and conditioning, methods without purposes." But the question remains: Is a faith that denies moral content capable of creating that which man appears to need—meaning and hope?

Therapy, then, represents a commitment to technology as a sacred of respect. It is a hierophanic form of the sacred of technology. In the dynamics of the sacred, however, the commitment is invariably to both poles of the axis. North argues that in the main, modern therapy assumes that "sex is a component and determinant of all human behavior" and that happiness is contingent upon sexual fulfillment. Before examining contemporary therapy's involvement in the sacred of transgression, first let us analyze Freud's contribution to the technologizing of sex.[52]

Psychoanalysis was one of the first therapies to gain a large following in the twentieth century, although more often than not psychoanalytical psychotherapy, rather than psychoanalysis per se, was practiced. Nevertheless, for our purposes both will be referred to as psychoanalysis. Rieff's brilliant interpretation of Freud's thought will be the basis for much of the following discussion.[53]

Freud's view of human nature was that of a nature at war with itself. Aggressive and sexual instincts were in conflict within the individual as well as between individuals. But he reasoned that our inherited Christian culture, while important in keeping these volatile instincts in check, had done so at too great a price—neurosis. An overdeveloped superego inhibited man from achieving what his abilities should have permitted. Man's conscience would not allow him to sublimate aggressive and sexual energy into creative and socially useful channels. Instead guilt had forced man to repress these forces, thereby increasing their intensity and making them more irrational. Psychoanalysis would enable man to face up to his aggressive and sexual nature in an honest way and allow him to use this energy in a rational and realistic fashion.

As part of the facing up, the patient was to discuss his aggressive and sexual feelings. In effect, psychoanalytical treatment became a time for deviant behavior, at least for its verbalization and dramatization. Those acts whose immediate and full expression civilization could not permit were given controlled release within therapy.

Freud, however, realized that relatively few people would have the money, time, and intelligence to benefit from psychoanalysis. Yet it was the one hope with which he indulged himself, for those who avail themselves of it would be able to adjust to themselves and the world as it was. Here lies the stoicism of Freud. He was antiutopian in believing that human nature had never really changed historically. Hence, the most that could be expected was that in compromising the immediate satisfaction of our most powerful instincts through sublimation, we could minimize collective suffering.

Freud's ambivalence toward psychoanalysis is the key to understanding therapy in the modern world. On the one hand Freud liked the idea of making psychoanalytical knowledge public as a means for individuals to exercise moral control over one another: if a knowledge of neurosis is public, we can pressure one another not to hide behind symptoms. On the other hand he feared that psychoanalysis would be institutionalized and in effect become a new state religion. Yet it appears, in light of the reality of modern societies, that informal moral control implies institutionalization. In this sense psychoanalysis would represent one vast initiation rite into the new moral order. What would that moral order be?

Freud assumed that there was no transcendent reality; he was an immanentist. He believed that the most we could hope for was a life in which suffering was minimal and that we could lessen suffering by lowering our ethical ideals. Adjustment and honesty were the norms to replace the unrealizable Christian norms. But this adjustment and honesty were in respect to the world as it *is*, not in respect to the world as it *should* be. In the modern world the moral order is increasingly a technological order; hence factual adjustment takes the form of technique. Psychoanalysis is a technique for living, a way of adjusting to one's instincts that results in the least suffering for oneself and others. Freud was the most antiutopian of the therapists, for subsequent therapies, without altering Freud's moral message of technical adjustment, have promised so much more—namely, happiness and self-fulfillment.

Where does Freud really stand on the issue of sex? It is nonsense, as Rieff notes, to associate him with the so-called sexual revolution. Freud advocated neither free love nor open sexuality, for he thought history had shown that sexual license inevitably led to enormous outbursts of aggression. The answer lies in his advocacy of talking about sex within the confines of therapy. Just as the festival was a sacred time for the transgression of taboos, an ordered disorder, so too is psychoanalysis the ordering of the sacred disorder of sex. Although Freud limited the disorder to verbal disorder, many modern therapists open it to sexual play-acting and even to actual sexual behavior. So even though Freud cannot be associated with the "wild communitas" of free love and open sexuality, he can be interpreted as supporting "normative communitas,"[54] its institutionalized counterpart. Certainly this is keeping with Freud's more modest, less utopian aims. Or perhaps we can see Freud's stand on sex as a transition from desacralizing the old Christian sexual taboo (sex as a sacred of respect) to its resacralization as a sacred of transgression in relation to technology. Certainly therapists after Freud have pushed sex as personal salvation and have advocated transgressive action, not merely transgressive talk.

Undoubtedly group therapy has been the dominant therapeutic force of the 1960s and 1970s. Carl Rogers claims that the "intensive group experience is perhaps the most significant social invention of this century."[55] Not sharing Rogers's enthusiasm, I nevertheless see it as the major therapeutic context for religiously transgressive acts.

The group is not the primary setting for sex therapy, but it is often an important aspect of the therapy. There spouses or lovers can openly discuss their sexual "problems." But even in groups that do not specialize in sex problems, the discussion often turns to sex. At the Esalen Institute in California, the home of the Human Potential Movement, one of the cardinal rules is total openness and honesty about sex. Then there are the nude encounter groups. But the most enthusiastic devotees of sex, of course, are the followers of Wilhelm Reich. Bioenergetic groups feature erotic touching both as a way of being "spontaneous" and as a vehicle for the release of "orgone" (universal biological energy). Orgone is at base sexual energy.[56]

The group therapies are pervaded by violence, not so much physical violence as psychological violence. Games involving physical aggressiveness were stressed in some encounter groups. One of the most violent encounters is that of the Leadership Dynamics Institute. Participants are punched and paddled. Stripped naked, the group scapegoat is humiliated and harassed, sometimes for hours at a time. Most groups stopped short of physical violence, relying instead on a more humane approach—psychological violence. Philip Slater, perhaps not intentionally, has documented this group phenomenon. Psychological scapegoating, group pressure on the individual to conform to group norms, and attacks upon the leader are all part and parcel of the group dynamics. Interestingly, the drug groups Synanon and Daytop are among the most violent of the therapy groups. As Malcolm points out, the ecstasy that all such groups seek can only occur with the destruction of individuality.[57]

Malcolm perceptively interprets the transgressions of group therapy in the following passage:

> [Encounter group leaders] offer a license to engage in behavior not ordinarily condoned in adult society. It is the belief of the encounterists that the breaking of a taboo will release a person from the restraint that is binding his human potential. Therefore they encourage the breaking of taboos for precisely the same reason that the practitioners of the black arts reverse every ritual of the church.[58]

The transgressions are thought by the therapists in question to be a source of creativity. This certainly aligns the therapy with a myth of renewal—sex, violence, and drugs allow creativity unshackled by inhibitions to come to full blossom. Transgression is invigorating for the individual and his "potential."

Therapy as a Rite of Initiation

Is therapy today more than a healing rite? Is it also, if not mainly, an initiation rite? The answers to these questions have been hinted at. In Eliade's formulation a ritual of initiation is the ceremonial representation of a myth by which an individual passes from one status to another. As van Gennep, Turner, and others have shown, the liminal (transition) phase of the three-stage initiation rite sometimes involves the transgression of taboos. Moreover, Eliade has clearly demonstrated that the initiation rite of the individual parallels the entire set of collective rites (order, transgression, expulsion, and so on) that act out cosmogonic myths.[59] It would not be surprising, then, to find that therapy, if it is truly a ritual of initiation, involves the transgression of taboos. I have attempted to show, however briefly, that indeed this is the case. Nevertheless, exactly what is the individual being initiated into?

A key to answering this rests in Kovel's observation about encounter groups, which applies to other group therapies as well: they are geared for "normal" people. By and large the group therapies aim to enrich the lives of tense and bored but otherwise normal people. If this is the case, then, the group therapies have to be seen in a different light. Therapy, group therapy in particular, is moving closer to the position Freud feared psychoanalysis might attain—institutionalization. Hendrik Ruitenbeek has analyzed the popularity of group therapy as reflective of the "other-directed" American character type David Riesman conceptualized several decades ago. For group therapy can at once integrate the individual into the group and allay, albeit momentarily, the anxiety and loneliness inherent in life in the technological society. Part of its effectiveness, no doubt, is its ability to place the client within the mythical structure the rituals of therapy embody.[60]

Although Freud's therapy did not promise happiness (which he regarded as a goal befitting animals), most other therapies did. Howard Mumford Jones's insightful account of the American preoccupation with happiness (defined more often than not in terms of individual pleasure) demonstrates how thoroughly it has been reduced to a technique.[61] Therapy has become one of the most important, if not the paramount, means of achieving happiness. As such, therapy links its clients to the myth of happiness, which is a subsidiary myth derived from the myth of progress.

Technology's importance to the happiness of the individual lies in the fact that it provides a plethora of consumer goods and services on the one hand and security on the other hand. Therapy is a technical service that promises happiness, a decrease in boredom and anxiety, and, when it occurs in a group context, the psychological consumption of and integration with others.

It is easy to underestimate the prevalence of therapy, especially if one restricts its definition to formal sessions conducted by psychiatrists and clinical psychologists. But almost everyone is into the act today. Businesses, schools, and churches are all involved in therapy, which is not intended just for the deviant. Many of these countless therapy groups, such as self-help and special interest groups, spend much of their time exploring members' feelings under the direction of an amateur group leader. This has led Rieff to characterize modern culture as therapeutic. Goethe anticipated this development in the late eighteenth century in forecasting not merely a society whose dominant institution was the hospital but even a society "turned into one huge hospital where everyone is everybody else's humane nurse."[62]

The reasons for this occurrence are twofold. On the one hand there has been the gradual displacement of religious fervor from a transcendent God whose will included a command to love and serve others to the immanental deity, man, whose ethical demand is narcissism, the "protestant ethic of modern times." It involves a preoccupation with one's feelings toward oneself and what one imagines other people's feelings toward oneself to be. If there is no purpose or meaning to life beyond what is, it follows that the reality of one's own person will be a major preoccupation, as Nietzsche's doctrine of the "overman" demonstrates. On the other hand, competitiveness and a loss of collective meaning and purpose have engendered anxiety. Riesman has brilliantly shown how the peer group has become the measure of all things and how competition in productivity has been rechanneled into competition in consumption, especially competition for friendship and peer approval.[63]

The logical conclusion of our preoccupation with therapy, as Rieff has noted, is a totally manipulating and manipulated society. For what else can immanentists do but adjust themselves to what is and adjust others to their version of what is? And the ritual of therapy attempts to accomplish these ends: it represents an initiation into the technological order.

Therapy has become a synthesis of healing and initiation in the modern world. The healing is not merely "normal" middle-class people attempting to escape boredom and discover happiness. It is also the healing made necessary by the repression of technology and the nation-state and by the lack of meaning and hope in modern culture. These assertions will be explored in greater depth in the next chapter.

The ritualistic synthesis of healing and initiation found in therapy has its counterpart in primitive society. Eliade has identified three major types of initiation rites: puberty initiation, initiation into secret societies, and shamanic rites.[64] The shaman is a figure comparable (in certain respects) to the sorcerer and medicine man. He is a healer whose initiation as a shaman often involved his healing himself. What could be more similar to Goethe's observation that in the modern world everyone was becoming therapist (humane nurse) to himself and others? We have all become shaman-therapists!

From "Wild Communitas" to Therapy

The relation of therapy and the media to transgression can instruct us about the basis of unity in modern societies. Primitive societies achieved a kind of mythical unity. By this I mean that the symbols of chaos and the symbols of order were both articulated within a single cosmogonic myth. Chaos was meaningful because it led to order. To return to the time of chaos was to begin the renewal of the cosmos. In this situation there were no competing myths, no antimyths, as I have termed them.

This cultural unity no longer exists, at least to the same extent and at the same level. It has been shattered. The antimyths of sex, violence, drugs, and revolution (the return to chaos) are articulated, not *within* the larger mythical unity (cosmogonic myth) of progress or technological utopianism but *against* it. They represent a renewal at odds with technological utopianism and progress.

But just as at a deeper level the sacred axis is one, so too is there an underlying commonality to the myth and the antimyth. For instance, technical goods and services (what progress is all about) are supposed to lead to happiness, but so is sex in that it leads to a more creative, self-fulfilled individual. Or again, the antimyth of revolution is apparently just the opposite of the myth of the progress of the nation-state, but yet both share in the political illusion—that politics as the be-all and end-all of existence can solve the problems of man. The deeper cultural unity of the myth and antimyth is not sufficient to overcome their manifest opposition. The net result is the experience of meaninglessness and contradiction, to which the structural arrangements of modern society also contribute.

If modern societies are not unified culturally, how then are they unified at all? The answer is social structure. What modern societies lack by way of cultural and mythical unity they more than compensate for in social structure. Technique is the basis of the social structure today. Its interface with the nation-state is the single most important sociological occurrence of the modern period. Our civilization, dominated as it is by technique, tends to exclude all that is not technique. The infrastructure of modern civilization, then, is technique; this is our unity. Yet like myth, the unity exists only at the superficial level of everyday news and consumption. Technique creates the impression of "future shock," of continual change and unlimited choice. Beneath this level of superficial change there is the monotonous and unrelenting movement of technique, which changes its cosmetics but not its face. New and better techniques always supplant older and less efficient techniques. Moreover, that which is not technique either becomes technique or disappears. A corollary of this is that each protest against the technological order, each disruption and inefficiency, each transgression, is eventually integrated into the technological order. Ellul, Jurgen Habermas, and Boorstin, among others, have shown this conclusively. This is the key to understanding the difference between primitive society's control of transgression and modern man's control: *primitive society exercised mythical control; modern society exercises technological control.* Of course, primitive man's rituals were a type of human technique, and modern man's technology has given rise to myth. So it is not an either-or choice, but a matter of relative emphasis.[65]

As human technique, therapy is an important step in the integration of transgression into the technological order. A few examples should illustrate this. In the 1960s there was a certain measure of spontaneity about the open-air rock concert. The orgy that accompanied it was not preordained. However, as speculators and investors saw a chance for a quick profit, the open-air rock concert was packaged and promoted. It was integrated into the entertainment industry. Farmers' fields were rented, the concert was advertised well in advance, and the police cordoned off the area. In providing policemen society was, although unconsciously, institutionalizing transgression. The next step in the transition from wild communitas to normative communitas was the rites of spring previously described. Here the orgy was even more a technique. As tame and harmless as most rites of spring were, there still was pressure to eliminate the chance of their becoming more harmful. Of course, an even more decisive step in normalizing transgression is to be found within those group therapies where the orgy is reduced to talking, play-acting, and touching.

A similar case can be made for violence. The urban riots and riots at sports events are spontaneous and contagious. On the other hand, assertiveness training, the recent emphasis on conflict as a positive force in family life, and the therapies advocating psychological and physical violence are normative. They represent the institutionalization and taming of violence by turning it into a technique.

The discotheque represents an important institutionalization of sex and violence. At the discotheque the music and dancing are highly eroticized. Some of the dance steps mimic sexual intercourse, others, sadistic-masochistic sex. The discotheque would thus appear to be a form of therapy in which, among other things, sex and violence are play-acted to music.

Most influential in the movement from wild communitas to normative communitas has been the "media festival." The media are preoccupied with sex and violence. And because television and the movies create images that are emotionally difficult to separate from reality, we are all permitted vicarious transgression. This is akin to the transgressive role-playing Freud envisioned psychoanalytical therapy providing. Perhaps it is an even more important source of transgression for most people than the spontaneous and therapeutic alternatives. It is certainly more readily available.

Transgression has assumed, then, three forms of ritual: full participation (open-air rock concerts, orgies, crowd violence at sports events, and so forth); dramatic enactment (discotheque and therapy); and vicarious experience (movies and television). The movement from the first form to the third represents the movement from wild communitas to normative communitas; moreover, it represents transgression made increasingly technical.

Therefore, the mythical control that modern societies cannot exercise over transgression is supplanted by technological control. This point has to be appreciated in order to understand the role of the sacred, myth, and ritual in modern societies. For, as Ellul has pointed out, given the "objective" force that technology and the nation-state are, it was inevitable that they would be sacralized and that a set of myths and rituals would develop around their sacred axes. Perhaps this extremely important happening can be understood by comparing nature with technology.

Primitive man's relationship to nature is analogous to modern man's relationship to technology. But this is only true up to a point, as with all analogies. It is true in the sense that primitive man was totally dependent upon nature for his existence, just as modern man is at the mercy of technology. Primitive man's relationship to nature was largely magical. But man's relationship to technology is his relationship with himself; for as McLuhan has pointed out so well, technology is but an extension of man. But technology can work objectively, not just subjectively as magic does.[66] Magic can affect only those who believe in it, whereas technology can act upon man independently of his consciousness and belief. Now it is true that some of our human techniques, the spiritual ones, are actually forms of magic. But many others act upon man in a largely physiological and biological manner. And is this not the direction we are moving, full steam ahead? Vance Packard's *The People Shapers* documents the plethora of material techniques to be used on humans: psychosurgery, genetic engineering, cloning, biofeedback, test-tube babies, drugs, electrodes in the brain—the list goes on and on. Is the end to be that prophesied in *A Clockwork Orange*—the total control of man's psychological and spiritual condition by physical means? For the spiritual human techniques, such as therapy, are the crudest and most inefficient techniques. And given the logic of modern society—efficiency drives out inefficiency—it should not be long before the magical, verbal therapies give way to those new "therapies" that control man's transgressions in a more direct and physical manner. Therefore, myth and ritual will continue to play second fiddle to technique. Still the sacred, myth, and ritual continue to remain important categories for understanding man's relationships to evil. They have not yet been eliminated, if indeed they ever will be.

CHAPTER SIX
Sacredly Transgressive Action:
Toward a Theory of Deviant Behavior
and Social Control

*This is the hidden reason for cultural decay: that men cannot use
their power over nature for the rational disposition of the earth but
must, under force of circumstance and inescapable manipulation,
surrender to blind individual and national egoism. This is why the
whole apparatus of amusement and education, including the human
studies, becomes an empty activity; this is why everyone is
looking for meaning. The whole has lost its sense of direction and, in
its restless movement, serves itself instead of men.*
MAX HORKHEIMER
Critique of Instrumental Reason

*Here lies the grimmest joke of our present American civilization.
The vast majority of us, deprived of any but an insignificant and
culturally abortive share in the satisfaction of the immediate wants of
mankind, are further deprived of both opportunity and stimulation to
share in the production of non-utilitarian values. Part of the time we
are dray horses; the rest of the time we are listless consumers of
goods which have received no least impress of our personality. In
other words, our spiritual selves go hungry, for the most part,
pretty much all of the time.*
EDWARD SAPIR
"Culture, Genuine and Spurious"

In this final chapter I wish to consider why certain deviant actions—
sacredly transgressive acts—are committed. The analysis so far has
indicated that sacredly transgressive acts are ritualistically demanded.

This is the cultural aspect. I will attempt to show that the social structure likewise exerts an influence on the commission of sacredly transgressive acts. But most important is the dialectical interplay between social structure and culture for a full understanding of sacredly transgressive acts. I think it appropriate to discuss my theory in the context of extant types of deviant behavior theory.

Control and Strain Theories of Deviance

In a well-argued chapter on sociological theories of deviance, Travis Hirschi identified three main types: strain, control, and cultural deviance theories.[1] Strain theory, assuming that man naturally conforms, looks for the motivation to commit the deviant act. On the sociological level it might emphasize the lack of legitimate opportunities to get ahead in a society that stresses success, or it might emphasize economic repression. On the psychological level the strain might be anxiety, re-sentiment, or sexual frustration.

Taken to its logical conclusion, control theory makes just the opposite assumption about human nature, namely, that man is naturally deviant. The question now becomes, Under what circumstances do people conform? Control theory argues that when society is not sufficiently present in individuals, when the individual has no stake in society, when his interests, beliefs, and emotional relationships run counter to those of "conventional" society, then the individual becomes "free" to commit a deviant act. The less society controls an individual, the more he does what comes naturally—deviance. Like strain theory, control theory can operate on the psychological level. Here one can theorize about the control of conscience, of ego, of reason, and so forth.

As Albert Cohen has pointed out, however, the two theory types that in their extreme form are contradictory are often found together.[2] For instance, in Freud, there is the strain of id and the control of superego. Or in Merton's anomie theory there is the strain of achieving a cultural goal whose legitimate opportunities for acquisition are blocked. This leads to the lack of control that is anomie.

Cultural deviance theory is in one sense a form of control theory. Rather than assuming one culture, one morality, as does control theory, cultural deviance theory assumes a plethora of interest groups, each with its own standards. A foremost proponent of this theory type, Edwin Sutherland, suggested that an individual in committing a crime might be deviant from the standards of some others but in conformity with those of his own group. As a variant of this theory type, cultural transmission theory suggested that in American society in the 1930s the divergent cultural and moral standards that were becoming more evident among lower-class immigrants was due to the paucity of legitimate opportunities for success. Consequently, some began to condone certain kinds of crime. In this argument the strain of the absence of opportunities gave rise to divergent moral positions. Now this was all well and fine to place the issue of strain and control in its historical context, but it is still not sufficient. For actually the issue is the weakness of the very classifications, strain and control.

For instance, Durkheim was not simply a "control" theorist. Certainly his assertion that egoism and anomie both represent the "insufficient presence of society in the individual" makes it impossible to deny this altogether. Yet in another sense he was a strain theorist. In his great work *Suicide* Durkheim talks about how the individual's appetites become excited in industrial society. It is not just the Hobbesian idea of man's evil nature being given free reign, but also the idea that society was deliberately fostering unlimited aspirations "by the very development of industry and the almost infinite extension of the market."[3] Now as Merton was to discover later, to be in a state of unlimited aspirations is to be placed in a stressful state, whether one's access to the legitimate opportunity structure is blocked or not; for by definition such aspirations are unrealizable. Furthermore, Durkheim suggests that those who do not succeed might become jealous of those who do.

Egoism presents a related but nonetheless distinct problem for the individual. On the sociological level it is the disintegration of the social group, whereas on the psychological level it is experienced as "man's no longer finding a basis for existence in life" or, in other words, the absence of meaning. Durkheim correctly perceives that individuals have a need to ascribe meaning to what they do and, moreover, that meaning is not something one can invent all alone (as in madness) but rather is something that must be defined and lived out in concert with others.

In essence the absence of control (society's insufficient presence in individuals) on the sociological level is experienced as strain on the psychological level (unlimited aspirations, absence of meaning). Durkheim's emphasis is on the individual's need for others (society) to help regulate his appetites and to make his world meaningful. Not blessed with Freud's insight about man's profound ambivalence toward his fellow societal members, Durkheim ends up overemphasizing the objective side of society and man's need for order.

Perhaps, however, we have been too hasty and facile in our criticism of him. For in a footnote in the chapter on anomic suicide, Durkheim points to a fourth type of suicide—fatalistic suicide, which is the "suicide deriving from excessive regulation, that of persons with futures pitilessly blocked and passions violently choked by oppressive discipline."[4] Certainly this indicates that Durkheim recognized that too much regulation and integration into society could be as much a problem as too little. Yet he dismisses its importance in industrial society, regarding it instead as a historical problem. For Durkheim control was principally a cultural phenomenon. And because he saw Christian morality in a state of decline and natural groups disintegrating, he thought he could dismiss fatalistic suicide as a contemporary problem.

But what if, as some have argued, control and meaning were passing from culture to what Habermas calls "subsystems of purposive-rational action?" Habermas describes the conditions under which a society might be characterized as traditional:

> "Traditional" societies exist as long as the development of subsystems of purposive rational action keep within the limits of the legitimating efficacy of cultural traditions. This is the basis for the "superiority" of the institutional framework, which does not preclude structural changes adapted to a potential surplus generated in the economic system but does preclude critically challenging the traditional form of legitimation.[5]

Habermas is suggesting that social institutions are dominated either by cultural traditions or by instrumental and strategic considerations. In traditional society, culture dominated technology so that each new technique or invention was legitimated or justified by existing cultural traditions or modifications of them within each institution. In modern society instrumental and strategic (efficiency) considerations supplant cultural traditions and are themselves the legitimating criteria. This is why Ellul, like Habermas, argues that technology has become autonomous, the actual basis of modern society. Technology at the material level gives rise to the ideology of technology at the spiritual level. The subsystems of purposive rational action have extended their dominion to the cultural level. If this analysis is sound, then along with taking stock of the collapse of culture and dissolution of natural groups (community and kinship) in the modern period, Durkheim would have needed to assess the control that technology and its ideology were exerting. In a sense, *The Division of Labor in Society* was an attempt to do this very thing. And, in his favor, it seems that in the nineteenth century the vacuum that the disappearance of a Christian culture had created was not adequately filled by the embryonic presence of the ideology of technology. It is necessary, I think, to separate the effect of technology from the effect of the ideology of technology. For, in fact, technology itself may be considered to be exerting a strong "control" today, even one meeting Durkheim's depiction of the stringent control capable of causing fatalistic suicide. But the ideology of technology may be so weak that the meaning of existence is left problematic.

In order to understand the workings of modern society, then, we must put Durkheim and Marx together. Durkheim's insight into industrial society—that meaning and purpose were disappearing—stands today. This is the cultural issue. Marx's brilliant understanding of the relationship between the forces and relations of production and the key role technology was playing is likewise still pertinent. This is the social structural issue. Naturally, one cannot apply their respective ideas willy-nilly, for social reality has changed considerably since their time.

Social Structure and Transgression

Social structure is *the* critical meeting ground for culture and psyche. As Ellul has noted, "Social structure gives meaning to life"—which is to say that social structure and social institutions have been the collective putting into practice of culture as theory.[6] If social structure contradicts culture to any great extent, the result on the psychological level is the experience of absurdity and meaninglessness. Whether such a major contradiction occurs has important consequences for the sacred festival. With this in mind I will begin to make a series of comparisons and contrasts between primitive society and modern technological society as representing near-polar types of social organization. The discussion will be general.

In primitive society there existed more or less a balance between the sociological and psychological levels of society. That is, the forces or structures that *controlled* man were meaningful to him psychologically and, moreover, allowed him to express his instinctual, ecstatic needs, as in the sacred festival. In primitive society, as Stanley Diamond has observed, man's survival needs were taken care of unless the entire society's survival was in question.[7] Private property was almost nonexistent, thus taking away a frequent cause of re-sentiment and envy. Certainly the wielding of political power is in itself a sufficient cause of strife, but the religious culture contained a myth or myths justifying the extant social structure. Furthermore, the cosmogonic myth often provided for a sacred festival in which the taboos could be violated and man's inherent need for ecstasy, revolt, and uninhibited behavior could be released. The individual was well integrated into the group, although societies differed in the competition they encouraged between groups such as moieties, secret societies, and clans. The structural and institutional arrangements of society provided a fit between culture and psyche. I do not wish to romanticize and idealize primitive society, for it neither possessed a true sense of individual worth nor did it accept serious dissent. However, there was a greater acceptance of less serious forms of deviation. It is a well-known fact that shamans and sorcerers were often recruited from those who were psychologically maladjusted.

In modern technological society, on the other hand, there exists a serious imbalance between the sociological and psychological levels of society.[8] Social structure and social institutions do not embody culture in a way that allows the individual to find meaning and purpose in life. Thus they repress man. But does not the loss of meaning and purpose vary inversely with the repression of social structure? As was previously noted, on the theoretical level we tend to see a Durkheimian emphasis on the loss of culture and a Marxian emphasis on the repression of social structure as mutually exclusive. And do we not perceive them to be politically antithetical as well? Even for those who do not insist that a Marxian or a Durkheimian view be superimposed on all of history, there is still, I think, a tendency to see the loss of cultural meaning and the repression of social structure as mutually exclusive.

For example, Turner's erudite work on communitas is illustrative. Turner is perhaps the only modern theorist to have fully explained how attacks upon the social structure can be both necessary and safe. Communitas or the ecstatic feeling of unity occurs most intensely when the extant order is temporarily suspended. People are shorn of their statuses and can relate as equals. Communitas can be either normalized as part of ritual or spontaneous (raw or wild). When normalized it often takes the form of a ritual of status reversal or of a festival. Raw communitas is a "phenomenon of major social change or it may be, sometimes a mode of reaction against too rigid a structuring of human life in status and role-playing possibilities." Therefore, both too little structure (major social change) and too much structure can facilitate wild communitas. However, Turner does not see both happening concurrently, nor does he envisage a situation in which wild communitas does not really threaten the social order.[9]

Turner's fellow anthropologist Mary Douglas might not agree with his conclusion about the relationship of structure to communitas. In her provocative and insightful book *Natural Symbols* she considers a society in which there is simultaneously both too little and too much structure. Her theory identifies two dimensions of social organization: grid and group.[10] Grid represents the entire system of classifications in a society—cultural and social structural—such as language, religion, and morality on the one hand and statuses, roles, and classes on the other hand. Grid is visualized on an axis whose poles are a system of shared classifications and a system of private classifications. The former system is so highly articulated that little divergence in interpretation is permitted. In the latter system the individual is "free" to construct his own world-view, his own system of classifications. Group is likewise visualized on an axis; its poles are strong social control by others and strong personal control over others. In the former case the individual is a social cipher whose life is almost completely controlled by others; whereas in the latter case the individual exercises maximum personal control over others. At the intersection of the two axes there is a point zero, where both grid and group are absent.

Douglas uses her diagram to plot the position of an entire society or, in many cases, the position of various groups within a society. Four distinct types are identified. The first, "high classification," is a society in which both grid and group are strong. Here the leaders do not truly exercise personal control over others because the shared classification system constrains them. This is the case of the integrated society, one in which all members' religious and moral beliefs are similar and in which the social structure does not unduly favor one group over another or one individual over another.

The second, "small group," is a society with two or more strongly integrated groups that are, however, in conflict with one another. The classification system is less clearly articulated, perhaps even ambiguous and contradictory. Each group's interpretation of the classification system serves as its boundaries. The leaders within each group are well integrated into the group, and their power, while greater than that of the high-classification leaders, is by no means either exploitative or absolute.

The third and fourth types occur in a society termed "strong grid." This society is characterized by one or more power elites that rule in a largely distant and impersonal manner. The multitude of powerless chafe under such rule, especially since the strongly articulated classification system fosters individual competition and individual success. Such a society, Douglas notes, suffers from an inherent moral weakness because egalitarian principles are so obviously not put into practice that the disenfranchised become susceptible to religious and political utopian movements that promise an end to injustice. In the strong-grid society the various powerful leaders have their own followings, but their power, while much greater than that in the other two types of society, is also more transitory. Hence the struggle for power is an ongoing process.

Modern industrial societies are characterized as strong grid by Douglas. Unfortunately her theory is not dialectical enough to grasp the complexity of the situation. She notes this herself, when in referring to several historical exceptions to her typology she observes, "The whole diagram becomes too complicated when the precepts of the renouncers are accepted by society at large and come to control the idiom of public classification."[11] Yet she fails to see that modern industrial societies fit this exceptional status.

But in order to elaborate on this point, we have to make a distinction between cultural classification and (social) structural classification. Douglas lumps together culture and social structure as classification, thereby assuming that they are directly related. I will argue that in contemporary technological societies part of culture directly reflects social structure and part of it contradicts it. In Douglas's theory, on the other hand, there is no room for a classification system to be contradictory. Only in the small-group society does the classification system become somewhat ambiguous and contradictory, and then only because multiple classification systems arise.

A similar problem appears with respect to the group variable when Douglas reduces this variable to the degree of human control that one exercises over others or has exercised over oneself. Douglas cannot handle the modern situation where control is increasingly centered in an abstract way in technique and the political state. This renders virtually everyone powerless in terms of the actual structural conditions but, paradoxically, permits maximum psychological manipulation of others on a more ephemeral level. Furthermore, propaganda facilitates simultaneously the integration of the nation (for example, in consumerism) and the integration of competing groups such as racial, ethnic, and interest groups within the larger whole. Yet propaganda renders the individual even more lonely and anxious at the very moment he is integrated into the group or the nation.

Criticisms notwithstanding, Douglas has rendered an important service. She has demonstrated that culture is not just control and superstructure but that it can and sometimes does satisfy man's need to live a meaningful existence without necessarily "exploiting" him. With Marxist assumptions so dominant today, anyone emphasizing man's need for meaning in a shared culture is automatically branded a conservative, and perhaps justly so. However, it should be pointed out that the present social arrangements repress man and actually prevent a livable culture from emerging.

As important and as well thought out as Douglas's work is, it is still too abstract and static to grasp the modern situation. In working through a theory of sacredly transgressive behavior, I wish to remind the reader that the theory is applicable only to the historical and existential conditions of modern society.

To begin with, I note that strain and control are dialectical concepts. When does strain become a form of control? Under what circumstances does too much control become strain? Are both too much control and too little control forms of strains? If we keep the dialectical and thus relative nature of these concepts in mind, the following discussion will seem less oblique.

Put very briefly, my argument goes something like this: technology and the nation-state as the basis of social structure in modern societies repress man, creating in him an intense need for the release of ecstasy. At the same time, technology and the nation-state are regarded as sacred on the cultural level, but without providing man with sufficient meaning; he therefore attempts to find meaning in their opposites (sacred of transgression)—sex and revolution. Therefore, sex and revolution, at one and the same time, meet man's increased need for ecstatic experiences and for meaning. In a situation where the basis of social structure is held sacred, a repressive social structure thus creates an increased need for sacredly transgressive acts. (This would seem to be a variant of Turner's observation that a repressive social structure creates a need for wild communitas.) In short, modern man is controlled through strain—the strain of a repressive social structure and the strain of meaninglessness on the psychological level. It is actually, we will see, the great tension technological societies generate that allows them to follow their logical development. The convulsions against the technological order ultimately strengthen its hold over us. The strain this order creates and our resistance to it are its dynamics.

The question of technology's impact upon man has been studied by Gabriel Marcel, McLuhan, and Ellul, among others.[12] But perhaps the earliest incisive analysis was Georg Simmel's brilliant essay "The Metropolis and Mental Life," which parallels in many important ways Robert Musil's great novel *The Man without Qualities*. Simmel notes early that the individual fights against "being leveled down and worn out by a social-technological mechanism."[13] The "social-technological mechanism" here is the metropolis. A number of reactions are in part or in whole attributed to the metropolis—the blasé attitude, antipathy toward others, the blunting of our powers of discrimination, intellectuality, and an overemphasis on the ephemeral, the unique, and the particular.

The metropolis proliferates and intensifies the "nervous stimuli," including "sensory mental imagery." The metropolis dweller is confronted with numerous human relationships, which by their sheer number cannot all be allowed to become deeply emotional. The tempo of life in the metropolis, schedules, the division of labor, and the impersonality of the money economy work to produce a reaction of intellect instead of habit or feeling: man "reacts with his head instead of his heart." Simmel comments on the origins of the blasé attitude, which is a defensive reaction: "Through the rapidity and contradictoriness of their change, more harmless impressions force such violent responses, tearing the nerves so brutally hither and thither that their last reserves of strength are spent: and if one remains in the same milieu they have no time to gather new strength. An incapacity thus emerges to react to new sensations with the appropriate energy."[14] This is only the "faithful subjective reflection of the completely internalized money economy." For money, as Marx noted earlier, mediates all relationships or, in Simmel's terms, becomes the "common denominator of all values." To react to all stimuli in a blasé fashion is only to re-create within oneself the leveling of all phenomena that the money economy creates objectively.

With regard to other people, however, the blasé attitude spills over into a "latent antipathy." Simmel argues that just as it would be unnatural to be easily and readily influenced by everyone in the metropolis, so too would the mere indifference toward the others be unnatural. Antipathy, then, is a protection against both.

Yet Simmel recognizes a side to psychological life in the metropolis that does not merely reproduce internally what the money economy and the other leveling techniques accomplish externally. Unable to accept his reduction to a social cipher, the individual exerts the "utmost in uniqueness and particularization in order to preserve his most personal care." Hence, at some point the individual ceases to be a microcosm of the external forces and becomes its inverse reflection.

In his discussion of how intellectuality, the blasé attitude, antipathy toward others, the blunting of our discriminatory powers, and an emphasis on the unique and particular protect the individual against overstimulation and emotional unrest, Simmel anticipated the work of McLuhan. In *Understanding Media* McLuhan compared technology's psychological impact upon the self to the physiological effect of injury or disease upon the central nervous system. When faced with stress or irritation, the organism has two principal means of restoring equilibrium to the central nervous system. The first is the elimination of the irritant by overcoming it or escaping it; the second is counterirritation in which the central nervous system "amputates" (that is, numbs) the affected limb or organ at the point of stress. Pleasure and therapy, McLuhan noted, are counterirritants, just as comfort is the elimination of stress or irritation. Physical shock and schizophrenia are extreme counterirritants: shock allows one to narcoticize physical stress, and schizophrenia "amputates" psychological stress. By way of analogy we can compare the self's handling of psychological stress to the central nervous system's control of physical stress. McLuhan argued that man has always been fascinated by extensions of himself. These extensions dull the perception until man becomes the "servomechanism" of his own extension in much the same way the Greek protagonist Narcissus becomes the slave of his own image reflected in the pool of water below him. Now the point of the story, as McLuhan observes, is that Narcissus died *not* knowing that it was his own image. McLuhan's application of the theory of counterirritation to technology is aptly illustrated in the following passage:

> The stimulus to new invention is the stress of acceleration of pace and increase of load. For example, the case of the wheel as an extension of the foot, the pressure of new burdens resulting from the acceleration of exchange by written and monetary media was the immediate occasion of the extension or "amputation" of this function from our bodies. The wheel as a counter-irritant to increased burdens, in turn, brings about a new intensity of action by its amplification of a separate or isolated function (the feet in rotation). Such amplification is bearable by the nervous system only through numbness or blocking of perception. This is the sense of the Narcissus myth. The young man's image is a self-amputation or extension induced by irritating pressures. As counter-irritant, the image produces a generalized numbness or shock that declines recognition. Self-amputation forbids self-recognition.[15]

Pleasure is a chief form of counterirritation. McLuhan cites sports, alcohol, and entertainment as examples. Ecstasy is perhaps the ultimate in pleasure. Following McLuhan's logic one would expect that the greater the extension of man in technology (the greater its tempo and pervasiveness), the greater the need for heightened or stronger pleasure, and hence for ecstasy. This is a major point of his *War and Peace in the Global Village*, for violence too is a form of ecstasy. In his remarkably insightful book *Fellow Teachers*, Rieff calls it the "ultimate therapy." In addition to these social-structural considerations is the fact that happiness defined in terms of pleasure has been a paramount cultural value in the West for two centuries. The search for sensual happiness leads to ecstasy.

Ellul, like McLuhan, has discussed the technology-ecstasy relationship, suggesting that an emphasis on ecstasy today is actually the result of society's having become overly technical. "It is a function," Ellul argues, "of the acceleration of the tempo of the technical society." [16] By this he means the rate of increase in the speed by which society is being technologized. Why should the tempo so repress man that ecstasy erupts?

To answer this we must first comprehend the nature of technique. As Ellul defines it, "*technique* is the *totality of methods rationally arrived at and having absolute efficiency* (for a given state of development) in *every* field of human activity." [17] Technique has become the infrastructure of modern society. All individual techniques are interrelated. The techniques of the present are radically different from those of the past in the sense that modern societies are *dominated* by technique, whereas in traditional societies technique was integrated into and subordinate to culture.

The mechanization of society reduces the ways in which instinctual energy can be released. Ellul comments:

> These observations confirm Roger Caillois' statement that the more restrictive the social mechanism, the more exaggerated are the associated ecstatic phenomena. The restrictions imposed by technique on a society reduce the number of ways in which religious energy can be released. In a nontechnical society there are a plurality of ways in which psychic energy can be channeled; but in a technical society there is only one. Technical restrictions eliminate all secondary objects. Human psychic energies concentrate, and there are no "leaks." The result is ecstatic phenomena of unparalleled intensity and duration. [18]

Man cannot tolerate living a completely mechanized existence. He needs to feel free even if he is not so. Technique represses the spontaneous in man because it represents order, efficiency, and planning. Ecstasy in this context is an impulsive breaking of the technical chains of restraint.

Insofar as the political state is necessary for the technique to develop and grow by funding and administering it, ecstasy is also directed against it and the nation. The political state has itself become highly technologized, that is, bureaucratized. Ecstatic phenomena are a response to the complex of technique and the nation-state.

If we bring together McLuhan's and Ellul's thoughts on technology and ecstasy we obtain the following: ecstasy is a counterirritant to the irritation that technology creates in the central nervous system and the psychic self by not permitting human impulses to be released and expressed. Technique is abstract; impulses are concrete. Technique is collective; impulses are individual. Technique denies all emotion and impulse, everything that is not technique.

Herbert Hendin's analysis of the experiences of students at Columbia University in the late 1960s illustrates the technology-ecstasy relation perfectly. Many young people unconsciously, and some even consciously, envied machines because machines can function without suffering. Knowing that they were regarded as burdens by their parents, often treated as objects of efficient socialization, these troubled young people were attempting to flee from strong emotions and passionate commitment. They desired instead to become machinelike on the one hand or to give themselves over to random sensations on the other hand. Often they fluctuated from the technological to the ecstatic adaptation. Hendin's findings parallel those of Karen Horney decades earlier. Horney argued that the Dionysian pursuit of pleasure often represented an attempt to allay neurotic suffering.[19]

At one point in his analysis, Hendin chides social scientists for seeing too direct a relationship between the economy and individual pathologies: "The burial of frustration and pain, the emphasis on function over feeling, the wish to flee from feeling entirely into pleasurable sensation or emotionless performance fill many students' lives and [might] seem to be designed for a society which stresses the technological virtues and consumer appetites."[20] The family, he argues, is an institution more or less independent of other institutions. It has its own logic.

Hendin's protest notwithstanding, I think that his findings actually support the position against which he is arguing. In case after case the parents of the troubled student took little genuine interest in their child's needs. Instead they attempted to control their child's behavior as efficiently and abstractly as possible. The qualities of this approach to child-rearing are analogous to those of technology and bureau-cracy—efficiency, impersonality, abstractness of relation. I would ar-gue that a society dominated by technology and bureaucracy is more likely to produce, especially among the wealthier classes, families that reflect these very tendencies.

Thus far our discussion of ecstasy does not distinguish its individual from its collective expressions. The latter is most needed today. Eliade has suggested that the orgy represents the method par excellence for experiencing the primordial totality, a condition of being undifferen-tiated from others.[21] Modern technological societies produce apathy, the blasé attitude, and extreme individualism; moreover, they make for a segmented and lonely existence. The orgy as a special form of ecstasy represents an attempt to make existence less lonely. The more alone one becomes the greater the need to lose oneself in a group. Therefore it is not merely ecstasy but group ecstasy that is in high demand.

In primitive society ecstasy was expressed in rituals, not only in the sacred festival but also in the liminal period of passage from one sta-tus to another (rites of passage). The sacred festival and rites of pas-sage were periods of both sensual and mystical ecstasy.

Technique, however, has accomplished the demise of ritual, at least traditional ritual. Human techniques contain a magical component, but, unrecognized as rituals, they do not allow the release of human impulses in a culturally defined and thus meaningful manner. The rituals of transgression in primitive society were meaningful because they were mythically related to and integrated with the rituals that up-held the social structure. They were necessary to revitalize the social order and were consciously perceived as such. Today the antirituals of transgression and the antimyths supporting them do not have the full, conscious support of society.[22] Thus the antirituals of transgres-sion reinforce the social order, not in a cultural, mythical way but only in a structural, technical way. Sex, violence, and revolution do not ac-tually threaten the extant social order; they only reinforce it. For the logic of the technological society, as Ellul and others have clearly shown, is that each disruption, each inefficiency, each disorder is eventually subject to and reduced to technique. Ecstasy breaks out in areas of life not yet fully technologized. We have already seen how sex and even violence have been reduced to techniques in therapy. Ec-stasy, even sensual ecstasy, is not an upheaval that threatens the technological order but an eruption necessary to its growth and development, the very dynamics of its continued existence.

Therefore it becomes apparent that widespread sensual ecstasy, far from being the result of too little control, is in fact a consequence of too much order, at least on the level of social structure. But what about on the cultural level? Here it is an entirely different matter.

Culture and Transgression

The problem of modern culture has been defined by countless social scientists over the past two centuries. There are four interrelated dimensions of this issue I wish to center upon: cultural contradictions, meaninglessness, reification, and hopelessness. Before doing so, however, it may prove helpful to make some preliminary remarks about Edward Sapir's brilliant article "Culture, Genuine and Spurious."

Sapir identifies three categories of definition of culture. The first, widely accepted today, defines culture as the sum total of man's creations and achievements, both material and spiritual. The second defines culture as the "high culture" that only certain individuals acquire. In so doing they become "cultured." The third defines culture in a spiritual and collective way, as in American culture, French culture, and so on.

Not accepting any of these definitions per se, he combines the second and third definitions in an ideal way. Genuine culture involves a dialectical movement of "communal culture" and the "individual incorporation of a cultured ideal." It provides its bearers a "sense of inner satisfaction, a feeling of spiritual mastery."[23] Furthermore, it relates the immediate end of survival to the more "remote ends" or spiritual values in a meaningful fashion without overemphasizing survival. Genuine culture, moreover, is respectful of the past, learns from and renews the best of it. Finally, it does not encapsulate the individual, but instead leaves him some room to contribute to that very culture of which he is the beneficiary.

Sapir identifies American culture as spurious. What he had to say about it in 1928 is even more true today. For instance, he points out something Marxists would agree with, namely, that the economic sphere of life is unable to provide people satisfaction and mastery in their work, in part because of extreme specialization. Consequently, they turn to nonutilitarian values in compensation. Even the otherwise astute critic David Riesman fell into this trap in *The Lonely Crowd* when he argued that creative leisure might provide compensation for alienated work. But as Sapir points out, the "remote end" or nonutilitarian values are outside our control as well, for we have become "listless consumers." The propaganda of advertising and human relations controls spiritual values in such a way that we are literally stuffed full of passive, standardized culture. This propaganda, of course, emanates from the nation-state. Small autonomous groups alone can provide the fertile ground for the proper cultural balance between individual and society to occur. Today, however, the "national-political unit tends to arrogate culture to itself."[24]

Sapir's incisive analysis correctly saw the problems technology and the nation-state were creating for culture. But there are other problems as well, such as cultural contradictions. In discussing cultural contradictions, we will also include contradictions between social structure and culture.

In her monumental work *The Neurotic Personality of Our Time*, Karen Horney identified three cultural contradictions. The first was between the emphasis on competition and success on the one hand and the emphasis on love and humility on the other hand. This represents, of course, part of the bourgeois synthesis between Christian morality and power. As Horney points out, one cannot take both admonitions seriously at the same time. One way out for the middle classes of the nineteenth century was to make a distinction between the public and private spheres of life. It is not difficult to figure out which ethic (success or humility, competition or love) went with which sphere. This was a sociological solution but hardly a psychological one. The second contradiction was the stimulation of wants versus the factual frustrations in realizing them. As Durkheim noted, the ambition to possess and dominate is insatiable in industrial society, especially today with its members being perpetually titillated by advertising. Contradicting this desire is the social structure, which denies most people's wants except on the rarest occasion. The third contradiction was the declaration of freedom for the individual as opposed to the enormous constraints under which he lives—technique, propaganda, the nation-state, and so on. Others that come readily to mind include an ideology of peace versus the perpetual cold war and nationalism versus extreme individualism.[25]

Daniel Bell sees modernism in conflict with the tradition of Western civilization, which is largely a synthesis of Greek philosophy and a Judaeo-Christian morality. Western civilization placed great importance upon reason, self-control, freedom with responsibility to others, and a sense of the common good. Modernism, on the other hand, is characterized, as Bell notes, by an "eclipse of distance" in all domains of life with a resultant emphasis on the "absolute presentness, the simultaneity and immediacy of experience," and by a deification of the self.[26]

Perhaps it would not be too much of an injustice to suggest the following synthesis of various cultural contradictions: there exists at least a three-way conflict among a traditional Christian morality that is being reduced to the rank of mere custom; a technological morality with its themes of success, power, and efficiency; and a counterculture protest against morality with an emphasis on ecstasy, revolution, and self-fulfillment. This three-way conflict makes life unbearable at the level of values and meaning.

Existentialists have been talking about the problem of meaninglessness for over a century. As Ellul notes, "The meaning of life does not reside in our imaginations but in a common purpose and common beliefs; if it is to be reliable, it must be communicable. It is a product of common sense. It cannot be decreed arbitrarily. Man cannot live without purpose, yet the individual is unable to provide himself with a stabilizing and satisfying one."[27]

Merely attributing a meaning to history as Marxism does is not a substitute for meaning as lived in concert with others. The former is abstract, the latter concrete. This is why Ellul has mentioned that it is social structure and not culture (at an abstract level) which gives meaning to life. Social structure is an attempt to put culture into practice. But as we have already seen, this is precisely the problem: social structure provides no satisfactory meaning today because it is an artifact of technique. Technique is pure form without content; it destroys content. It is means without an end. Ellul has suggested that the question of meaning arises in a society when three factors are present: "(1) a high abstractness of social relation, (2) a breaking of the causal nexus in regard to acts we do and results which are essential to life, (3) a multiplicity of interpretations of social conduct."[28]

The first point—the abstractness of social relation—is commonly recognized by now. Well over a century ago Karl Marx analyzed how money came to mediate people's existence and interrelationships. While money still has this effect today, an even more important source of mediation is technique, which is itself abstract. After Weber we know of the abstractness of bureaucracy (technique of organization). Increasingly, social relations are bureaucratized, under state control, technologized. Consumer goods and services are a major source of reification, as money used to be. The individual, in becoming just one more consumer good, is made abstract.

The second point touches on the fact that modern society is increasingly guaranteed. That is, everything important is taken care of by the state and technique: witness insurance, retirement plans, public education, social security, military security, and so on. At the same time, the acts we do perform are superficial; that is, they are unrelated to crucial physical and spiritual concerns. Work and leisure have been made trivial. Ellul would seem to be alluding here to a condition of alienation. For just as Marx saw a hiatus between labor and its products under capitalism, Ellul is pointing to dysfunction between actions and their results in a technological civilization. Technique mediates my life to the point that I myself am no longer *responsible* for the consequences of my acts. As Max Born once noted, the complexity of a technological society is such that one cannot even discover what the consequences of actions are, let alone be responsible for them.

The third requires little discussion, for it refers to cultural contradictions on the one hand and the cult of the self on the other. The term cultural contradictions implies that one of several collective interpretations can be given an act, whereas the cult of the self suggests that the individual becomes "free" to interpret actions as he sees fit. But as Victor Frankl points out, meaning that is not arrived at in communion with others is psychologically debilitating. Frankl's experiences both in a concentration camp and as a therapist indicate that the lack of meaning is man's greatest problem today.[29] Of course, therapy by itself is insufficient to meet this need.

Still, does not the fact that technology and the nation-state are regarded as sacred suffice for meaning? The political ideologies of capitalism, socialism, and communism all promote progress, and the common goal of progress is to make man happy, that is, to increase his consumption capabilities. But this is false meaning. A consumption-oriented lifestyle permits but a temporary abatement of this problem—the fleeting pleasure of a new consumer good or service. Boorstin refers to consumer goods and services as "self-liquidating ideals."[30] Advertising is always creating new needs and more prestigious needs. The old ethic of saving has been replaced by an ethic of consuming, of using up. These goods and services must be used up so that the economy can be renewed. To turn us into the good little consumers our economy demands, advertising has helped to foster goods and services as ideals—but ideals that must be destroyed in the interest of progress. Individual consumption achieved through destructive competition hardly provides a basis for meaning shared in communion with others. Consumption, moreover, creates the illusion of total cultural heterogeneity. For if each individual is "free" to consume both materially and spiritually what he desires, then individuals will differ in the accidental details of what and how they consume. These differences are mistaken as decisive signs of disunity because the larger unifying fact of consumption is overlooked.

A related issue is that of the relation of power to values. As Nietzsche observed, in the past moral restraints were always placed on the exercise of power. These moral restraints were themselves an important component of community. Because we have mandated the pursuit and acquisition of individual power, community has tended to disappear, and with it meaning. Hence, there appears to be, as numerous writers have observed, an inverse relation between power and values. Or, more precisely, where power is pursued for its own sake, it becomes the sole value.

Consumption does not merely make for self-liquidating ideals, it also leads to reification. Marx saw perfectly how in the nineteenth century the money economy led to reification: man's being turned into a money object and money's being turned into a living deity. The human individual is supplanted by a reified universe of money according to which man himself is operationalized and evaluated. Money, strange as it may seem, has lost its sacred status to consumer goods and services. When the economy demanded an ethic of saving, money was hoarded as a sacred object. Now that the economy necessitates spending, the technical goods and services we consume have been turned into sacred objects (totems). In other words, the process of reification now centers on consumption. Ellul has observed in this context: "As the person withers, objects become more and more autonomous and mutually strengthen one another. The person is replaced by a reified universe of objects of which the person itself is one.

This is the concrete situation of man in a highly developed consumer society."[31]

One need only look around on a crowded street corner or in a department store to see reified humans advertising themselves as products. Sweatshirts and undershirts with the names and emblems of products abound. The prestige and power of the product rub off on its advertiser. Then too there are the slogans and clichés we wear on our clothes and the bumper stickers we display on our cars—once again, a case of "things" with printed messages. As a reified object, man can hardly help sustain a genuine culture; rather he can only conform to a spurious culture.

In this sense the crimes of consumerism—property crimes—can be seen as conformity to our technological society. Marx understood this: in his essay on money he argued that the possessor of money is presumed to be honest. The only important thing is that one has money (nineteenth century) or has goods and services (twentieth century). Most observers miss the point that property crimes involve the using up of sacred objects, which is an ethical imperative in a consumer-oriented society.

Finally, profound cultural contradictions, meaninglessness, and reification, together with the repression of technique and the state, produce an unconscious hopelessness that is perhaps the worst problem of all. We must not be deceived by answers on public opinion polls indicating that most people consider themselves happy and are optimistic about the future. This is nothing but an expression of people's commitments to the myths of happiness and progress. In our civilization one is supposed to be happy and optimistic—it is a moral obligation. Therefore, to be normal (moral) one must at least pretend that one is happy and optimistic. So the hopelessness operates, as Fromm notes, unconsciously. This hopelessness is a feeling that the present is intolerable and the future is closed. It is evidenced today by widespread cynicism, the perversion of traditional values, a sense of the absolute absurdness of life, cruel humor, scorn for and derision of others, the cult of the irrational, and the destruction of language. A sense of hopelessness and the loss of meaning is omnipresent in modern literature. Joseph Heller's *Something Happened* only takes to an extreme what many other writers have been pointing to since the time of Virginia Woolf and Camus, among others.[32]

The questions of meaning and hope, so intertwined, arise in Colin

Turnbull's brilliant ethnography *The Mountain People*. The IK tribe in East Africa has been starving to death for several generations now. Concurrent with the starvation, but by no means simply its result, is a loss of meaning and hope. The IK religion and ritualistic observances have largely fallen into disuse. Good is operationalized as having food. In the individual competition for food, the IK laugh at everything we assume to be tragic—death, disease, accidents. This chilling portrait suggests a people so totally without hope that they are without love, having become completely apathetic to others, existing without feeling toward one another. They are, as Freud well knew, giving into an impulse that can appear "attractive" when all meaning and hope dissipate. Ellul's description of the loss of hope fits the IK, although it was written about us:

> The end of hope . . . is discrete and silent. It is an open vein in a warm bath, draining out all the blood, bringing sleep without pain and without reaction. It gives rise to nothing. It is scarcely aware of itself. . . . There is nothing tragic about it. One succumbs to it simply because there is no reason not to do so. One stops resisting the death impulse with will, energy, sexual appetite, and the love of life. One fades away because, where there no longer is any hope neither is there any form or being. But this is at such a deep level that there is nothing at first glance to indicate what is taking place.[33]

In the last chapter of his book Turnbull compares us with the IK. Some readers have thought this unfair, but it is an apt comparison if we remember that the IK's hopelessness has progressed further than ours. Theirs is manifest. In modern technological societies there are still attempts to find meaning and some source of hope, largely in going against the technological-state order. But only at times. For often we only experience ennui, a condition of bored resentment, one step removed from total apathy.[34] This psychological condition, which itself leads to ecstasy and violence, is a product of social repression and cultural meaninglessness.

The import of this is enormous. For now sacredly transgressive acts share a larger burden in providing meaning and hope than they did in primitive society. In primitive society the social structure was meaningful, and there was a myth justifying and necessitating sacredly transgressive acts as well. But today the social structure is meaningless; therefore, sacredly transgressive acts are an attempt to restore meaning in a meaningless situation. Moreover, the antimyths related to sacredly transgressive acts (sex, violence, drugs, and revolution) are not integrated with technological utopianism and the myths of history and science on an overt cultural level. Not all utopians are manifest worshippers of technology. Utopians such as Reich and Rozak attack technology in the name of human creativity, communion with nature, and the like. Yet what they suggest as a goal for man is actually only a technological utopia with its negative features removed: not a *1984* nor even a *Brave New World*, but the aesthetic paradise of Marx.[35] To be "free" to take drugs whenever and wherever one pleases, to have sex with whomever one pleases, and to vent one's anger openly does not imply a perfect relationship with nature but a totally controlled social environment.

The lack of *overt* cultural agreement about technology and sacredly transgressive acts means that our myths are fragmented and in conflict. There is no unifying myth, then, to give direction and purpose to life. Our unification is only technologically enforced. But this is how it must be, given both the repression of social structure and its lack of meaning.

Sacredly transgressive acts, then, are a consequence both of the repression of technique and of an attempt to find meaning. By itself the repression of technique gives rise to ecstasy—but not necessarily sexual and revolutionary ecstasy. The social structure's lack of meaning, however, suggests that the attempt to find meaning will be diametrically opposed to the extant social order, which is regarded as sacred—technology and the nation-state. Hence sex and revolution as the sacred of transgression will be primary sources of meaning. Sacredly transgressive acts are also a response to the repression and meaninglessness of our social structure. It is in this sense that we can talk of modern society's being characterized by too much control (the repression of technique and the state in denying man's spontaneity and the expression of his instincts) and by too little control (cultural contradictions, meaninglessness, reification, and hopelessness). Both the repression of social structure and the decline of culture are related to sacredly transgressive acts and related in dialectical fashion.

Hence our society is caught in a vicious circle in which the desire for sacredly transgressive acts grows, and as it does, the original conditions that gave rise to it are exacerbated. The dynamics are as follows:

the repression of social structure increases the need for transgression (ecstasy) and furthers the decline of culture (loss of meaning and purpose); concurrently the decline of culture intensifies the need for both sacredly transgressive acts (as a source of meaning and renewal) and the repression of social structure (to compensate for the lack of cultural control); finally, widespread transgression leads to increased control by social structure (as transgression *appears* to threaten the extant order) and to the decline of culture (transgression being unable by itself to provide sufficient meaning). The dialectic continues without interruption but always with increased intensity. That is, the repression of social structure, the decline of culture, and the need for transgression all become more pronounced over time. Therefore, both in its conscious social structures (technology and the state) and in its unconscious structures (the sacred, symbol, myth, and ritual), society demands and instigates more and more sacred evil.

But in order to remedy this situation, one must work in different directions simultaneously (something which will please neither conservatives nor radicals). One must work against the totalitarian order of technique and the state and attempt to restore a common meaning to life in concert with others. But given the complexity and strength of the present order, to engage in only one of the two approaches will be to doom one's efforts to failure.

The Sporadicity of Modern Rituals and the Evolution of the Sacred of Transgression

*Violence is the therapy of therapies . . . there is
less and less to inhibit this final therapy, least
where the most progressively re-educated classes seem
ready to go beyond their old hope of deliverance,
from violence as the last desperate disciplinary
means built into the interdicts, as punishment,
to violence as a means toward a saving
indiscipline, as self-expression.*
PHILIP RIEFF
Fellow Teachers

Many primitive rituals occurred periodically, often yearly. The sacred festival and rituals for the expulsion of evil were end-of-the-year phenomena, symbolizing and reenacting the passage from chaos to cosmos (creation). Today this is not the case, unless one wishes to argue that New Year's Eve is a festival. Actually it is only a ghostly facsimile of the real thing. Those things I have previously identified as rituals of transgression (with the exception of the rites of spring) appear to have no pattern. Critics might even point out that many of my examples are drawn from the late 1960s and early 1970s. Perhaps then my analysis has value only for this limited period. Is it already passé?

I think not, if one is willing to adopt a longer time frame as a reference point. That is, is it possible that today rituals signifying chaos (transgression, expulsion, etc.) are cyclical, occurring not on a yearly basis but over decades? My hypothesis is that the period from the late

1960s through the early 1970s was one of intense transgression—sex, violence, drugs, and revolution—and of ritualistic scapegoating—the persecution of drug users and pushers, anti–Vietnam War demonstrators, civil rights advocates, and violent revolutionaries—but that the present period is one in which the rituals of order are more pronounced. As a society we are fluctuating back and forth between the opposite poles of each sacred axis.

Let me be explicit. I am not suggesting that it is an all-or-nothing affair; rather, it is a matter of emphasis. The rituals of transgression and expulsion have not disappeared, only some of their wilder manifestations. Urban riots, open-air rock concerts, and the rites of spring, for example, are less in evidence now than ten or fifteen years ago. The media and therapy have claimed transgression for themselves and in so doing have tamed it. Similarly, the ritual persecution of drug users and pushers and political revolutionaries has fallen off.

On the other hand, patriotism has made a strong comeback, as has out-and-out technological materialism. People, some of whom were eager participants in earlier transgressions, are unabashedly "into" consumer goods and services once again, as if the events of the 1960s had never happened. This has led many observers to regard the earlier period as an anomaly. Now, it is argued, things are back to normal. Or one sees the late 60s and early 70s as akin to the 1920s, a period of both radicalism and hedonism. Even in this latter interpretation, the larger pattern of order-transgression is not clearly perceived.

However, the question remains: Why the sporadicity of the sacred rituals, especially rituals of transgression and of expulsion? First, there is the lack of mythical unity that would on a conscious level make sense of transgression within the festival. As a consequence, transgression appears more radical and serious than it truly is. Second, there is the ambiguity of sacred value. Both technology and sex and both the nation-state and revolution are sacred. Third, these sacred values are inherently unstable in that they are incapable of providing sufficient meaning and hope. Therefore, as a society we fluctuate from pole to pole. Because of the ambiguity of the sacred and our commitment to it, we are incapable of decisively going against the social order. And because of the lack of cultural meaning and hope at either pole of the sacred, we swing erratically from pole to pole in the vain expectation of being fulfilled. After years of attacking America and technological materialism, we have desperately embraced them once again as if we were in danger of losing them.[1] If my hypothesis has any merit, I would expect that before long we will be embroiled in another period of wild transgression. This time the transgressive acts might prove even more unbridled.

In my estimation violence is in the course of being sacralized by our society. It has not yet reached the point of widespread advocacy as has sex, but this is coming. The recent glut of horror movies is illustrative of our fascination with violence, especially sexual violence. In many of these films the victim is an attractive woman, sometimes a prostitute, and the killer is a male psychopath. The killing is brutal, bloody, and quite explicit. Consider, if you will, how humor has gone cruel. Not just sarcasm, cynical remarks, and "black humor," but also the straight-forward humiliation of others. Don Rickles, Monty Python, *The Gong Show*, *The Cheap Show*, the *$1.98 Beauty Contest*, Mr. Bill on *Saturday Night Live*, *National Lampoon*—these are only the most obvious examples of psychological violence.

Equally telling is the content of advertising, which is the key to the "collective unconscious." At the level of subliminal perception, advertising is replete with sexual and violent material.[2] It is evident that for some time sex has surfaced from the subliminal level to that of conscious perception. Now this is happening to violence. The women's high-fashion industry is beginning to emphasize conscious, violent themes. Selzer provides the example of an ad in which a beautiful woman's wrist is being chewed by a Doberman pinscher, thereby highlighting a bracelet on her wrist. An ad in *Vogue* shows a voluptuous woman kicking and destroying electronic equipment with shoes for the new fashion season. The ad was captioned "The Killer."[3] This ad is a perfect example of the technology/sex-violence sacred axis.

Wilson Bryan Key's research on subliminal perception in advertising and the media concluded that "violence is a merchandising staple for every mass communication media in America—every bit as virulent as sex, perhaps even more so."[4] He went on to suggest that sex and violence are frequently used together in movies, television, and popular music.

Then too there is the support of marital and familial conflict by psychologists and psychiatrists. Husbands and wives, parents and children, should have it out with one another. It is only honest to say whatever comes to mind, no matter how cruel and humiliating to others. Assertiveness training is the therapeutic expression of this. It sanctions making human relationships even more competitive and manipulative. But will it stop with media and psychological violence? In the 1968 French student uprising, this sign appeared: BE CRUEL, BE VIOLENT.[5]

Violence is, after all, as Rieff has argued, the ultimate therapy.[6] By this he means the most extreme act of individualism without regard for others, the supreme form of "self-fulfillment." When fully sacralized, violence will overlap with sex, especially in acts of sexual violence such as rape, sadism, masochism, necrophilia, and certain forms of "kinky" sex.

Likewise it will overlap with revolution, as in many forms of modern terrorism. It is possible to make the case, as Laqueur does, that there has been some shift away from terrorism as a revolutionary tactic of the poor toward terrorism as a form of tyranny by those who aspire to power for its own sake. In becoming freed from an ideological context, the violence of terrorism also becomes more an end in itself. Terrorism, then, can simultaneously be enlisted in the cause of either revolution or tyranny and of personal violent ecstasy. On this latter point, Laqueur claims that among insiders the "explosion of a bomb has come to be regarded as something like an ersatz orgasm."[7]

The underlying basis of the technology/sex axis is possession, the spirit of conquest, and power. The technology/sex axis appeals to the individual's natural selfishness and resentment of others. Violence fits in here very well, although, psychologically speaking, it is often a consequence of actual powerlessness, especially in the Nietzschean sense of a lack of self-control (self-overcoming).[8] Violence, which manifestly suggests power, is sometimes latently a sign of a lack of mastery over one's environment, personal impotency, boredom, and meaninglessness. In this sense violence represents an even more extreme reaction to the repression of technical-state mechanism and the meaninglessness and hopelessness of modern culture.

My argument should not be mistaken, however, for that of René Girard.[9] His argument about the origins of the sacred is indeed exciting; nevertheless, it is misplaced. He finds that the sacred is grounded in and arises from man's violent nature. Stressing the ambiguity of the sacred and the importance of festivals and ritualistic scapegoating, he builds a strong case. Still, he overemphasizes the negative side of the sacred in perceiving the positive side as only its rationalization. Thus it is the violence and breaking of taboos that is most desired.

However, I think his theory possesses several flaws. First, he defines human nature as violent and tries to demonstrate this cross-culturally. From a scientific viewpoint this is dubious. All attempts to define human nature or history in metaphysical terms are doomed to failure, for the empirical evidence invariably contradicts them. Second, he misinterprets the evidence to some extent. For example, Eliade has demonstrated the variations among cultures in respect to orgies, scapegoating, and so forth. Some societies seem to have greater need for such activities, as I have tried to indicate in the previous chapter. The repression of social structure and loss of culture can create an exaggerated need for orgies, violence, and revolution, which may be universal but whose meaning and pervasiveness are hardly constant.

As a matter of fact, I think it very likely that Girard's theory is itself a reflection of the gradual sacralization of violence taking place today. If our human nature is inevitably violent, what else is there to do but make the most of it, even enjoy it? For today the normal has replaced the moral or, better yet, become the moral.

One should not draw the conclusion from the sacralization of violence, however, that the present social order is in danger. Quite the contrary! Widespread violence will only lead to a tightening of the political state's and of technology's hold over us. Burgess's *A Clockwork Orange* is prophetic in this respect. Alex's violence, which was sacred to him as a means of self-fulfillment, only led to the development of a therapeutic technique (Ludivico's treatment) sponsored by the government, which was capable of eliminating evil by preventing it from ever occurring. Whenever Alex felt a violent impulse, he became nauseated.

But is not this what the myth of progress and technological utopianism have promised all along—the total elimination of evil? Of course its elimination portends a bleak future in which everything and nothing are equally present. With no distinction between good and evil possible, we can all settle back into a bland existence directed by the technical-state mechanism. All transgressions will have been reduced to therapeutic techniques. But this is just as Huxley foresaw in *Brave New World*: the individual was reduced to a therapeutic role-player before transitory and faceless groups.

NOTES

Chapter 1. Advertising and the Media

1. Stanley Diamond, *In Search of the Primitive*, especially chap. 1.

2. Mircea Eliade, *Myth and Reality*, pp. 113, 184–87.

3. Victor Turner, *The Ritual Process*; see also Victor Turner, *Dramas, Fields, and Metaphors*, especially chaps. 6 and 7.

4. Lancelot L. Whyte, *The Unconscious before Freud*, pp. 20–21.

5. Philip Rieff, *Freud: The Mind of the Moralist*, pp. 253–54; Peter Berger and Thomas Luckmann, *The Social Construction of Reality*.

6. Arnold Gehlen, *Man in the Age of Technology*, chap. 7.

7. Marshall McLuhan, *Understanding Media*, chap. 4.

8. Jacques Ellul, *The Technological Society*, pp. 402–5.

9. On the distinction between oral and literate cultures see especially Walter Ong's articles "Technology Outside Us and Inside Us" and "Literacy and Orality in Our Times." See also Ong's books *The Presence of the Word* and *Interfaces of the Word*.

10. Ong, "Literacy and Orality," p. 3.

11. Edmund Carpenter, *Oh, What a Blow That Phantom Gave Me!*, pp. 43–47.

12. Clifford Geertz, *The Interpretation of Cultures*, chap. 4.

13. See McLuhan, *Understanding Media*; Carpenter, *Oh, What a Blow*; Jacques Ellul, *Propaganda*.

14. If the mass media can be reasonably termed an oral culture, this designation would appear to apply to television, radio, and the movies but not to newspapers and popular magazines. Important, however, is the fact that the last two media have come to resemble the first three in several ways. First, they tend to be dominated by advertising; second, they tend to be superficial in the ideas they communicate. A literate culture most distinguishes itself from an oral culture by its cultivation of the higher learning. Newspapers and popular magazines in their emphasis on the factual, the spectacular, and the superficial can be thought of as appendages to television, radio, and the movies, whose primary impact upon people is immediate and unconscious. Hence, we will consider newspapers and popular magazines to be more truly a part of the oral side of our culture than of the literate side.

15. Max Horkheimer and Theodor Adorno, "The Culture Industry as Mass Deception."

16. Ibid.; see also Ellul, *Propaganda*.

17. Marshall McLuhan, "Myth and Mass Media," p. 290.

18. Carpenter, *Oh, What a Blow*, pp. 61–66.

19. Ibid., p. 47.

20. Daniel Boorstin, *Democracy and Its Discontents*, p. 41; Horkheimer and Adorno, "Culture Industry," pp. 161–67; McLuhan, *Understanding Media*, p. 232.

21. Carpenter, *Oh, What a Blow*, p. 60.

22. McLuhan, *Understanding Media*, p. 228.

23. Max Horkheimer, "Traditional and Critical Theory."

Chapter 2. The Sacred of Transgression

1. If the book were to be written in methodological order, that is, following the steps of discovery the social scientist employs, then this chapter on the sacred would come after those on symbol, myth, and ritual. What is sacred or is being sacralized cannot be apprehended directly, but only indirectly from symbol, myth, and ritual. Yet I have reversed the order of discovery because, in my judgment, the argument makes more sense if the sacred is identified at once.

2. Robin Williams, Jr., *American Society*, p. 379.

3. Ibid., p. 381.

4. Robert Merton, *Social Theory and Social Structure*, p. 318.

5. Philip Rieff, *The Triumph of the Therapeutic*, pp. 4, 232–33.

6. Ibid., p. 212.

7. Jacques Ellul, *The New Demons*, chap. 3; much of this chapter is but an elaboration of his ideas.

8. Mircea Eliade, *The Quest*, pp. 81–86.

9. Technique and technology will be used interchangeably in the course of this book. Ellul defines technique as the "*totality of methods rationally arrived at and having absolute efficiency* (for a given stage of development) in every field of human activity" (*Technological Society*, p. xxv). The emphasis here is on the unity that all the various techniques together form. Moreover, there is the suggestion that this totality of techniques is increasingly the basis of the social order. Little escapes its grasp and influence. Technology, however, is the more common English term used to refer to the various methods of efficiency Ellul describes, although the term is quite ambiguous in meaning. Thus these terms, technique and technology, will be treated as synonymous. But the reader should note that even if technology or technique is used in its more isolated, less sociological sense, for example, *a* technology or *a* technique, it implies the larger sociological environment of technique.

10. Maurice North, *The Secular Priests*, p. 229.

11. Dennis Brissett and Lionel Lewis, "The Big Toe, Armpits, and Natural Perfume: Notes on the Production of Sexual Ecstasy," p. 73.

12. Wilson Bryan Key, *Subliminal Seduction*, p. 108, and *Media Sexploitation*, p. 15.

13. Bernice Martin, "The Sacralization of Disorder: Symbolism in Rock Music," p. 121.

14. Hunter Thompson, *Hell's Angels*; Marshall McLuhan, *The Mechanical Bride*, p. 84.

15. Andrew Greeley, "Symbol, Myth and Ritual in the Modern World"; Greeley quotes Dichther on p. 24. I wish to thank my colleague Rob Dirks for calling my attention to the advertising in medical journals.

16. McLuhan, *Mechanical Bride*, p. 96. McLuhan devotees would point out that in our electronic age the machine with its specialization and assembly line is outmoded, but the important aspect is the technique behind the machine. Just because machines

have become computerized does not change this. A recent ad, for instance, shows a voluptuous woman in underwear and high heels next to a computer.

17. Joachim Wach, *Sociology of Religion*, chaps. 4 and 7; Reinhold Niebuhr, *The Nature and Destiny of Man*, 1:83.

18. Alexis de Tocqueville, *Democracy in America*, p. 60.

19. Some would argue that the attempt of certain ethnic groups within the nation to become autonomous and related attempts at decentralization make my argument less plausible. One must keep in mind, however, that the insurgent ethnic group inevitably desires to establish itself as a nation. Hence the nationalism of the ethnic group has merely been relocated.

20. José Ortega y Gasset, *The Revolt of the Masses*, pp. 120–21.

21. Tocqueville, *Democracy in America*, p. 670.

22. Jacques Ellul, *The Betrayal of the West*, p. 180.

23. Eric J. Hobsbawm, *The Age of Revolution, 1789–1848*, p. 163.

24. Jacques Ellul, *Autopsy of Revolution*, chap. 4.

25. Elias Canetti, *Crowds and Power*, p. 174.

26. The discussion of the sacred as power and of the secular manifestations of the sacred is based on Mircea Eliade, *The Sacred and the Profane*, pp. 11–13.

27. Mircea Eliade, *Patterns in Comparative Religion*, chap. 1.

28. Ellul, *New Demons*, p. 48.

29. Eliade, *Patterns in Comparative Religion*, p. 39.

30. Roger Caillois, *Man and the Sacred*; Eliade, *The Sacred and the Profane*.

31. Rudolf Otto (*The Idea of the Holy*) was the first to study in detail man's psychological ambivalence toward the holy.

32. Caillois, *Man and the Sacred*, p. 59.

33. See, for instance, Norman Snaith, *The Distinctive Ideas of the Old Testament*, chap. 2.; Caillois, *Man and the Sacred*. Eliade (*Patterns in Comparative Religion*, p. 15) cites a number of studies, in addition to providing some examples himself.

34. My use of Caillois's concept of the sacred of transgression may give the appearance of a structuralist approach—the sacred of transgression as the dialectic of the sacred and profane. But in reality Caillois's discovery that in many societies there were three terms—sacred of respect, sacred of transgression, and profane—and not merely two terms, sacred and profane, for dealing with good and evil, predated the structuralist approach. Moreover, Caillois noticed that the sacred was a dynamic relation between two poles of the sacred and not a static entity. The point of this is that while I will seem to be applying the structuralist method, I do so in a nondogmatic way. I am suggesting neither that this logic is invariant nor that it is determined by the structure of the brain, but only that it applies to how modern societies solve the dilemma of good and evil.

35. The ambiguity of the sacred is seriously questioned by some anthropologists and other students of religion, who doubt its universality. For example, Mary Douglas (*Purity and Danger*, chap. 1) argues that the full-blown ambiguity of the sacred, restricted to a handful of cases, is essentially a linguistic problem. Therefore, she goes on to say that for those anomalous cultures in which the same word is used to designate both the holy and that which defiles it, there is a simple solution: change the vocabulary. Douglas assumes that ambiguity is unusual and, moreover, a sign of stupidity. Hence to suggest that a culture has a decidedly ambiguous concept of the sacred is tantamount, in her eyes, to demeaning it. Quite the contrary! Caillois, Eliade, and Ellul all conclude that the ambiguity of the sacred is inherent in man's use of the

concept: in the dialectical nature of language, in man's basic ambivalence toward good and evil, and in man's need to control evil.

I have no illusions about solving this problem, which is both an empirical and a conceptual one. But a few observations may provide leads. Later in the chapter desacralization will be examined in a historical context. Is it possible that some historians and anthropologists have at times confused what was formerly sacred with what is currently sacred? Moreover, the ambiguity of the sacred need not be expressed in language; it depends in part on how abstract the language in question is and on how much the unconscious ambivalence toward the sacred is allowed to surface. It is also possible that the degree to which good and evil are ambiguous varies directly with the degree of sacralization of a society.

36. Ellul, *New Demons*, p. 57.

37. Mircea Eliade, *Myth of the Eternal Return*.

38. Ibid., p. 44.

39. Eliade, *The Quest*, p. 87; Victor Turner, *Dramas, Fields, and Metaphors*, p. 254.

40. Ellul, *New Demons*, pp. 58–64.

41. The relation between the sacred and morality is complex. In general, social morality tends to increase in importance as the intensity of commitment to the sacred begins to wane. Social morality insures that things will be done that formerly were done out of fear and respect for the sacred. The logic is *not* "moral is to sacred of respect as immoral is to sacred of transgression." To transgress sacred taboos can be a "moral" obligation during the festival; at other times it is evil. Likewise to follow the path of holiness too fanatically can be regarded as evil. Therefore, involvement in both the sacred of respect and sacred of transgression may be either "moral" or "immoral" depending on the circumstances.

On the relationship between technology and morality, see Jacques Ellul, "Technological Morality."

42. Paul Ricoeur, *The Symbolism of Evil*, pp. 28–29; Gabriel Vahanian, *God and Utopia*, p. 9.

43. Geoffrey Ashe, *Do What You Will*.

44. Ortega y Gassett, *Revolt of the Masses*, p. 118; Vahanian, *God and Utopia*.

45. Bertrand de Jouvenel, *On Power*.

46. Ortega y Gasset, *Revolt of the Masses*, p. 123; Ellul, *Autopsy of Revolution*, p. 202.

47. Cited in Ellul, *Autopsy of Revolution*, pp. 202, 163.

48. Anders Nygren, *Agape and Eros*, p. viii.

49. Michel Foucault (*The History of Sexuality*, vol. 1, *An Introduction*) has vividly portrayed how sex gradually became institutionalized and technologized from the seventeenth century to the present. Unfortunately, he has failed to see how sex symbolically represents a going against the technological order.

50. Mary Douglas, *Natural Symbols*, chap. 5.

51. Ellul, *Technological Society*.

52. Vahanian, *God and Utopia*, pp. 99–125.

53. Canetti, *Crowds and Power*, pp. 354–58. Some have argued that in an age of relative scarcity we are beginning to turn away from the consumption of material goods under the ideology of scarcity (see Rolf Meyersohn, "Abundance Reconsidered"). Others have argued that we have simply turned our consumerism away from material goods toward services, for example, lifestyles, experiences, and relationships. This latter position recognizes that consumerism is still virulent; it has simply changed its form (see David Gutmann, "Killers and Consumers: the Terrorist and His Audience."

As consumption becomes more "spiritual" and less material, there will be, no doubt, a corresponding increase in the importance of human technology. As certain resources of nature become more scarce, technology directs its attention to the unlimited resources of the human. Human techniques to mediate one's relationship to others or even to one's self (for example, mysticism) provide a plenitude of spiritual consumption. Still there remains plenty of old-fashioned material consumption to go around.

54. Ellul, *New Demons*, p. 121. Eliade (*Patterns in Comparative Religion*) argues that on occasion the sacred was general; that is, all of nature was seen as sacred. This is the case today, I think, where technology as a whole is seen as sacred.

55. Canetti, *Crowds and Power*, pp. 348–58.

56. Eliade, *Patterns in Comparative Religion*, p. 397.

57. Ibid., p. 446.

58. Will Herberg, *Protestant Catholic Jew*, especially chaps. 5 and 11. The quotations are from pp. 265–67.

59. Thomas Luckmann, *The Invisible Religion*, pp. 102–6.

60. Ellul, *New Demons*, chap. 5.

61. Daniel Boorstin, *The Americans: The Democratic Experience*, pt. 2.

62. Simondon's work is discussed in Ellul, *New Demons*, pp. 200–202.

63. See Jacques Ellul, *The Political Illusion*, on these points.

Chapter 3. Sociological Symbols of Evil

1. Jacques Ellul, *A Critique of the New Commonplaces*, pp. 15–16.

2. See, for instance, Charles Ellwood, *Sociology and Modern Social Problems*, pp. 20–21; and Edward Hayes, *Sociology and Ethics*, chap. 3. As late as 1947, George Lundberg (*Can Science Save Us?*) was advocating this idea.

3. See Friedrich A. Hayek, *The Counter-Revolution of Science*, and Albert Salomon, *The Tyranny of Progress*.

4. Richard Weaver, *The Ethics of Rhetoric*, pp. 197–98.

5. The following discussion of metaphor and symbol is taken from Paul Ricoeur, *Interpretation Theory: Discourse and the Surplus of Meaning*, chap. 3. Religious symbols may be either concrete or abstract. In the former case an object or event serves as a symbol; in the latter case the *word* that points to the object or event becomes the symbol. In this chapter the focus will be on literary symbols of evil.

6. Mircea Eliade, *The Sacred and the Profane*, pp. 129–32.

7. Ellul, *New Demons*, pp. 91–92.

8. Ibid., pp. 92–97.

9. Ricoeur, *Symbolism of Evil*, pp. 162–63.

10. Ibid., p. 152.

11. The following discussion of defilement, sin, and guilt is taken from Ricoeur, *Symbolism of Evil*, pt. 1.

12. Hans Kelsen, *Society and Nature*.

13. Earl Rubington and Martin Weinberg, eds., *The Study of Social Problems*; Irving Tallman, *Passion, Action, and Politics*; Ritchie Lowry, *Social Problems*; Malcolm Spector and John Kitsuse, *Constructing Social Problems*.

14. See among others, Willard Waller, "Social Problems and the Mores"; Louis Wirth, "Ideological Aspects of Social Disorganization"; C. Wright Mills, "The Professional Ideology of Social Pathologists"; Albert H. Hobbs, *The Claims of Sociology: A*

Critique of Textbooks, chap. 9; Irving Louis Horowitz, *Professing Sociology*, pp. 80–100; Spector and Kitsuse, *Constructing Social Problems*.

15. Thomas Szasz, *Ideology and Insanity*.

16. Carl Becker, *The Heavenly City of the Eighteenth Century Philosophers*, p. 55.

17. See Berger and Luckmann, *Social Construction of Reality*, especially pp. 89–92, for a brief but competent treatment of the topic.

18. Barbara Wootton, *Social Science and Social Pathology*, p. 317.

19. David Rothman, *The Discovery of the Asylum*.

20. Hobbs, *Claims of Sociology*, chap. 9.

21. Among others, see Arnold Green, *Social Problems: Arena of Conflict*, chap. 1; and Gwynn Nettler, *Social Concerns*, p. 5.

22. Gabriel Marcel, *Man against Mass Society*, p. 90.

23. Bertrand de Jouvenel, *The Pure Theory of Politics*, p. 207; see also Ellul, *Political Illusion*, chap. 6.

24. Hayek, *Counter-Revolution of Science*, especially chaps. 9 and 10; and Friedrich A. Hayek, *The Constitution of Liberty*, chap. 2.

25. Horowitz, *Professing Sociology*, pp. 93–94.

26. Michel Foucault, *The Birth of the Clinic*, p. 23.

27. Jessie Bernard, *Social Problems at Midcentury*, p. 133. Erving Goffman ("The Insanity of Place") argues that the conception of individual mental illness is inherently social. Its symptoms ultimately refer to infractions of social rules and to failures to live up to others' expectations, both of which are disruptive of social institutions.

28. For an interesting view of this subject see A. J. I. Kraus, *Sick Society*.

29. De Jouvenel, *On Power*, p. 53.

30. Ibid., p. 54.

31. Ibid., pp. 44–51.

32. Raymond Williams, *Keywords*, pp. 189–92.

33. Quoted in Bernard, *Social Problems at Midcentury*, p. 135.

34. Rubington and Weinberg, *Study of Social Problems*, chap. 5; Robert Merton, "Social Problems and Sociological Theory," p. 843.

35. Among the writings that helped to crystalize the movement were Howard Becker, *Outsiders: Studies in the Sociology of Deviance*; and Erving Goffman, *Stigma: Notes on the Management of Spoiled Identity*.

36. See Friedrich Nietzsche's books *Beyond Good and Evil*, *The Will to Power*, and *On the Genealogy of Morals*.

37. Jacques Ellul, *The Ethics of Freedom*, p. 194; see also Ellul, *Technological Society*.

38. Ellul, *Political Illusion*, p. 55, and *Propaganda*, pp. 202–12.

39. Irving Louis Horowitz and Martin Liebowitz, "Social Deviance and Political Marginality: Toward a Redefinition of the Relation between Sociology and Politics."

In this book I am mainly dealing with American society; hence to attempt to prove that, despite ideological differences among capitalists, socialists, and communists, all accept the same basic myths would lead us far afield. I think a plausible case for this position has been made by Ellul in *Critique of the New Commonplaces*.

40. Jerome G. Manis, *Analyzing Social Problems*, p. 11.

41. Hayek, *Constitution of Liberty*, pp. 56–67.

Chapter 4. From the Myth of Progress to Technological Utopianism

1. The following discussion of Spencer is taken from Richard Hofstadter, *Social Darwinism in American Thought*, chap. 2. Although the symbol of social pathology was explicit in Spencer's writings, its synonyms, maladjustment and nonadaptation, seemed to appear even more frequently. This is probably because Spencer's thought was influenced more by biology than by medicine.

2. Karl Marx and Frederick Engels, *The German Ideology*, pp. 43–46.

3. Ibid., p. 53.

4. Karl Marx, *The Economic and Philosophic Manuscripts of 1844*, p. 169.

5. Eliade, *Myth and Reality*, p. 184.

6. Eric Voegelin, *Science, Politics, and Gnosticism*, pp. 23–25.

7. Eliade, *Myth and Reality*, p. 184; Karl Lowith, *Meaning in History*, chap. 2; and Robert Tucker, *Philosophy and Myth in Karl Marx*, especially chaps. 11 and 15. See also Ellul, *Autopsy of Revolution*; Joseph Schumpeter, *Capitalism, Socialism, and Democracy*, chap. 1; Voegelin, *Science, Politics, and Gnosticism*, pp. 23–28; Mircea Eliade, *Myths, Dreams, and Mysteries*, pp. 25–26.

8. See for instance, Peter Sedgwick, "Mental Illness *Is* Illness."

9. Stanislav Andreski, introduction to *Principles of Sociology*, by Herbert Spencer, pp. xxiv–xxix.

10. Richard H. Tawney, *The Acquisitive Society*, p. 8; Ernst Cassirer, *An Essay on Man*, pp. 228–32; Andreski, introduction to *Principles of Sociology*, pp. xxviii–xxix.

11. Richard Weaver, *Visions of Order*, pp. 28ff.

12. This term comes from John Dewey. It means "a *pronounced character* of the mind." Kenneth Burke, *Permanence and Change*, pp. 44–47, discusses technological psychosis as the dominant outlook in the modern world. It tends to regard life as one enormous experiment.

13. Emile Durkheim, *The Rules of Sociological Method*, p. 64.

14. Emile Durkheim, *Suicide*, pp. 300–306.

15. Durkheim, *Rules of Sociological Method*, p. 58.

16. Steven Lukes, *Emile Durkheim: His Life and Work*, p. 30.

17. William Goode, *Explorations in Social Theory*, pp. 64–94.

18. Charles Van Doren, *The Idea of Progress*, chaps. 15–25.

19. E. R. Dodds, *The Ancient Concept of Progress*, pp. 24–25.

20. The following discussion is based upon Becker, *Heavenly City*.

21. Ernest Tuveson, *Redeemer Nation*.

22. Gabriel Vahanian, *The Death of God*, p. 230.

23. Becker, *Heavenly City*, p. 27.

24. Theodore Roszak, *The Making of a Counter Culture*, chap. 7.

25. Kelsen, *Society and Nature*, chap. 6.

26. Ellul, *Critique of the New Commonplaces*, pp. 240–48.

27. Kelsen, *Society and Nature*, p. 266.

28. Becker, *Heavenly City*, pp. 37–38.

29. In this section I am drawing heavily upon Vahanian's brilliant book *God and Utopia*. For Vahanian technological utopianism is potentially either positive or negative. When it is enslaving, it becomes technocracy, a totalitarian utopia. My use of the term technological utopianism is in keeping with this totalitarian version of utopia, which is the sociological form technological utopianism most often assumes in the modern world.

30. The following two paragraphs are based upon Eliade, *Myth of the Eternal Return.*

31. Lowith, *Meaning in History.*

32. Edward Tiryakian, "The Time Perspectives of Modernity"; Jurgen Moltmann, "American Contradictions." Social Darwinism and Marxism are of course more reflective of the myth of progress, whereas functionalism with its static perspective is tied to technological utopianism. Still, the earlier point remains: functionalism implies evolutionism and thus progress. The myth of progress eventually leads to technological utopianism and is, at bottom, similar in its basic assumptions about man.

33. Peter Berger, Brigette Berger, and Hansfried Kellner (*The Homeless Mind*, p. 51) argue that predictability is an assumption of bureaucracy. In this sense bureaucracy is utopian in aim.

34. Eliade, *Myth of the Eternal Return*, chaps. 1 and 2.

35. Kelsen, *Society and Nature*, p. 259.

36. Cassirer, *An Essay on Man*, p. 230.

37. Deviance as a symbol of evil is indirectly related to progress and technological utopianism, as we have seen. It refers to the ephemeral side of modern society—public opinion—whereas social problem refers to the necessary side—the logic of technique.

Chapter 5. The Magical and Ritualistic Control of Deviant Behavior

1. Mircea Eliade, *Myths, Rites, Symbols*, vol. 1, ed. Wendell C. Beane and William G. Doty, p. 164.

2. Geoffrey Kirk, *Myth*, pp. 23–25; Clyde Kluckhohn, "Myths and Rituals: A General Theory," p. 78.

3. Claude Levi-Strauss, *Structural Anthropology*, pp. 229–38.

4. Ellul, *New Demons*, p. 121.

5. The following discussion of magic and technique is taken from Ellul, *Technological Society*, pp. 23–27.

6. Quoted in Ellul, *Technological Society*, p. 25.

7. Arnold van Gennep, *The Rites of Passage.*

8. Mircea Eliade, *Rites and Symbols of Initiation*, pp. ix–xv.

9. Turner, *Ritual Process*, p. 94.

10. Daniel Boorstin, *The Americans: The Democratic Experience*, pp. 159, 164.

11. W. Lloyd Warner, *American Life: Dream and Reality*, chap. 1; see also Boorstin, *Americans*, chap. 42.

12. Ellul, *New Demons*, pp. 190–97.

13. Edward Norbeck, "African Rituals of Conflict," p. 197. See especially Max Gluckman, *Custom and Conflict in Africa*, and *Order and Rebellion in Tribal Africa.*

14. Norbeck, "African Rituals of Conflict," pp. 198–99.

15. Turner, *Ritual Process*, p. 167.

16. Norbeck, "African Rituals," p. 222; Turner, *Ritual Process*, p. 128.

17. As an example of guidebooks to group sex, see Caroline Gordon, *Beginner's Guide to Group Sex*. The advice on how to avoid emotional entanglements is from Gilbert Bartell, *Group Sex*, p. 122.

18. Gordon, *Beginner's Guide to Group Sex*, pp. 111–16.

19. Hunter Thompson, "Hell's Angels: Hoodlum Circus and Statutory Rape of Bass Lake," p. 143.

20. Richard Cloward and Lloyd Ohlin, *Delinquency and Opportunity*, pp. 43ff; David Dawley, *A Nation of Lords*, pp. 24–25.

21. Dawley, *Nation of Lords*, pp. 42–43.

22. Thompson, "Hell's Angels," p. 143.

23. Robert Conat, *Rivers of Blood, Years of Darkness*, pp. 178–79.

24. Associated Press, 18 October, 1971, cited in Harold L. Nieburg, *Culture Storm*, p. 139.

25. Becker, *Outsiders*, chap. 3.

26. Bruce Jackson, "White-Collar Pill Party," p. 264.

27. Caillois, *Man and the Sacred*, pp. 165–66.

28. J. Bowyer Bell, *On Revolt*, p. 228.

29. Nieburg, *Culture Storm*, pp. 146–47.

30. Norbeck, "African Rituals of Conflict," pp. 221–22.

31. Eliade, *Myth of the Eternal Return*; Eliade, *The Quest*, p. 80.

32. North, *Secular Priests*, chap. 8.

33. See Jacques Ellul, *Violence*, chap. 3, for a discussion of Sorel; Franz Fanon, *The Wretched of the Earth*.

34. Kneale's view is cited in North, *Secular Priests*, p. 248. See McLuhan, "Myth and Mass Media," pp. 288–99, for an excellent discussion of the media's psychological impact upon man.

35. James G. Frazer, *The Golden Bough*, 6:227.

36. Thomas Szasz, *The Manufacture of Madness*, pp. 260–75, and *Ceremonial Chemistry*.

37. Although recent studies (see Chap. 1, notes 12–16) have indicated that efficiency is the main consideration of our various agencies and institutions of social control, this does not mean that these agencies do not practice magic. Spiritual human techniques, as we have already seen, are not dissimilar from magical techniques. Nevertheless, the magic of human technique is quite different from that of ritual, as will become apparent later in this chapter.

38. Kai Erikson, *Wayward Puritans*.

39. See Ellul, *New Demons*, pp. 58–59, for a brief but illuminating discussion of the Bible as sacred.

40. Walter Connor, "The Manufacture of Deviance: The Case of the Soviet Purge, 1936–1938," pp. 242–43.

41. Norman Zinberg and John Robertson, *Drugs and the Public*, pp. 201, 217, 28–30; William O'Neill, *Coming Apart*, p. 240.

42. Orrin Klapp, *Collective Search for Identity*, p. 56.

43. John Helmer, *Drugs and Minority Oppression*, pp. 141–42. Szasz (*Ceremonial Chemistry*) stresses the symbolism of drug use and the symbolism of the persecution of drug users. However, his interpretation of the political implications of the ritualistic persecution is limited to placing the persecution in the context of medicine (psychiatry especially) and science as systems of political control. He would, no doubt, disagree with my interpretation.

44. Frazer, *Scapegoat*, p. 225; Eliade, *Rites and Symbols of Initiation*, p. xiii.

45. Caillois, *Man and the Sacred*, p. 102.

46. Claude Levi-Strauss, *Structural Anthropology*, p. 174.

47. Victor Turner, *The Forest of Symbols*, pp. 359–93.

48. Jerome Frank, *Persuasion and Healing*, p. 164; North, *Secular Priests*, chap. 1.

49. Thomas Szasz, *The Ethics of Psychoanalysis*, chaps. 2–4; Andrew Malcolm, *The*

Tyranny of the Group; North, *Secular Priests*; Frank, *Persuasion and Healing*; Ari Kiev, ed., *Magic, Faith, and Healing*.

50. Perry London, *Behavior Control*, p. 39; Malcolm, *Tyranny of the Group*, chap. 2.

51. Joel Kovel, *A Complete Guide to Therapy*, p. 69.

52. Ellul, *Technological Society*; London, *Behavior Control*, p. 70; North, *Secular Priests*, chap. 8.

53. Psychoanalytical psychotherapy is used on patients with limited resources of money and time; it tends to focus on more manageable everyday problems and to be more directive. See Kovel, *Complete Guide to Therapy*, pp. 76–78. Rieff, *Freud*, chaps. 6–10.

54. Victor Turner's distinction between "wild communitas" and "normative communitas" is helpful here. Often the result of a repressive social structure or a decaying religion, wild communitas is spontaneous. Communion and ecstasy are born out of immediate transgressions. But very quickly it becomes normative; that is, myth and ritual rise up around it. See Victor Turner, *Dramas, Fields, and Metaphors*, pp. 231–71.

55. Quoted in Malcolm, *Tyranny of the Group*, p. ix.

56. Ibid., pp. 59–60; Hendrik Ruitenbeek, *The New Group Therapies*, pp. 186–201, 146–65.

57. Malcolm, *Tyranny of the Group*, pp. 102, 169–72; Philip Slater, *Microcosm*; Ruitenbeek, *New Group Therapies*, pp. 166–85.

58. Malcolm, *Tyranny of the Group*, p. 113; see also Kovel, *Complete Guide to Therapy*, p. 167, for a similar observation.

59. Van Gennep, *Rites of Passage*, p. 11, argues that all three stages are not necessarily present or equally present in any single ritual. Eliade, *Rites and Symbols of Initiation*.

60. Kovel, *Guide to Therapy*, p. 166; Ruitenbeek, *New Group Therapies*, pp. 58–71.

61. Howard Mumford Jones, *The Pursuit of Happiness*, pp. 131–65.

62. Quoted in Rieff, *Triumph of the Therapeutic*, p. 24.

63. Richard Sennet, *The Fall of Public Man*, pp. 333–36; David Riesman, *The Lonely Crowd*, especially chaps. 2 and 3.

64. Eliade, *Rites and Symbols of Initiation*. Those groups devoted to sex (group sex clubs), violence (conflict street gangs), and drugs may be thought of as secret societies. As we have already shown, their initiation rites and myths suggest that personal renewal and creativity are tied to the consumption of sex, violence, and drugs.

65. The discussion of technology is heavily indebted to Ellul, *Technological Society*. See Jurgen Habermas, *Toward a Rational Society*, pp. 81–122; Boorstin, *Americans*. We usually think of technology with respect to the control and manipulation of our natural environment. But the question of human technology (techniques for the control of man) has been profitably explored. See London, *Behavior Control*; Vance Packard, *The People Shapers*; and Ellul, *Propaganda*. The split in modern consciousness between science and myth and between technique and ritual is indicative of modern man's inability to live in a totally rationalized existence. Also indicative of this are irrational acts against bureaucracies, a seeming protest against excessive instrumental rationality.

66. Subjective belief in magic can have objective consequences and can even cause one's death, as in voodoo. It is likewise true that many physical techniques work on man in a "psychosomatic" manner.

Chapter 6. Sacredly Transgressive Action

1. Travis Hirschi, *Causes of Delinquency*, chap. 2.

2. Albert Cohen, *Deviance and Control*, chap. 5.

3. Durkheim, *Suicide*, pp. 258, 255.

4. Ibid., p. 276.

5. Habermas, *Toward a Rational Society*, p. 95.

6. Ellul, *Ethics of Freedom*, p. 463. This is not the time to take a definitive stand on the concept of culture. I would argue that culture is both abstract and concrete. The concrete aspect of culture includes social institutions and social structure. Culture as abstract contains various configurations of signs, metaphors, and symbols, which, while meaningful in the abstract, need to be put into practice in order to be made fully meaningful.

Now rather than regarding social structure as a product or culture as a product of social structure, I think it preferable to regard each as dialectically related. Culture determines social structure and, as well, is determined by it. This position Marx argued in an extreme way. Culture becomes a mere epiphenomenon, a justification of social structure. This is the realist position. The idealist position is that culture determines social structure. One need not choose between realist and idealist positions if one recognizes that both contain an element of truth and that each position is more or less true depending on the society in question and the historical period.

7. Diamond, *In Search of the Primitive*, chap. 1.

8. Ellul, *Ethics of Freedom*, pp. 423, 480.

9. Turner, *Ritual Process*, and *Dramas, Fields, and Metaphors*, p. 254.

10. Douglas, *Natural Symbols*, chap. 4.

11. Ibid., p. 178.

12. Marcel, *Man against Mass Society*; McLuhan, *Understanding Media*; Ellul, *Technological Society*.

13. Georg Simmel, *The Sociology of Georg Simmel*, p. 409.

14. Ibid., p. 414.

15. McLuhan, *Understanding Media*, pp. 42–43.

16. Ellul, *Technological Society*, p. 421.

17. Ibid., p. xxv.

18. Ibid., p. 422.

19. Karen Horney, *The Neurotic Personality of Our Time*, pp. 270–80.

20. Herbert Hendin, *The Age of Sensation*, p. 314.

21. Eliade, *The Quest*, pp. 77–87.

22. The issue of unconscious cultural patterns has been profitably explored by Edward Hall in *Beyond Culture*. In an argument that parallels McLuhan's, Hall maintains that extensions of ourselves such as technology affect us in ways which our models and theories do not fully grasp. When we forget that these extensions are our own creation, they become part of objective reality, something to which we adjust by becoming their servomechanisms. The collective repressive effect of these extensions results in our blocking their actual functions out of our consciousness. Consequently, these extensions become, to some extent, unconscious.

23. Edward Sapir, "Culture, Genuine and Spurious," pp. 104–5.

24. Ibid., p. 117.

25. Horney, *Neurotic Personality of Our Time*, chap. 15.

26. Daniel Bell, *The Cultural Contradictions of Capitalism*, p. 47.

27. Ellul, *Autopsy of Revolution*, p. 241.

28. Ellul, *Ethics of Freedom*, p. 463.

29. Victor Frankl, *Man's Search for Meaning*.

30. Boorstin, *Democracy and Its Discontents*, pp. 96–99.

31. Karl Marx, *The Economic and Philosophical Manuscripts of 1844*, pp. 165–69; Ellul, *Ethics of Freedom*, p. 309.

32. Erich Fromm, *The Revolution of Hope*, pp. 10–13. The evidence of hopelessness is found in Jacques Ellul, *Hope in Time of Abandonment*, chaps. 1 and 2. For the sense of hopelessness in literature see Erich Auerbach, *Mimesis: The Representation of Reality in Western Literature*, p. 515. The same polls that report that people seem happy often indicate many specific sources of dissatisfaction and pessimism, but in answering a general question about his life, the interviewee feels compelled to be optimistic and happy. Jeremy Seabrook's *What Went Wrong? Why Hasn't Having More Made People Happier?* suggests that the unhappiness of the English working class is becoming more self-evident. Studs Terkel claims that this applies to the American working class as well. Perhaps the middle classes have been able to conceal their unhappiness better because their greater wealth has enabled them to remain more active, leaving them little time to ponder their situation. The work of Robert Coles and especially that of Herbert Hendin would seem to indicate the children of the middle classes are suffering from a loss of a sense of purpose and from disquietude.

33. Ellul, *Hope in Time of Abandonment*, p. 70.

34. Ralph Larkin (*Cultural Crisis of Suburban Youth*) discovered that the most pervasive and intense psychological characteristic among middle-class high school students was boredom.

35. Ellul, *Betrayal of the West*, p. 151.

Epilogue

1. The 1960s were a period of economic prosperity. With consumer goods and services at everyone's beck and call, the spiritual emptiness of a life devoted to consumer goods and services was very much in evidence. In the 1970s and into the 1980s, a period of recession and inflation, it seems at times that consumer goods and services just might disappear. So once again they become objects of adulation and desire.

2. Key, *Subliminal Seduction*.

3. Michael Selzer, *Terrorist Chic*, chap. 3.

4. Key, *Media Sexploitation*, p. 209.

5. Cited in Ellul, *New Demons*, p. 140.

6. Philip Rieff, *Fellow Teachers*, p. 50.

7. Walter Laqueur, *Terrorism*, p. 167.

8. See especially Erich Fromm, *The Anatomy of Human Destructiveness*, and Rollo May, *Power and Innocence*, on this topic. In suggesting that cruelty and destructiveness are often borne out of powerlessness and impotency (in the general sense), their respective arguments confirm what Nietzsche had suggested in the nineteenth century.

9. René Girard, *Violence and the Sacred*.

BIBLIOGRAPHY

Andreski, Stanislav. Introduction to *Principles of Sociology*, by Herbert Spencer. Hamden, Conn.: Shoestring Press, Archon Books, 1969.

Ashe, Geoffrey. *Do What You Will*. London: W. H. Allen, 1974.

Auerbach, Erich. *Mimesis: The Representation of Reality in Western Literature*. Translated by Willard Trask. Princeton, N.J.: Princeton University Press, 1968.

Bartell, Gilbert. *Group Sex*. New York: New American Library, Signet Books, 1971.

Becker, Carl. *The Heavenly City of the Eighteenth Century Philosophers*. New Haven, Conn.: Yale University Press, 1932.

Becker, Howard. *Outsiders: Studies in the Sociology of Deviance*. New York: Free Press, 1963.

Bell, Daniel. *The Cultural Contradictions of Capitalism*. New York: Basic Books, 1976.

Bell, J. Bowyer. *On Revolt*. Cambridge, Mass.: Harvard University Press, 1976.

Berger, Peter; Berger, Brigette; and Kellner, Hansfried. *The Homeless Mind*. New York: Random House, 1974.

Berger, Peter, and Luckmann, Thomas. *The Social Construction of Reality*. Garden City, N.Y.: Doubleday, Anchor Books, 1967.

Bernard, Jessie. *Social Problems at Midcentury*. New York: Holt, Rinehart & Winston, Dryden Press, 1957.

Boorstin, Daniel. *The Americans: The Democratic Experience*. New York: Random House, 1973.

————. *Democracy and Its Discontents*. New York: Random House, 1974.

Brissett, Dennis, and Lewis, Lionel. "The Big Toe, Armpits, and Natural Perfume: Notes on the Production of Sexual Ecstasy." *Society* 16 (1979): 63–73.

Burke, Kenneth. *Permanence and Change*. Rev. ed. Los Altas, N.M.: Hermes, 1954.

Caillois, Roger. *Man and the Sacred*. Translated by Meyer Barash. New York: Free Press, 1959.

Canetti, Elias. *Crowds and Power*. Translated by Carol Stewart. New York: Viking Press, 1962.

Carpenter, Edmund. *Oh, What a Blow That Phantom Gave Me!* New York: Holt, Rinehart & Winston, 1973.

Cassirer, Ernst. *An Essay on Man*. New York: Bantam Books, 1970.

Cloward, Richard, and Ohlin, Lloyd. *Delinquency and Opportunity*. New York: Free Press, 1960.

Cohen, Albert. *Deviance and Control*. Englewood Cliffs, N.J.: Prentice-Hall, 1966.

Conat, Robert. *Rivers of Blood, Years of Darkness*. New York: Bantam Books, 1967.

Connor, Walter. "The Manufacture of Deviance: The Case of the Soviet Purge." In

The Collective Definition of Deviance, edited by F. James Davis and Richard Stivers. New York: Free Press, 1975.

Cooley, Charles. *Social Organization*. New York: Schocken, 1962.

Dawley, David. *A Nation of Lords*. Garden City, N.Y.: Doubleday, Anchor Books, 1973.

de Jouvenel, Bertrand. *On Power*. Translated by J. F. Huntington. Boston: Beacon Press, 1962.

———. *The Pure Theory of Politics*. New Haven, Conn.: Yale University Press, 1963.

Diamond, Stanley. *In Search of the Primitive*. New Brunswick, N.J.: Transaction Books, 1974.

Dodds, E. R. *The Ancient Concept of Progress*. Oxford: Clarendon Press, 1973.

Douglas, Mary. *Natural Symbols*. New York: Random House, Vintage Books, 1974.

———. *Purity and Danger*. London: Routledge & Kegan Paul, 1978.

Durkheim, Emile. *The Rules of Sociological Method*. Translated by Sarah Solovay and John Mueller. New York: Free Press, 1964.

———. *Suicide*. Translated by John Spaulding and George Simpson. New York: Free Press, 1951.

Eliade, Mircea. *Myth and Reality*. Translated by Willard Trask. New York: Harper & Row, Colophon Books, 1975.

———. *The Myth of the Eternal Return*. Translated by Willard Trask. Princeton, N.J.: Princeton University Press, 1971.

———. *Myths, Dreams, and Mysteries*. Translated by Philip Mairet. New York: Harper & Row, Colophon Books, 1975.

———. *Myths, Rites, Symbols*. Vol. 1. Edited by Wendell C. Beane and William G. Doty. New York: Harper & Row, Colophon Books, 1976.

———. *Patterns in Comparative Religion*. Translated by Rosemary Sheed. New York: New American Library, 1974.

———. *The Quest*. Chicago: University of Chicago Press, 1969.

———. *Rites and Symbols of Initiation*. Translated by Willard Trask. New York: Harper & Row, Torchbooks, 1965.

———. *The Sacred and the Profane*. Translated by Willard Trask. New York: Harper & Row, Torchbooks, 1961.

Ellul, Jacques. *Autopsy of Revolution*. Translated by Patricia Wolf. New York: Alfred A. Knopf, 1971.

———. *The Betrayal of the West*. Translated by Matthew O'Connell. New York: Seabury Press, 1978.

———. *A Critique of the New Commonplaces*. Translated by Helen Weaver. New York: Alfred A. Knopf, 1968.

———. *The Ethics of Freedom*. Translated by Geoffrey Bromiley. Grand Rapids, Mich.: Wm. B. Eerdmans, 1976.

———. *Hope in Time of Abandonment*. Translated by C. Edward Hopkin. New York: Seabury Press, 1973.

———. *The New Demons*. Translated by C. Edward Hopkin. New York: Seabury Press, 1975.

———. *The Political Illusion*. Translated by Konrad Kellen. New York: Random House, Vintage Books, 1972.

———. *Propaganda*. Translated by Konrad Kellen and Jean Lerner. New York: Alfred A. Knopf, 1965.

———. "Technological Morality." In *The Collective Definition of Deviance*, edited by F. James Davis and Richard Stivers. New York: Free Press, 1975.

————. *The Technological Society*. Translated by John Wilkinson. New York: Random House, Vintage Books, 1964.

————. *Violence*. Translated by Cecelia Gaul Kings. New York: Seabury Press, 1969.

Ellwood, Charles. *Sociology and Modern Social Problems*. New York: American Book, 1910.

Erikson, Kai. *Wayward Puritans*. New York: John Wiley & Sons, 1966.

Fanon, Franz. *The Wretched of the Earth*. Translated by Constance Farrington. New York: Grove Press, 1968.

Foucault, Michel. *The Birth of the Clinic*. Translated by A. M. Sheridan Smith. New York: Random House, Vintage Books, 1975.

————. *The History of Sexuality*. Vol. 1, *An Introduction*. Translated by Robert Hurley. New York: Random House, Vintage Books, 1980.

Frank, Jerome. *Persuasion and Healing*. New York: Schocken Books, 1974.

Frankl, Victor. *Man's Search for Meaning*. New York: Washington Square Press, 1963.

Frazer, James G. *The Golden Bough*. Vol. 6, *The Scapegoat*. New York: Macmillan, 1935.

Fromm, Erich. *The Anatomy of Human Destructiveness*. Greenwich, Conn.: Fawcett Crest Books, 1973.

————. *The Revolution of Hope*. New York: Harper & Row, Colophon Books, 1968.

Geertz, Clifford. *The Interpretation of Cultures*. New York: Basic Books, 1973.

Gehlen, Arnold. *Man in the Age of Technology*. Translated by Patricia Lipscomb. New York: Columbia University Press, 1980.

Gennep, Arnold van. *The Rites of Passage*. Translated by Monika B. Vizedom and Gabriella L. Caffee. Chicago: University of Chicago Press, 1960.

Girard, René. *Violence and the Sacred*. Translated by Patrick Gregory. Baltimore: Johns Hopkins University Press, 1977.

Gluckman, Max. *Custom and Conflict in Africa*. Glencoe, Ill.: Free Press, 1955.

————. *Order and Rebellion in Tribal Africa*. New York: Free Press, 1963.

Goffman, Erving. "The Insanity of Place." In *Relations in Public*. New York: Harper & Row, Colophon Books, 1972.

————. *Stigma: Notes on the Management of Spoiled Identity*. Englewood Cliffs, N.J.: Prentice-Hall, 1963.

Goode, William. *Explorations in Social Theory*. New York: Oxford University Press, 1973.

Gordon, Caroline. *Beginner's Guide to Group Sex*. New York: Pocket Books, 1974.

Greeley, Andrew. "Symbol, Myth and Ritual in the Modern World." *Critic* 20 (December 1961–January 1962): 18–25.

Green, Arnold. *Social Problems: Arena of Conflict*. New York: McGraw-Hill, 1976.

Gutmann, David. "Killers and Consumers: The Terrorist and His Audience." *Social Research* 46 (Autumn 1979): 517–26.

Habermas, Jurgen. *Toward a Rational Society*. Translated by Jeremy Shapiro. Boston: Beacon Press, 1970.

Hall, Edward. *Beyond Culture*. Garden City, N.Y.: Doubleday, Anchor Books, 1977.

Hayek, Friedrich A. *The Constitution of Liberty*. Chicago: Henry Regnery, 1960.

————. *The Counter-Revolution of Science*. New York: Free Press, 1955.

Hayes, Edward. *Sociology and Ethics*. New York: Appleton, 1921.

Helmer, John. *Drugs and Minority Oppression*. New York: Seabury Press, 1975.

Hendin, Herbert. *The Age of Sensation*. New York: W. W. Norton, 1975.

Herberg, Will. *Protestant Catholic Jew*. Rev. ed. Garden City, N.Y.: Doubleday, Anchor Books, 1960.

Hirschi, Travis. *Causes of Delinquency*. Berkeley and Los Angeles: University of California Press, 1969.

Hobbs, Albert H. *The Claims of Sociology: A Critique of Textbooks*. Harrisburg, Pa.: Telegraph Press, 1951.

Hobsbawm, Eric. *The Age of Revolution, 1789–1848*. New York: Mentor Books, 1962.

Hofstadter, Richard. *Social Darwinism in American Thought*. Boston: Beacon Press, 1955.

Horkheimer, Max. "Tradition and Critical Theory." In *Critical Theory*, translated by Matthew O'Connell et al. New York: Herder & Herder, 1972.

———, and Adorno, Theodor. "The Culture Industry as Mass Deception." In *Dialectic of Enlightenment*, translated by John Cumming. New York: Herder & Herder, 1972.

Horney, Karen. *The Neurotic Personality of Our Time*. New York: W. W. Norton, 1937.

Horowitz, Irving Louis. *Professing Sociology*. Chicago: Aldine, 1968.

———, and Liebowitz, Martin. "Social Deviance and Political Marginality: Toward a Redefinition of the Relation between Sociology and Politics." *Social Problems* 15 (Winter 1968): 280–96.

Huxley, Aldous. *The Doors of Perception*. New York: Harper & Row, 1970.

———. *Island*. New York: Harper & Row, 1962.

Jackson, Bruce. "White-Collar Pill Party." In *Observations of Deviance*, edited by Jack Douglas. New York: Random House, 1970.

Jones, Howard Mumford. *The Pursuit of Happiness*. Cambridge, Mass.: Harvard University Press, 1953.

Kelsen, Hans. *Society and Nature*. New York: Arno Press, 1974.

Key, Wilson Bryan. *Media Sexploitation*. Englewood Cliffs, N.J.: Prentice-Hall, 1976.

———. *Subliminal Seduction*. New York: New American Library, 1973.

Kiev, Ari, ed. *Magic, Faith, and Healing*. New York: Free Press, 1964.

Kirk, Geoffrey. *Myth*. Berkeley and Los Angeles: University of California Press, 1973.

Klapp, Orrin. *Collective Search for Identity*. New York: Holt, Rinehart & Winston, 1969.

Kluckhohn, Clyde. "Myths and Rituals: A General Theory." *Harvard Theological Review* 35 (1942):78.

Kovel, Joel. *A Complete Guide to Therapy*. New York: Pantheon Books, 1976.

Kraus, A. J. I. *Sick Society*. Chicago: University of Chicago Press, 1929.

Laqueur, Walter. *Terrorism*. Boston: Little, Brown, 1977.

Larkin, Ralph. *Cultural Crisis of Suburban Youth*. New York: Oxford University Press, 1979.

Leary, Timothy. *The Politics of Ecstasy*. New York: Putnam, 1968.

———. *Psychedelic Prayers*. Kerhonkson, N.Y.: Poets Press, 1966.

Levi-Strauss, Claude. *Structural Anthropology*. Translated by Claire Jacobson and Brooke Grundfest Schoepf. Garden City, N.Y.: Doubleday, Anchor Books, 1967.

London, Perry. *Behavior Control*. New York: Harper & Row, 1969.

Lowith, Karl. *Meaning in History*. Chicago: University of Chicago Press, 1949.

Lowry, Ritchie. *Social Problems*. Lexington, Mass.: D. C. Heath, 1974.

Luckmann, Thomas. *The Invisible Religion*. New York: Macmillan, 1967.

Lukes, Steven. *Emile Durkheim: His Life and Work*. New York: Harper & Row, 1972.

Lundberg, George. *Can Science Save Us?* New York: Longmans, Green, 1947.

McLuhan, Marshall. *The Mechanical Bride*. Boston: Beacon Press, 1967.

———. "Myth and Mass Media." In *Myth and Mythmaking*, edited by Henry Murray. New York: George Braziller, 1960.

————. *Understanding Media*. New York: McGraw-Hill, 1964.

————. *War and Peace in the Global Village*. New York: Bantam Books, 1968.

Malcolm, Andrew. *The Tyranny of the Group*. Totowa, N.J.: Littlefield, Adams, 1974.

Manis, Jerome. *Analyzing Social Problems*. New York: Praeger, 1976.

Marcel, Gabriel. *Man against Mass Society*. Translated by G. S. Fraser. Chicago: Henry Regnery, 1962.

Martin, Bernice. "The Sacralization of Disorder: Symbolism in Rock Music." *Sociological Analysis* 40 (1979): 87–124.

Marx, Karl. *The Economic and Philosophical Manuscripts of 1844*. Translated by Martin Milligan. New York: International, 1964.

————, and Engels, Frederick. *The German Ideology*. Translated by W. Lough et al. New York: International, 1970.

May, Rollo. *Power and Innocence*. New York: W. W. Norton, 1972.

Merton, Robert. "Social Problems and Sociological Theory." In *Contemporary Social Problems*, edited by Robert Merton and Robert Nisbet. 3rd ed. New York: Harcourt Brace Jovanovich, 1971.

————. *Social Theory and Social Structure*. New York: Free Press, 1968.

Meyersohn, Rolf. "Abundance Reconsidered." In *On the Making of Americans: Essays in Honor of David Riesman*, edited by Herbert Gans et al. Philadelphia: University of Pennsylvania Press, 1979.

Mills, C. Wright. "The Professional Ideology of Social Pathologists." *American Journal of Sociology* 49 (September 1943): 165–80.

Moltmann, Jurgen. "American Contradictions." *Center Magazine* 9 (November–December 1976): 59–65.

Niebuhr, Reinhold. *The Nature and Destiny of Man*. Vol. 1. New York: Charles Scribner's Sons, 1941.

Nieburg, Harold L. *Culture Storm*. New York: St. Martin's Press, 1973.

Nietzsche, Friedrich. *Beyond Good and Evil*. Translated by Walter Kaufmann. New York: Random House, Vintage Books, 1966.

————. *On the Genealogy of Morals*. Translated by Walter Kaufmann. New York: Random House, Vintage Books, 1969.

————. *The Will to Power*. Translated by Walter Kaufmann and R. J. Hollingdale. New York: Random House, Vintage Books, 1968.

Norbeck, Edward. "African Rituals of Conflict." In *Gods and Rituals*, edited by John Middleton. Garden City, N.Y.: Natural History Press, 1967.

North, Maurice. *The Secular Priests*. London: George Allen & Unwin, 1972.

Nygren, Anders. *Agape and Eros*. Translated by Philip Watson. Philadelphia: Westminster Press, 1953.

O'Neill, William. *Coming Apart*. Chicago: Quadrangle Books, 1971.

Ong, Walter. *Interfaces of the Word*. Ithaca, N.Y.: Cornell University Press, 1977.

————. "Literacy and Orality in Our Times." *ADE Bulletin*, no. 58 (September 1978), pp. 1–7.

————. *The Presence of the Word*. New Haven, Conn.: Yale University Press, 1967.

————. "Technology Outside Us and Inside Us." *Communio* 5 (1978): 100–121.

Ortega y Gassett, José. *The Revolt of the Masses*. New York; W. W. Norton, 1957.

Otto, Rudolph. *The Idea of the Holy*. Translated by John Harvey. New York: Oxford University Press, 1958.

Packard, Vance. *The People Shapers*. Boston: Little, Brown, 1977.

Ricoeur, Paul. *Interpretation Theory: Discourse and the Surplus of Meaning*. Fort Worth: Texas Christian University Press, 1976.

———. *The Symbolism of Evil.* Translated by Emerson Buchanan. Boston: Beacon Press, 1969.

Rieff, Philip. *Fellow Teachers.* New York: Harper & Row, 1973.

———. *Freud: The Mind of the Moralist.* Garden City, N.Y.: Doubleday, Anchor Books, 1961.

———. *The Triumph of the Therapeutic.* New York: Harper & Row, 1966.

Riesman, David. *The Lonely Crowd.* Abridged ed. New Haven, Conn.: Yale University Press, 1969.

Rosen, Richard. *Psychobabble.* New York: Atheneum Publishers, 1977.

Roszak, Theodore. *The Making of a Counter Culture.* Garden City, N.Y.: Doubleday, Anchor Books, 1969.

Rothman, David. *The Discovery of the Asylum.* Boston: Little, Brown, 1971.

Rubington, Earl, and Weinberg, Martin, eds. *The Study of Social Problems.* 2nd ed. New York: Oxford University Press, 1977.

Ruitenbeek, Hendrik. *The New Group Therapies.* New York: Avon Books, 1970.

Salomon, Albert. *The Tyranny of Progress.* New York: Noonday Press, 1955.

Sapir, Edward. "Culture, Genuine and Spurious." In *Culture, Language and Personality,* edited by David Mandelbaum. Berkeley and Los Angeles: University of California Press, 1970.

Schumpeter, Joseph. *Capitalism, Socialism, and Democracy.* 3rd ed. New York: Harper & Row, Torchbooks, 1962.

Seabrook, Jeremy. *What Went Wrong? Why Hasn't Having More Made People Happier?* New York: Pantheon Books, 1978.

Sedgwick, Peter. "Mental Illness *Is* Illness." *Salmagundi* 20 (Summer–Fall 1972): 196–224.

Selzer, Michael. *Terrorist Chic.* New York: Hawthorn Books, 1979.

Sennett, Richard. *The Fall of Public Man.* New York: Alfred A. Knopf, 1977.

Simmel, Georg. *The Sociology of Georg Simmel.* Translated and edited by Kurt Wolff. New York: Free Press, 1950.

Slater, Philip. *Microcosm.* New York: John Wiley & Sons, 1966.

Snaith, Norman. *The Distinctive Ideas of the Old Testament.* New York: Schocken Books, 1964.

Sorel, Georges. *Reflections on Violence.* Translated by T. E. Hulme. 3rd ed. New York: B. W. Huebsch, 1941.

Spector, Malcolm, and Kitsuse, John. *Constructing Social Problems.* Menlo Park, Calif.: Cummings, 1977.

Spencer, Herbert. *Principles of Sociology.* Hamden, Conn.: Shoestring Press, Archon Books, 1969.

Sutherland, Edwin, and Cressey, Donald. *Criminology.* 9th ed. Philadelphia: J. B. Lippincott, 1974.

Szasz, Thomas. *Ceremonial Chemistry.* Garden City, N.Y.: Doubleday, Anchor Books, 1975.

———. *The Ethics of Psychoanalysis.* New York: Dell Publishing, Delta Books, 1965.

———. *Ideology and Insanity.* Garden City, N.Y.: Doubleday, Anchor Books, 1970.

———. *The Manufacture of Madness.* New York: Harper & Row, Colophon Books, 1970.

Tallman, Irving. *Passion, Action, and Politics.* San Francisco: W. H. Freeman, 1976.

Tawney, Richard H. *The Acquisitive Society.* New York: Harcourt, Brace & World, Har-

Thomas, William, and Znaniecki, Florian. *The Polish Peasant in Europe and America.* Boston: R. G. Badger, 1918.

Thompson, Hunter. *Hell's Angels.* New York: Random House, 1967.

———. "Hell's Angels: Hoodlum Circus and Statutory Rape of Bass Lake." In *Observations of Deviance*, edited by Jack Douglas. New York: Random House, 1970.

Tiryakian, Edward. "The Time Perspectives of Modernity." Paper read at American Sociological Association meeting, 1977, Chicago.

Tocqueville, Alexis de. *Democracy in America.* Translated by George Lawrence. Garden City, N.Y.: Doubleday, Anchor Books, 1969.

Troeltsch, Ernst. *The Social Teaching of the Christian Churches.* 2 vols. Translated by Olive Wyon. London: George Allen & Unwin, 1950.

Tucker, Robert. *Philosophy and Myth in Karl Marx.* Cambridge: Cambridge University Press, 1971.

Turnbull, Colin. *The Mountain People.* New York: Simon & Schuster, Touchstone Books, 1972.

Turner, Victor. *Dramas, Fields, and Metaphors.* Ithaca, N.Y.: Cornell University Press, 1974.

———. *The Forest of Symbols.* Ithaca, N.Y.: Cornell University Press, 1967.

———. *The Ritual Process.* Ithaca, N.Y.: Cornell University Press, 1977.

Tuveson, Ernest. *Redeemer Nation.* Chicago: University of Chicago Press, 1968.

Vahanian, Gabriel. *The Death of God.* New York: George Braziller, 1961.

———. *God and Utopia.* Translated by Paul Lachance et al. New York: Seabury Press, 1977.

Van Doren, Charles. *The Idea of Progress.* New York: Praeger, 1967.

Voegelin, Eric. *Science, Politics, and Gnosticism.* Chicago: Henry Regnery, 1968.

Wach, Joachim. *Sociology of Religion.* Chicago: University of Chicago Press, 1962.

Waller, Willard. "Social Problems and the Mores." *American Sociological Review* 1 (December 1936): 924–30.

Warner, W. Lloyd. *American Life: Dream and Reality.* Chicago: University of Chicago Press, 1953.

Weaver, Richard. *The Ethics of Rhetoric.* Chicago: Henry Regnery, 1953.

———. *Visions of Order.* Baton Rouge: Louisiana State University Press, 1964.

Weber, Max. *From Max Weber.* Translated and edited by Hans Gerth and C. Wright Mills. New York: Oxford University Press, 1946.

Whyte, Lancelot L. *The Unconscious before Freud.* London: Tavistock, 1962.

Williams, Raymond. *Keywords.* New York: Oxford University Press, 1976.

Williams, Robin, Jr. *American Society.* 3rd ed. New York: Alfred A. Knopf, 1960.

Wirth, Louis. "Ideological Aspects of Social Disorganization." *American Sociological Review* 5 (August 1940): 472–82.

Wootton, Barbara. *Social Science and Pathology.* London: George Allen & Unwin, 1959.

Zinberg, Norman, and Robertson, John. *Drugs and the Public.* New York: Simon & Schuster, 1972.

INDEX

DATE DUE

APR. 20. 1989			

HIGHSMITH 45-220